Career Success of Disabled High-Flyers

of related interest

A Supported Employment Workbook
Using Individual Profiling and Job Matching
Steve Leach
Forewords by Stephen Beyer, Deputy Director, Welsh Centre for Learning Disabilities
and Dave Willingham, Supported Employment Co-ordinator for Hartlepool
ISBN 1 84310 052 5

Helping People with a Learning Disability Explore Choice
Eve and Neil Jackson
ISBN 1 85302 694 8

From a Different Viewpoint
The Lives and Experiences of Visually Impaired People
Sally French and John Swain
Published with the Royal National Institute for the Blind
ISBN 1 85302 551 8

The Views and Experiences of Disabled Children
and Their Siblings
A Positive Outlook
Clare Connors and Kirsten Stalker
ISBN 1 84310 127 0

Brothers and Sisters of Disabled Children
Peter Burke
ISBN 1 84310 043 6

Ageing with a Lifelong Disability
A Guide to Practice, Program and Policy Issues for Human
Services Professionals
Christine Bigby
Foreword by Gordon Grant
ISBN 1 84310 077 0

Career Success of Disabled High-Flyers

Sonali Shah

Jessica Kingsley Publishers
London and Philadelphia

Epigraph on p.21 from *Man or Superman* by George Bernard Shaw, published by Penguin Classics, London, 2001. Reproduced with kind permission of The Society of Authors, on behalf of the Bernard Shaw Estate.

First published in 2005
by Jessica Kingsley Publishers
116 Pentonville Road
London N1 9JB, UK
and
400 Market Street, Suite 400
Philadelphia, PA 19106, USA

www.jkp.com

Copyright © Sonali Shah 2005

Library of Congress Cataloging in Publication Data
Shah, Sonali, 1973-
    Career success of disabled high-flyers / Sonali Shah.-- 1st American pbk. ed.
      p. cm.
    Based on author's thesis (doctoral).
    Includes bibliographical references and index.
    ISBN-13: 978-1-84310-208-3 (pbk.)
    ISBN-10: 1-84310-208-0 (pbk.)
    1. People with disabilities--Employment. 2. People with disabilities--Vocational guidance. I. Title.
    HD7255.S485 2005
    650.1'087--dc22
                            2005004516

British Library Cataloguing in Publication Data
A CIP catalogue record for this book is available from the British Library

ISBN-13: 978 1 84310 208 3
ISBN-10: 1 84310 208 0

Printed and Bound in Great Britain by
Athenaeum Press, Gateshead, Tyne and Wear

Contents

LIST OF TABLES

Acknowledgements

This book could not have been written without the support and generosity of many people out there.

I would like to thank the Barrow Cadbury Trust for funding the PhD research on which this book is based. The credit for talking me into converting my PhD into this goes to Dr Cheryl Travers, who has given me some helpful pointers over the years.

This research would not be possible without all of the disabled high-flyers who took part in it and so generously took the time to share their stories with me. My thanks and best wishes to you all. The disabled high-flyers will appear under pseudonyms in this text.

Several friends, both academics and practitioners, have given me helpful advice, supportive chats and friendly ears. So thanks for this, folks, especially Rebecca Calcraft, Martin Deaney and Mark Priestley. Also cheers to my research assistant Nicola Kilvington who has been a great asset to my work over the past six months.

Above all, I am indebted to my partner Jonathan who has been a tower of strength during the past year, coping with my fluctuating moods and motivating me to persevere and finish even when the going seemed impossible. Also much love and appreciation to my mother and father who have always been the key people in my life and enabled me to be who I am today. Thanks for supporting me and guiding me through life, and encouraging me to strive high.

Finally, many sincere thanks to Professor John Arnold for his honest, positive and encouraging attitude towards myself and my work, and for his patient and rigorous editing.

CHAPTER 1

Career Success of Disabled High-Flyers

Science is organised knowledge, wisdom is organised life.
Immanuel Kant

INTRODUCTION

Over the past ten years organisations have tended to rethink the way in whichthey operate. Increasing globalisation and continuous moves towards a multicultural society have sharpened competition for organisations to become more organic and responsive to change (Legge, 1995). As a consequence of this, much interest has been placed on the contributions of the employees. As has been argued by Kandola (1995), the multinational success of organisations has stemmed from the diversity of their workforce. Similarly, Woodhams and Danieli (2000) argue that a diverse workforce is more representative of a diverse customer base and able to get closer to the customer, understand their needs and so increase the company's market share.

By appreciating the value of a more diverse public work place in terms of race, gender and disability, organisations become better equipped with specific skills and knowledge to compete in the labour market (Cassell, 1997; Dickens, 1994). For example, Duckworth (1995) argues that disabled people living in a predominantly inaccessible world have to develop highly refined problem-solving skills that can be seen as valuable to today's economic development.

In the UK much has been done in recent years to improve the employment situation of disabled people and encourage their inclusion in the mainstream labour market. Legislation such as the Disability Discrimination Act (1995), the Human Rights Act (1998), and the Special Educational Needs and Disability Act (2001) enshrines the legal tradition of treating all individuals equally, so that they have a stake in policy-making processes and their views are given due weight. This includes making decisions about their occupational futures, which is not only important to the individual concerned, but to the future survival of society as a whole. Although this legislative framework has undoubtedly provided increasing employment opportunities for disabled people, while reducing discrimination in the work place, it tends to depend on a measure of homogeneity within disabled groups of employees in order to produce effective remedies (Woodhams and Danieli, 2000). This presents problems for disabled people, who are a heterogeneous group with different needs according to the type and severity of their impairment. Therefore no single inclusion strategy is universally applicable to all disabled workers.

On the other hand, other governmental initiatives such as Access to Work or PACT (Placement and Counselling Team) do tend to operate on a more individualised basis, working to empower disabled employees by providing financial assistance for reasonable accommodations to be made. In addition, these initiatives have promoted the uptake of flexible employment opportunities, which new technologies make possible to disabled people whose credentials were previously overlooked due to work being based on manual labour.

Nevertheless, despite these policy-led innovations to promote an integrated and diverse workforce, other issues have to be addressed about how disabled people's individual life experiences and characteristics drive them to be successful in their careers, and the influence that constant attributes such as gender and onset of disability have on disabled people's life experiences. Therefore further attention needs to be given to their childhood background and socialisation which will usually have a significant influence on their career choice and occupational achievement (see White, Cox and Cooper, 1992). Social class and parental occupation have been found, over the years, to play a critical role in determining the career orientation of non-disabled people. Similarly parental expectations and childhood events have a lasting influence on how disabled children grow and develop, and the direction they take in adult life (e.g. Cox and Cooper, 1988; Shah, Arnold and Travers 2004).

An individual's personality also has an important influence on their occupational choice, on whether they achieve success or failure in their job and on whether they are likely to work hard to overcome obstacles to achievement or give up in the face of adversity. The personality of every individual is unique and determines whether they are inclined to be self-controlled or controlled by others, how strong their need for achievement is and the goals that they are likely to aspire to and achieve. It is important to understand how individuals behave in certain circumstances and what motivates them to do so.

Education has been considered to be strongly linked to vocational participation (Giddens, 1997). Schools and colleges help to motivate some individuals towards achievement and success, while discouraging others who find their way into low-paid jobs. The level and subject of education has a general connection to the accessing of employment opportunities, especially since employers use academic credentials as a means of narrowing down the field of applicants. The type of educational institution an individual attends influences their psychosocial, cognitive, and academic experiences and development, which in turn can contribute to their economic future. This is particularly the case for disabled students who have attended segregated educational institutions with a limited choice of subjects and low expectations, or mainstream education with limited funding to provide appropriate support and total inclusion. This is discussed further in Chapter 5.

Occupational success

Managing a diverse workforce entails organisations having a greater understanding of what their employees want from their career and what it means to them (Sturges, 1996). This is particularly the case for certain minority groups such as people with disabilities who, as this study will show, for various reasons, may hold different ideas about career success than those which are traditionally held. One explanation for this could be that disabled people are often restricted from climbing the career ladder due to the 'glass ceiling' (Barnes, Thornton and Maynard Campell, 1998, p.33). True barrier removal for disabled people would cost organisations too much in terms of disruption, specialist advice, training and money (Woodhams and Danieli, 2000). Moreover, this examination of work procedures and activities is unlikely to be truly beneficial to all disabled employees.

However, the disappearance of 'career by advancement' (Sturges, 1996) and the emergence of a 'boundaryless' career, which moves across the boundaries of separate employers and is independent of conventional organisational career principles (Arthur, 1994; Mirvis and Hall, 1994), places greater value on individual perceptions of career success. It may offer organisations a better idea of what people actually want from their careers and thus provide some indication of potential alternative focuses for future career development initiatives. As argued by Gattiker and Larwood (1986, p.78): 'Any understanding of career paths and effective personnel management is substantially reduced if the subjective side of career success is ignored.'

They also argue that the examination of subjective perceptions of success is important for some groups in today's society, especially groups who are unlikely to measure success in objective terms, as they might reveal that individuals feel differently about their accomplishments than an outsider might expect. Disabled people are one of these groups who are likely to place a great importance on internal subjective measures of career success. One reason may be that they are susceptible to being victims of 'glass ceiling' advancement and pay inequity, and could be, therefore, less likely to be recognised as externally successful.

AIMS OF THIS BOOK

Governmental legislation has indeed provided disabled people with the opportunity to contribute to the economic development of society. Also, more flexible notions of careers may create a climate that is more favourable towards disabled people. In the light of this potential opportunity for disabled people to reach positions of power and influence, it seems appropriate to explore the issues facing disabled men and women as they strive for career success. The focus of this book is on the process of career development among a unique group of disabled people who have achieved career success. It aims to understand the characteristics of those disabled people who make it to the top and successfully achieve their own personal and professional goals.

The correlation between disabled people's life experiences and their career development is a very important subject area, but has received very little attention to date. The literature on career development and success has traditionally been largely based on non-disabled men (Cox and Cooper, 1988; Super, 1957), and, only recently, their female counterparts (Sturges, 1999; White et al., 1992). Therefore the research reported in this book aims to contribute to this limited knowledge by demonstrating how a group of disabled high-flyers perceived their life experiences and personal attributes, and how significant people have influenced their life, career development and choices. It explores how the areas considered to be significant to the career success of a non-disabled high-flyer (such as childhood, personality, education, and career choice and progression) contribute to the disabled person's career development and success. In addition, it will reveal the similarities and differences that occur as a consequence of gender and onset of disability. In looking at the experiences of disabled high-flyers, this book identifies significant turning points in their journeys to career success, routes they took to reach their success goals, the barriers they encountered along the way and specific strategies adopted to combat them. It is hoped that the findings may reveal practical recommendations which may help employers, support service workers and society in general have a greater understanding of what disabled people feel can help or hinder them to achieve their potential. Such recommendations could help to inform policy and practice in educational services by giving an understanding of significant educational experiences, needs and opinions of disabled people. With this, mainstream institutions and gatekeepers are made aware of what disabled people can achieve, and how their worth is valuable to the development of a multicultural global economy.

A general aim of this book is for it to be used to provide role models for young career-minded people with disabilities. All girls and boys need positive role models, which are essential for the development of their self-esteem and self-worth. Many children, however, grow up never having met a disabled adult and so do not understand what growing up will mean for them. Disabled children may grow up more isolated than other children because most disabled children are born to non-disabled adults, and therefore do not necessarily come into contact with disabled adults. It is hoped this work will be involved, in some way, in the education of disabled children by reporting the inspiring stories of the disabled high-flyers' journey from disabled childhood to successful adulthood.

The book demonstrates that disabled high-flyers have different ideas about what success means to them, and consider subjective success to be as important as objective success. It indicates that if disabled people are to become high-flyers in their fields, employers seriously need to recognise the importance of internal success.

THE DISABLED HIGH-FLYERS

The terms 'disabled high-flyer' and 'disabled high-achiever' are used interchangeably in this study, to refer to physically disabled individuals who have achieved a recognised standard of power and prestige in their professional lives. These individuals have achieved and secured employment at levels far beyond what is considered to be the norm for disabled people in Britain.

Further, the terms 'disabled people', 'people with physical disabilities' or 'people who are physically impaired' are also used interchangeably in this book, to mean individuals with mobility, dexterity and/or speech impairments whose life development has been influenced by their individual differences as well as social and physical barriers in society. Such a definition is appropriate to the current study as it includes the disability imposed by societal institutions and the disability taken on board as part of an individual's identity. It also can be used as one of the selection criteria to identify potential respondents for this study.

The sample studied for this research consisted of 31 disabled high-flyers; 19 men and 12 women, with physical impairments acquired from birth or in their early adulthood. They all lived in the United Kingdom and were born between 1940 and 1970. All these people were well established in their careers by the 1990s, working in professions classified in accordance with either Social Class I or II of the Registrar General's Scale of occupations by social class. The sample is illustrative rather than representative of the ways in which disabled men and women participate in the labour market. As the aim was to gain an insight into the professional and personal experiences of disabled high-flyers, a diversity of career areas was desirable. These professions included politics, the arts, media, business, medicine and academia. Due to the fact that the majority of disabled employees do tend to work in the lower end of the service sector, it was not simple to target potential respondents who worked in Social Class I or II type occupations. Therefore because of the lack of time and resources to find a large enough sample of disabled employees in such occupations, one or two of the respondents selected for the study held occupations that could not be classified in terms of Social Class I or II. These respondents worked in specialist non-manual areas and also were considered, by others, to have exceeded societal expectations of disabled people. These disabled people (from different social and ethnic backgrounds) with congenital or acquired impairments perceived themselves as successful in terms of their career development and life achievements, compared to other disabled people and, in a few cases, non-disabled people. They all believed they had built a record of educational and professional achievements that exceeded societal expectations of disabled people.

The disabled high-flyers were recruited into the study via various channels. These included well-established disability organisations, registered charities, the researcher's social network, the media and networks in different regions of the country, and as a result of successful 'snowballing' (i.e. getting to know subjects and having them introduce the researcher to others). Details of the high-flyers, including their name, nature of disability, their gender and their occupation (at the time the research was carried out) are summarised in Table 1.1. All real names have been changed to ensure anonymity.

INFLUENCE OF THE DISABLED RESEARCHER

It may be argued that the acquisition of rich quality data, during this study, was facilitated by the fact that the interviewer and the participants came from the same minority group, that is, both parties shared experiences of physical impairment and life development. This is supported by Leicester (1999), who suggests that by interviewing individuals with similar experiences, empathy encourages richer interview responses. It was also thought that this shared culture and background was helpful in accessing potential respondents, building a rapport with them, reducing any suspicions and encouraging them to be more open. However, no research is completely free of bias. It is recognised that the closer our subject matter is to our own life, the more we can expect our own world view to enter into and shape our work, to influence the questions we pose and the interpretations we generate from our findings. As Wheatley points out:

> Ethnographic relations, practices and representations as well as the metaphors we use to make sense of them are contextually contingent – their character is shaped by who we look at, from where we look, and why we are looking in the first place. (1994, p. 422)

Table 1.1 Disabled high-flyers

Name	Nature of disability	Occupation
Sam	Congenital	Sports development officer
Greg	Congenital	Actor/Singer/Songwriter
Ed	Congenital	TV Critic/Writer
Marty	Congenital	Dancer
Sunny	Congenital	Actor – stage and screen
Tom	Congenital	Vicar
Bob	Congenital	Financial planning advisor
Christian	Congenital	Parliamentary officer
Jonathan	Congenital	TV Presenter/Freelance journalist
Timmy	Congenital	Church minister
Harry	Congenital	Senior computer analyst
Mary	Congenital	Solicitor (retired)/Disability consultant
Rachel	Congenital	Member of Parliament
Katey	Congenital	Freelance journalist
Kay	Congenital	Disability strategy manager
Anna	Congenital	Professional wheelchair athlete
Jude	Congenital	Vicar
Lara	Congenital	Artistic director of theatre company/Actress
Maria	Congenital	Speech and language therapist
Corin	Congenital	University lecturer
Clint	Acquired	Trade finance advisor
Roger	Acquired	University professor
Kenny	Acquired	Management accountant
Ali	Acquired	Barrister
Amil	Acquired	Computer programmer and analyst
Adrian	Acquired	Senior architect
Nick	Acquired	Careers officer
Cane	Acquired	Theatre director
Pauline	Acquired	Project manager
Judith	Acquired	Education and training officer/Visual artist
Amanda	Acquired	Artistic director of dance company/Dancer

Nevertheless, only part of my life history resembled that of each respondent, so I still could retain a fair level of objectivity. Also, I kept in mind the danger of assuming too much commonality of perspective with respondents.

In this study, there were particularly marked differences in age and cultural background between disabled high-flyers and myself, the researcher. All of them were older than I was and most were British Caucasian, whereas I call myself British Indian. Only some of our life experiences were indeed similar, and even these were not identical. So, although I could empathise with the participants with regards to living as a disabled person and thus interpret the data in a non-oppressive manner, many differences did exist between us that helped me to avoid bias when doing this.

Cultural and age differences aside, my status as a disabled person definitely made a difference in terms of accessing potential respondents to talk to. Several openly admitted that had I not been disabled they would have refused to be interviewed. As one of the high-flyers, Cane, confessed: 'When I realised you were disabled I put your letter to the top of the pile!'

I sensed that several of the respondents became less guarded and more open when they realised we had something in common. Some shared my impairment. For others, identification occurred in terms of our shared experiences of segregated education and partial integration rather than our shared impairment status. Several of the respondents attended the same residential college as myself, although at different times, and we bonded over our shared liking of some 'care' and academic staff and our dislike of others. I also discovered, especially during interviews with some of the disabled women, that we shared a determination to succeed by working twice as hard as non-disabled peers and not giving up in the face of oppressive barriers.

THE STORY OF THE AUTHOR AND THE RESEARCH

My decision to pursue a PhD research project in this particular subject matter was greatly influenced by the Asian achievement-oriented culture within which I was born and brought up; growing up as a disabled person; and working against disabling barriers to meet mainstream goals in education, employment and society as a whole.

My brain was starved of oxygen during the first 30 minutes of my life. Had this not happened I would not be physically disabled with athetoid cerebral palsy and my life would have undoubtedly taken a different course. It is almost certain that I would have pursued my childhood career aspirations of being a medical doctor like my father. However, although I still had these ambitions as a disabled child, I soon learned the realities of growing up with a disability in a predominately non-disabled world, and various powerful people (including teachers and medical professionals) forced these aspirations to become dormant. This was not the first time my aspirations have been quashed as a consequence of disability discrimination and definitely will not be the last during my lifetime. One particular instance, which will always remain with me, possibly because it was an important transitional period in my life, after graduating from university, was being rejected from a diploma course in journalism. Such a course would qualify me to achieve an ambition I had (after realising that I could never be a medical doctor) to pursue a career in newspaper journalism. However, despite being awarded a bursary to study the course, and passing the initial examination successfully, I was not given a place because the employers thought that my disability would prevent me from achieving and coping with the work required. This was seen as a significant turning point in my future professional orientation. The fact that the decision to do a postgraduate degree was made after my experience of disability discrimination when striving to meet my aspired career goals meant that this was an obvious topic for me to investigate. As Marshall (1995) asserts, research can often be linked with the researcher's life process as they pursue topics of personal relevance and hope to achieve life development as well as intellectual insight.

The direction of my research, on which this book is based, changed somewhat since my initial PhD proposal. Originally I intended to explore the impact of information technology on the employment of disabled people. However, after a brief literature search I realised that such a subject had been investigated several times in various ways, therefore I would not be adding anything new to knowledge. Nevertheless, the experiences of myself, of friends and of other people with disabilities living in a mainstream society continued to motivate me. I was eager to develop work that reflected my belief that every person has the right to their personal freedom, and to make personal choices, in accordance with their personal credentials, and not be stereotyped in any way. It was at this point that I was exposed to the idea of investigating the career success of disabled high-flyers.

The five years I spent working on this research, kindly funded by the Barrow Cadbury Trust, has proved to be a crucial period of personal development for me. It has not only taken me into new avenues of competence, and exposed me to great inspirations, but also taught me that there is truth in the famous proverb, 'Where there's a will there's a way.' Although this work was demanding and challenging, often leaving me exhausted, frustrated and wanting to quit, I was greatly inspired by the disabled high-flyers who participated in my study. Like them, I believe that everyone can exercise control over their own destiny, that successes and failures are the result of one's own behaviour, that it takes personal ability to work hard to create opportunities, and personal ability to capitalise on these opportunities when they present themselves. It was this belief, coupled with the support of a handful of people, that drove me to overcome the various stumbling blocks that were put in my path and finish what I started. I am not joking when I say this involved much blood, sweat and tears, especially after I submitted my whole thesis for the first time. I was so relieved and excited when I saw all seven chapters of my work printed and bound together with pink covering that I never imagined the end was not yet in full view. The end was, in actual fact, another year away, which I discovered after spending two and a half hours trying to defend my thesis to a couple of strangers, only to get referred and given another year to rewrite the whole thing and submit it again. This was a killer, but now people call me Dr Shah.

COLLECTING THE DATA

It was decided that an investigation about the careers of successful disabled men and women would best be conducted by collecting detailed information about a relatively small number of disabled adults. This approach was considered more likely to produce deep, rich quality data about the dynamics of disabled people's journeys through life to career success than could be obtained by a more quantitative, questionnaire-based study. As Lofland and Lofland (1984) suggest, the objective of qualitative research is to collect the richest data that is achievable using techniques like semi-structured interviewing. Also, it calls for subjective judgements as well as bringing into play my own consciousness, experience of career development and disability.

The interview schedule used in the research was influenced by the works of Sonnenfeld and Kotter (1982), White, Cox and Cooper (1992), and Cox and Cooper (1988) who identified the areas deemed most significant to a non-disabled individual's career development and success.

Research setting

The time and place of the interviews were arranged according to the respondents' convenience. Most of them took place at their own homes or work places, although in two instances the most convenient setting was a public bar or cafe. The decision to carry out the research in the home or work environment was made because either setting was thought to offer a relaxed and accessible environment for the respondent to function comfortably, thus providing the opportunity to assemble data most likely to answer the research questions.

The data collected are integrated with existing theory and discussed in the following chapters.

Conceptions of success

This was concerned with the disabled high-flyers' subjective perceptions of career success. It explores internal and external measures of success.

Childhood

There is extensive discourse on the effects of childhood events, and parental and sibling relationships, on later life. Therefore the principal focus here was on the significance of parent–child relationships and parental expectations on the career success and orientation of high-flyers, in particular disabled high-flyers. The role of childhood socialisation was also examined, particularly critical childhood events and the influence of social class.

Education

Education is an important prerequisite to vocational success. This section concerns itself with the level and subject of education. Furthermore, data was obtained on the type of education received (i.e. segregated or mainstream) and how this was believed to influence the career pursuits of disabled individuals. The issue of whether the acquisition of qualifications was part of a long-term career plan was explored.

Personality, motivation and work centrality

The objective here was to identify significant personality traits, conceptualised by the respondents to be the most beneficial to their career success. The investigation concentrates on three major areas of personality and motivation, namely *locus of control*, *need for achievement* and *work centrality*, which were all examined using qualitative measures.

Locus of control – concerned with the individuals' perception of how their received rewards are controlled, either internally (i.e. by hard work and determination) or externally (i.e. by luck or fate).

Need for achievement – assessed using Murray's (1938) definition. The aim was to seek information on the respondents' desire to achieve, by identifying what motivates and satisfies them, and the main things they require from a job.

Work centrality – examines the amount of time and effort the respondent spends on work-related activities and the extent to which their work is central to their life.

Although quantitative scales are usually used to measure locus of control (e.g. Career Locus Questionnaire designed by Makin, 1987), this research measures it qualitatively via a semi-structured interview. Respondents were asked specific open-ended questions, influenced by psychological literature such as: which of their characteristics did they perceive to be beneficial to their career success; what did they do when faced with an obstacle; what motivates them; and what satisfies them in terms of their career.

Career choice, progression and turning points

This is concerned with the concepts of career choice and career progression, recognising the impact of differential life roles and life events on individual career choice and orientation. Particular attention was paid to the career patterns adopted by disabled people, attempting to uncover which career paths they are most likely to follow and the reasons behind this.

Disability and gender played a significant part in each phase of the high-flyers' lives, and are therefore discussed, to a certain extent, in every section.

CHAPTER 2

The Role of Disabled People in the Workplace

The reasonable man adapts himself to the world, the unreasonable man persists in trying to adapt the world to himself. Therefore, all progress depends on the unreasonable man.

George Bernard Shaw, Man or Superman

WHAT IS DISABILITY?

The definition of 'disability' follows the growing orientation of disability rights and disability politics that developed from active groups of disabled people in society, particularly from the 1970s. Arguments over definitions are often reduced to technical issues, but they are, in effect, fundamental to the whole issue of equal opportunities and legitimise one way of thinking over another (Swain *et al.*, 1993).

Prior to the emergence of the politics of disability, disability was construed as a purely medical phenomenon, reducing it to a problem of the individual. All professions, especially the medical profession, failed to involve people with disabilities in decisions that affected them, but instead treated them as passive objects of intervention, treatment and rehabilitation (Oliver, 1990). French (1986) contends that people with disabilities believe that medical professionals are unable to perceive them other than as people needing help, and that they become disturbed if their diagnosis is contradicted.

There is ample evidence to suggest that disabled people are frequently dissatisfied with the care they receive. Sutherland (1981) discovered that many disabled people have recollections of medical staff treating them in a patronising and alienating manner.

According to the traditional individualistic medical model, the reason why disabled people encounter inequalities and discrimination in their daily lives is because they deviate from the societal norm. So, in this respect, disability is explained in terms of individually based functional limitations. Such a notion maintains that disability is seen as a personal tragedy, an approach that is recognised as considerably harmful to disabled people, causing a downward spiral of the social and economic position of this minority group. Furthermore, this approach encourages the development of social policies which attempt to compensate victims for the misfortune that has befallen them and which do not accord them many of the basic rights to citizenship; thus encouraging dependency. Segregated education and the benefits system were cases in point (Oliver, 1996). For instance, the provision of segregated education was seen as beneficial for disabled children as it offers them specialist teaching and access to small classes with suitable facilities. Further, it has been argued to protect disabled children from the 'rough and tumble' of a 'normal' environment (Barnes, 1991; Middleton, 1999). However, Barnes (1991) argues that being in a segregated school community shields individuals from the realities of society, socially isolating them and failing to teach them the skills necessary to grow up and lead an autonomous life. As argued by the BCODP (British Council of Disabled People, 1986), segregated education reinforces the myth that disabled people are 'eternal children'. The benefits and drawbacks of segregated education will be discussed at greater length in Chapter 5.

As argued by Hendey (1999), disabled people can and do face problems as a direct result of their physical impairment. Individuals can develop painful muscle spasms and respiratory tract disorders (Bax and Smyth, 1989; Chamberlain, 1993; DCDP, 1992; Morris, 1989). These may place a severe burden upon the individual in terms of pain, reduced mobility and increased dependency, and associated difficulties in achieving adult status through employment, having an active social life or enjoying a romantic partnership. Therefore it is important to stress that not all the problems faced by disabled people are social in origin. Some are directly linked to an individual's impairment and the management of such.

Hendey (1999) maintains that although disability does have a personal cost that cannot be omitted from the equation, it is not the sole cause of the difficulties encountered by disabled people. The medical perspective of disability fails to acknowledge the extent to which disability results from the restrictions and disabling barriers caused by the social construction of a society designed to meet the needs of the non-disabled majority. This supports Hahn (1988), who recognises that the fundamental restrictions of a disability may be located in the surroundings people encounter rather than in the disabled individual. Swain *et al.* (1993) argue that disabled people are often denied full citizenship due to the barriers in attitudes, institutions, language and culture, organisation and delivery of support services, and the power relations and structures that constitute society. So, these perspectives can be combined to support Barnes' (1991) definition of disability as being 'the loss or limitation of opportunities to take part in the normal life of the community on an equal level with others due to physical and social barriers'(p.2).

This perspective rejects the personal tragedy approach taken by the medical model. The theory of disabled people being victims of social oppression is, undeniably, having an influence on society's motivations to create full democratic participation by the twenty-first century.

Wood's (1981) individual-based perspective of disability, like the medical model, sees the inability to perform an activity as the result of a problem with the individual. It has been identified as being particularly useful in differentiating the social consequences of the impairment from the impairment itself. However, Croxen (1984) criticises the approach for attempting to depoliticise what is essentially a political issue. She argues that because Wood's classification is largely blinkered by the assumed benevolent neutrality of medical knowledge, its vision fails to capture the degree to which disability is socially constructed. This social interpretation of disability emerged in the early 1970s during the combined struggles of disabled people living in residential institutions and the community. The focus was on strengthening the spontaneous demands of disabled people for full integration into all aspects of mainstream society. Some years later the social interpretation of disability was developed and explained by Mike Oliver (1990), a disabled academic, as a 'social model of disability'. However, although the social model helped spread the idea that the way society is organised is disabling, the fact that being 'normal' is still very important for employment, promotion and gaining an independent livelihood means that the medical model also remains extremely significant to the lives of disabled people.

The perspectives discussed above are central to the understanding of the lives and career development of disabled people, an important focus of this book. As reported in the literature reviewed, and evidenced by the voices of the disabled high-flyers in Chapter 4, the medical model of disability had a significant influence on what was expected of disabled children by their parents, the medical profession and society as a whole. According to the medical interpretation of disability, individuals with impairments are helpless, dependent and incapable of making their own decisions (Shearer, 1981). Therefore the medical perspective invariably influenced the childhood socialisation of the disabled high-flyers, in terms of what their parents expected of them, gender socialisation or lack of it, the experiences they had as children and the relationships they developed with others. Further, it encouraged the decision for disabled children to be educated in segregated institutions, seen to permit intensive one-to-one attention and instruction in an environment free from the intervention of mainstream barriers, although it is criticised for creating artificial barriers between disabled and non-disabled peers (Barnes, 1991). So, as education and childhood are seen as important to occupational choice and achievement, one can argue that the medical perspective of disability had an important part to play in understanding what influenced the disabled high-flyers' career development and success.

This book also recognises that, for disabled people, their impairment is an important part of their self, and does invariably have an impact on how and when their life moves from one stage to another, and the range of choices available to them. For example, young disabled people may experience frequent periods of hospitalisation and treatment, due to their medical condition, which can cause severe disruptions to their education and future orientations.

However, this book has also undeniably been inspired by the social model of disability to highlight how the social and physical organisation of society has contributed to the disabling of individuals with physical impairments, and serves to hinder their democratic participation in mainstream activities such as education and employment. For instance, an article in the *Psychologist* (Cornwall, 1995) reported how potential undergraduate students with disabilities still had to apply to physically accessible universities with appropriate facilities, rather than those with the most suitable courses. Similarly, Preece (1995), in a survey of the educational experiences of 44 disabled adults, identified barriers to course attendance at both attitudinal and practical levels, often resulting in underachievement.

DISABLED PEOPLE AT WORK

An individual's status in economic society is somewhat determined by the expectations and ideologies of many agents of socialisation and the psychosocial structure of society (that is, the social factors and individual interactive behaviour that influence the composition of society). Information about an individual's professional status indicates their social and political beliefs and their resultant placement in the social system. Furthermore, it attributes various characteristics, expectations of others and patterns of behaviour to the individual. As Vroom (1964) postulates, a person's occupational status greatly influences the way in which other people respond to them. For instance, according to Young (1981), doctors are often viewed as God-like figures; strong, powerful, clever and in control of some kind of magic. This popular, socially approved image of health professionals can itself be a barrier for disabled people, who are generally perceived as being too weak and ineffective to succeed as health and care professionals (French, 1986). It is possible that some of these negative perceptions of disabled people may colour professional attitudes, albeit unconsciously, and thus cause an otherwise conventional career path to be redirected.

Numerous studies suggest that, like women and people from ethnic minorities, disabled people are particularly influenced by others' perceived acceptance or rejection of their achievements (Freeman, 1971; Horner, 1972). According to Government statistics (Department for Education and Employment, 1996; Office of Population Census and Surveys, 1988) and research projects, they come out extremely badly on nearly every aspect of mainstream life. Such aspects include employment (Barnes, 1991), education (Barton, 1988; Disability Rights Commission, 2000) and social class (Borsay, 1986).

There is little dispute that people with disabilities are more likely to be out of work than their non-disabled contemporaries (DRC, 2000). In the mid-1960s the general unemployment rate was below 2 per cent while among disabled people it was over 7 per cent. In the early 1980s the gap narrowed somewhat, not because unemployment among disabled people declined but because of the rise in unemployment generally (Grover and Gladstone, 1982). The Labour Force Survey (LFS) consistently demonstrated that people who have a health problem or a disability that limits the kind of work they can do have high rates of unemployment (EOR, July/August 1994). Its statistics show that in the summer of 1993, 25 per cent of men and 18 per cent of women in this category were unemployed, compared with unemployment rates of 12 per cent and 8 per cent respectively in the working population as a whole.

In some cases disabled people are discouraged, by explicit UK governmental regulations, from accepting employment for fear of their welfare income or subsidised medical coverage and attendant care being deducted or taken away altogether (McCarthy, 1988). However, current initiatives aimed at tackling barriers to paid employment faced by disabled people are welcome, in particular the recent decision to disregard earnings when assessing charges to be made for community care services (including direct payments) and eligibility for Independent Living Grants. The introduction of Joint Investment Plans (JIPs) have a role in tackling a range of barriers experienced by young disabled people, including making sure that community care assessment accounts for employment needs and that delivery of support services facilitate employment (Morris, 2002). The Department of Health, the Department for Education and Skills, and the Department for Work and Pensions all have a responsibility to encourage local agencies to make sure their JIPs do this.

The Government's Disability Discrimination Act, implemented in December 1996, provides a number of new rights to disabled people, attempting to illegalise their segregation from various spheres of mainstream society, including employment, goods and services, and accommodation. The Act makes all UK employers of 20 or more employees legally liable for discriminating against disabled persons in recruitment, promotion, training, working conditions and dismissal. Clause 6 of the Act imposes a duty on the employer to make reasonable accommodations in cases when working arrangements or physical features of the work place put the disabled person concerned at a substantial disadvantage in comparison with non-disabled persons.

However, even with such legislation there are a substantially lower percentage of disabled people, compared to non-disabled people, in employment. According to recent evidence, reported in the Labour Force Survey (2001), the economic activity rate for people with disabilities was approximately half that of non-disabled people. It also shows that disabled people are nearly eight times as likely as non-disabled people to be out of work and claiming benefits. However, the survey indicates that the differentiation between the two groups is less substantial in the actual type of employment, although disabled people are slightly more likely to work in non-manual jobs or be self-employed. Quantitative data generated from the survey demonstrate that the likelihood of pursuing part-time employment is similar for people with and without disabilities.

The Employer's Forum on Disability states that only 9 per cent of disabled people report themselves as actively looking for work. However, according to Lysaght, Townsend and Orser (1994), many disabled people classified as 'economically inactive' might be seeking work if appropriate conditions were available. These may involve work schedule modification, and making adaptations to existing premises, work places and equipment. Such measures need not necessarily be complicated or expensive.

When disabled people do find work, the majority find themselves in poorly paid, low-skilled, low-status jobs which are both unrewarding and undemanding (Burchardt, 2000). They are likely to be unemployed for longer periods than non-disabled people, despite equivalent qualifications. In addition, the earnings of disabled people are on average one-quarter less than those who are non-disabled, and they are often underemployed, that is doing work that does not fully utilise their skills (Jolly, 2000). Also, disabled workers are likely to endure sub-standard working conditions and they have fewer chances for promotion (Jolly, 2000). According to official statistics from the Labour Force Survey (2001), 19 per cent of the population of working age are disabled and approximately half of those are in paid employment. Disabled workers hold 11 per cent of managerial and senior official positions (434,443 posts out of a total of 3,994,968 positions), and 10 per cent of positions in professional occupations (321,273 posts out of a total of 3,221,809 positions).

In their study of successfully employed women with disabilities, Hayslip (1981) and Johnson (1983) found that the majority had achieved careers at the lower end of the service sector and very few of them were employed in managerial or professional occupations. French (1986), in a content analysis of the career literature of 26 health and caring professionals, discovered that disabled people were never specifically invited to apply for the jobs, yet ten of these occupations sought candidates with the ability to empathise and understand ill and disabled people.

Despite the strong body of evidence to suggest that disabled people are as efficient, if not more efficient, than their non-disabled counterparts, they are frequently assumed to be less capable than non-disabled workers, to have a relatively high rate of absenteeism and to be more accident-prone (Kettle, 1979). Furthermore, it is believed that disabled people do not possess the appropriate communication skills required to adopt a professional role. Many of these negative conceptions of disability stem from the Bible and nineteenth and early-twentieth century fiction which, Reiser and Mason (1990) suggest, can have a powerful influence on public beliefs and perceptions. Classical literature used for education, such as *Treasure Island* and *Heidi*, which portray characters with impairments as pitiful, sad and dependent on others, can generate prejudicial attitudes against people with disabilities which can have a negative influence on how their lives develop in a non-disabled society.

Women, disability and employment

While people with disabilities experience an obvious disadvantage in the labour market, both disabled and non-disabled women are less likely to be employed than their male counterparts. In 1984, Kutner found marked differences in both groups. Blaxter's (1976) study illustrated, through case studies, the obstacles encountered by female job seekers, with and without professional qualifications. It was found that, despite the considerable sexism in the employment sector, the greatest obstacle proved to be physical disability. This implies that, for a disabled woman, the disability plays a predominant role in the formulation of identity status and that gender is secondary to this. For instance, when a feminist woman who is disabled decides not to act out the feminine role, her behaviour will not be recognised as a positive act, but as part of being disabled (Campling, 1981). However, according to Low (1996), a non-disabled identity can be achieved if people with disabilities successfully negotiate the physical environment.

Perry's (1984) research found a tendency for women with disabilities to feel they are less likely than non-disabled women to attract a supportive spouse and, consequently, experience greater pressure to take on the breadwinner role than other women. Furthermore, one of the most common assumptions made about disabled women is that they are asexual (Hayslip, 1981; Matthews, 1983). They are not expected to engage in romantic relationships and, if they do, long-term relationships are expected to dissolve as a consequence of the disability. It can be argued that women with disabilities try to compensate by being better at their work, and by becoming superachievers (Hayslip, 1981). This need for disabled women to excel themselves in work can be argued to be engendered by their desire to find a purpose to their life. As they are denied the opportunity to fulfil traditional wife/mother roles, they may go down another avenue to discover their life's purpose. By pursuing high-status careers, women with disabilities may have the opportunity to override their ascribed status and develop an identity that is respected by society. Slappo and Katz (1989) indicated that the 170 women in their survey of women with disabilities in non-traditional careers were predominately unmarried and had a great deal of personal initiative, persistence and assertiveness. Although the women with disabilities in professional occupations were not dissimilar to their non-disabled counterparts in terms of their characteristics and drive, the obstacles to their careers differed. It was found that the women with disabilities experienced prejudice concerning their disabilities whereas the career journeys of the non-disabled women were hindered by their gender.

Social stratification and class

The concept of social stratification refers to any arrangement of structured inequality among social groups and is derived from the multilayered structure of society. In modern societies, the most important of these layers is social class, which is used to compare, categorise and differentiate individuals and groups on the basis of their occupation. As defined by Reid (1981, p.6): 'social class is a grouping of people into categories on the basis of their occupation.'

In Britain, the best known hierarchy of stratification, based on social class, is the Registrar General's Scale of Social Classes. The Registrar General had a list of 20,000 separate occupational titles which were grouped into 223 occupational units and categorised into five social classes. Occupations entered in a given class are, as far as possible, of comparable general standing in the community. Educational and economic factors are of great importance in deciding which class a particular occupation is allocated. There is a strong correlation between a person's income, their educational achievement and their social class. According to the Registrar General's Classification of Occupations (1970), social class I is exclusively non-manual (professional), and V exclusively manual (unskilled). Classes II and IV are mixed, although the former is predominantly non-manual and the latter predominantly manual. Persons whose basic occupational status is class IV or V, but who have achieved foreman or managerial status, are allocated to class III.

Occupation and income are obviously important determinants of possessions, style of life and place of living in a society based on a cash nexus (Reid, 1981). Since for much of society income is the main source of wealth, occupation is a good indicator of the economic situation of a person and a family. Furthermore, pursuing an occupation takes up a considerable amount of people's time and life, and typically places them in a situation where they interact with particular groups of people in particular ways. Thus it is inevitable that an individual's experience of work influences his/her perception of the world. This is emphasised by the words of Adam Smith:

> The very genius which appears to distinguish men of different professions, when grown up to maturity, is not upon many occasions so much the cause, as the effect of the division of labour. (cited in O'Donnell, 1981, p.124)

He contends that the differentiation of lifestyles of middle-class and working-class citizens is more a consequence of nurture than nature. This can be illustrated from data collected by the American National Opinion Research Center that discussed the relationship between family income, father's occupation and education, and the student's plans for graduate study. Of those participants whose fathers' occupational status was classified 'professional', 38.5 per cent of them had plans for further study, compared to 21.8 per cent whose fathers were farmers. Judging by these statistics it seems that family background, in terms of social class, can have an influence on occupational aspirations and social participation.

Gottfredson (1981) argues that children's differential occupational aspirations can be explained by differences in social class groups. She notes that individuals from lower social class backgrounds are more positive about lower-level jobs than are individuals from higher social classes. This is similar to the findings of Sewell and Shah (1968) who demonstrated a significant positive correlation between social class and aspirations. Their study evidenced that the higher social class youngsters, within all ability groups, have the higher aspirations. Similarly Bowles and Gintis (1976) insisted on the unimportance of the genetic inheritance of IQ and the prime importance of socio-economic background in explaining economic success. The best hope for obtaining a high income, they maintain, is to be born into a high socio-economic background. Although social class is not static throughout an individual's life, the social class background into which they are born is undoubtedly a major factor in their future life status. It is an influential agent for the type of education, peer group, interests and activities pursued, as well as occupational choice and success.

Although class is an extremely powerful determinant of occupational status, the strength of its influence is diluted if the other psychosocial variables in the individual's make-up do not conform to those of the social expectations. Although disability is more common in the working class (Wedge and Prosser, 1973), disabled people are still more likely to be unemployed and in low-paid jobs when class is held constant. For instance, a middle-class disabled man may not share the same privileges and opportunities as a middle-class non-disabled man. However, Pfeiffer (1991) reports that the social class structure that enables white males to have access to education, high-status occupations and high income still prevails in the disability community. According to his study, disabled white men from middle-class backgrounds still have certain advantages over their working-class counterparts in their quality of life and diversity of opportunities. They are more likely to have financial support, and thus greater access to health care, assistive technology and specialised equipment and services that enable them to participate in mainstream society.

It can be confidently stated that the higher the social class from which an individual comes, regardless of their physicality, the greater the probability that he/she will aspire to those occupations that society has defined as the most socially prestigious and economically rewarding. Larson (1977) argues that the superiority over, and distance from, the working class is one of the major characteristics that all professionals and would-be professionals have in common. Furthermore, Sutherland (1981) contends that it is much easier to counteract the stereotyped issues of disability on which discrimination is founded if one has a middle-class background and accent, a university education, and the particular type of articulacy and confidence these factors produce. Therefore it is fair to say that the power of class still predominates in the disability community and is recognised as a major determinant of occupational status.

PROSPECTS FOR DISABLED PEOPLE IN THE TWENTY-FIRST CENTURY

As discussed earlier in the chapter, disabled people are far more likely than non-disabled people to be economically inactive. This stems from the fact that the majority of people in the former group are only too aware of the physical and social obstacles facing them in their search for work. They are also more likely than their non-disabled counterparts to be underemployed or to work in the secondary labour market where jobs have low wages, low skill levels, poor working conditions, little job security, and few if any possibilities for promotion and advancement. Routine office work, general labourers, catering jobs and cleaners would fall into this category (McCrudden, 1982). There is not only a problem with getting employed; staying employed has also been seen to be a problem for disabled people. The findings of a recent study by the Joseph Rowntree Foundation, reported in *Disability Now* (December 2000), revealed that one in three disabled people lose their jobs within a year of starting.

However, it is widely recognised that people are the key to success in any work arena. Talented people, whether disabled or non-disabled, are a valuable commodity and worth the investment of time and resources (Foster and MacLeod-Gallinger, 1999). The fact that a person has a disability does not necessarily mean they do not possess the skills required to become economically active and proficient in a particular line of work. While society is never free of discrimination and different forms of prejudice, certain individuals have the ability to combat the prejudice, turn the obstacles into opportunities and achieve success against the odds. Although each disabled person may have been driven to achieve success by different personal attributes or experiences, empowerment of the disability culture may also be facilitated by various societal developments. One is information technology, which is increasing in influence and importance in the corporate world. Cornes (1988) reported that technology has changed the nature of jobs in a typical organisation and has created opportunities for people with disabilities, who are usually at a disadvantage when competing for jobs with their non-disabled contemporaries. Many studies have confirmed that this minority group share a vested interest in technology which provides them with the means to overcome communication barriers and neutralise the effects of many kinds of disablement (Hawkridge, Vincent and Hales, 1985). Cornes (1988) suggests that the new technologies create jobs in which physical requirements are replaced by electronic skill and precision, and which are particularly suitable for people with disabilities.

The introduction of telecommunications systems has enhanced the globalisation of industrial activities over international boundaries, while at the same time reducing the need to travel on a regular basis. This shift towards the 'mobile worker' has created opportunities for people with disabilities in the employment sector as the telecommunication links between individual remote terminals grant access to communication worldwide from one physical location. Therefore technology has permitted individuals with physical impairments to succeed in employment as it allows them to establish global connections without the need to travel and it enables disabled people to deliver lectures without the need to speak.

A number of changes and developments have been made in UK society, over the years, to help increase the participation of disabled persons in the labour market. These include implementing legislation such as the Civil Rights (Disabled Persons) Bill, originally enforced in 1993 and amended in 1996. This engendered the use of 'reasonable accommodations', including acquisition or modification of equipment or devices; provision of qualified readers, personal assistants or interpreters; reduction in working hours; and reallocation of certain secondary duties. These accommodations were seen, by governmental legislation, as a way of providing workers with disabilities with the means to achieve their most desirable goals. Work schedule modification was thought to enhance the success of employees with severe disabilities who may have limited tolerance for 'productive work activity' (Lysaght *et al.*, 1994). An investigation conducted by Lysaght *et al.* (1994) indicated that, in many instances, the occupational success of people with disabilities is partly attributed to work schedule modification. The investigation revealed that the process of job schedule modification has positive implications for this minority group, in that it not only enhances their quality of life, but also leads to an improvement in job performance. Therefore although, as argued by Milton Friedman (1970), the primary social responsibility of a business may be to maximise profits, the workforce has to be presented with desirable social processes with which an increase in profits can be achieved.

Another important factor in this optimism regarding the career success of disabled people is the strong, vibrant and international disability movement (Oliver, 1990). The sheer size of the disability problem has engendered the establishment of organisations and companies that create opportunities for disabled people, who were rejected by mainstream employers, to work and build a career of their choice. Such companies include Graeae, a national touring theatre company for disabled people which employed some of the high-flyers, who feature in this book, before they moved into more mainstream work. Another such company is Candoco, an international integrated dance company. This professional dance company of disabled and non-disabled dancers was established and is managed by a disabled woman, another one of the high-flyers in this study.

The increasing emergence of disability-related organisations such as Scope, RADAR and Skill, which seek to serve and represent disabled people, also creates new employment opportunities for people with disabilities at all levels of the organisational hierarchy, including managerial and professional levels. Furthermore many of the strategies implemented by customer service organisations to serve the needs of the disabled population have called for the advice of, and consultation with, disabled people themselves. The growth of both disability organisations and of disability-related work in mainstream organisations provides opportunities for disabled people to use their skills and experience to help a disabled customer base, while building a career for themselves. This is demonstrated in this book by the career situations of some of the high-flyers.

Finally, the appearance of many more disabled people in general mainstream social situations is beginning to change public consciousness concerning their ability. It has been suggested that people within society might become more tolerant of accepting disability if they were more aware and had greater understanding of it. Increased integration of disabled people into mainstream activity would facilitate this process. Furthermore, it would serve to disprove traditional stereotypes and misrepresentation of disability in the media and popular discourse. As mentioned earlier in the chapter, disabled people have historically been represented as passive, destructive, dependent and tragic. However, their recent inclusion and involvement in economic production and mainstream culture have served to dilute such negative images and generate more positive interpretations of disability. This book shows disabled people in prestigious professional positions in mainstream society, and tells their real stories.

CHAPTER 3

Meanings of Success for High-Flyers

Success is counted sweetest by those who ne'er succeed.

Emily Dickinson, 'Success'

It is becoming more apparent that the ways in which people perceive, think about and explain success can vary tremendously (Colwill, 1984). Lewis (1998) contends that for many, the desire for success is the driving force in their lives; some will achieve it through coincidence or luck, but for others it requires careful planning and hard work. It can be large of scale and high in profile or it can be created in smaller, but no less valuable, nuggets of satisfaction – hidden from the outside world – that come from reaching personal goals. For example, for Evelyn Glennie, world famous solo percussionist who was classified profoundly deaf at the age of 12, success has two dimensions: '...the private personal side of success where happiness needs to be achieved. Then there is what the public sees – "the Evelyn Glennie success"' (Lewis, 1998, p.416).

Further, success is driven by the individual and their perception of what it represents to them. Each person has his/her own preferences, perspectives and expectations. As cited in Lewis (1998), success for David Blunkett, the former Home Secretary, is concerned with fulfilling desired aspirations and looking beyond obstacles. The *Concise Oxford Dictionary* (1997) defines success as 'The accomplishment of an aim; a favourable outcome; the attainment of wealth, fame, position; a thing or person that turns out well'.

This definition suggests that success has external and internal dimensions. Therefore, it implies that success can be seen not only as something that can be quantified through external criteria such as hierarchical position and salary level (e.g. Melamed, 1995; O'Reilly and Chatman, 1994), but can also incorporate factors that are internal to the individual, such as accomplishment of a personal goal. This two-dimensional definition of success will be explored in more detail later in the chapter.

Success is a broad concept which can be applied to a variety of situations and contexts. One such situation is careers, the focus of this book.

TRADITIONAL CONCEPTUALISATIONS OF CAREER SUCCESS

Organisational careers have been traditionally conceptualised as linear trajectories where individuals advance hierarchically within a single organisation over the course of their careers. For example, Driver (1988) discusses 'steady state' and 'linear' careers marked by a common work role for life and upward mobility.

In the past a career was defined as an organised path taken by an individual across time and space (Van Maanen and Schein, 1977). Although this definition does not imply success or failure, it is usually perceived as reflecting systematic progression in any occupation (Hall, 1976). However, post-entrepreneurialism is hastening the demise of the traditional hierarchical career. Recently scholars have started building new models to understand the changing nature of careers. Given today's more volatile and unstable organisational environment, individuals can no longer expect lifetime employment within one organisation or a steady climb up the corporate ladder. Increasingly, individuals are experiencing involuntary job loss, lateral job movement both within and across organisational boundaries, and career interruptions (Arthur and Rousseau, 1996; Eby and De Matteo, 2000; Sullivan, 1999). According to Kanter (1989), people no longer climb the career ladder, but instead become multi-skilled by moving from job to job. This has led to changes in the nature of careers and in the meaning of career success.

Derr (1986) defines career success as being able both to live out the subjective and personal values one really believes in and to make a contribution to the world of work. This incorporates both psychological success, which Hall and Mirvis (1996, p.26) describe as 'a feeling of pride and personal accomplishment that comes from knowing one has done one's personal best'. Alternatively, as Jasolka, Beyer and Trice (1985) noted, career success is an evaluative concept, so judgements of career success are dependent on who does the judging.

In a body of previous writings, an individual's career success was said to be measured according to the judgement of others, on the basis of relatively objective and visible career accomplishments and using the metrics of pay and ascendancy (Judge and Bretz, 1994; London and Stumpf, 1982). Furthermore, research suggests that job tenure and total time in one's occupation are both positively related to career attainment (Cox and Harquail, 1991; Gutteridge, 1973).

According to various theories of career success (as mentioned above), positive work-related outcomes or achievements are a consequence of both intrinsic and extrinsic factors. As extrinsic and intrinsic aspects of career success are conceptually and empirically distinct, many theorists, including Judge and Bretz (1994), stress that it is important to consider both in order to provide a broad measure of career success. As Boudreau, Boswell and Judge (2001) argue, career success reflects the accumulated interaction between a variety of individual, organisational and societal norms, behaviours and work practices.

Occupational title

In the research literature, career success has often been defined in terms of a person's occupational position (e.g. Kotter, 1982). Researchers often refer to this type of career success as 'objective success' because it can be measured by objectively observable metrics such as income level and hierarchical position (Gattiker and Larwood, 1988; Judge and Bretz, 1994; Kotter, 1982). In the popular press, a selection of discourses on careers imply that individuals enjoy 'successful' careers by virtue of occupational status, which is guaranteed through certain career strategies, education and the 'proper' entrance requirements. Thus, for example, although there may be no particular formula for success, professionals may be considered 'successful' as they are required to undergo extensive specialised training and tend to excel in particular fields of expertise. This was the criterion used by Lewis (1998) when selecting professionals to interview for his popular discourse, *Reflections on Success*. They were considered to have been successful in one or more particular fields, ranging across business, politics, art, entertainment, sport and journalism.

Carr-Saunders and Wilson (1944) suggested that the major criterion for professional status is the presence of an intellectual technique, acquired by special training, which performs a service for society and is unavailable to the lay person. In Western society, as individuals progress up the occupational hierarchy as a result of increasing specialisation, they are likely to experience upward mobility in terms of their social status and income, and are ascribed a corresponding label that informs others of their achievement of objective success.

Even the most untrained observer will recognise the connection between occupations and social status. An individual's occupational status defines them with respect to their position in society and becomes the source of motivation for career striving, which facilitates the setting and attainment of various goals. Knowledge of what a person does provides handy indicators of what a person has achieved and thus where they fit within the social system. This may be the reason why researchers, including Cooper and Hingley (1985) and White *et al.* (1992), used occupational status to identify their target sample. White *et al.*, who conducted an investigation into female high-flyers, defined a 'successful woman' as one who had advanced up the organisational ladder to occupy executive or managerial positions in high-status occupations. Thus their sample included lawyers, management consultants, high-level politicians and accountants. Similarly Cooper and Hingley's (1985) 'change makers' were professionals who had made or were continuing to make a lasting change in attitudes within their own particular sphere of activity. These representatives were drawn from politics, industry, business, the arts and medicine. They included 32 individuals who were identified by their high-status occupational titles such as a managing director, Chairman of British Rail and President of the National Union of Mineworkers. For Cox and Cooper (1989), in their study of the 'High Flyers', a successful manager was defined as one who had reached the top of a major organisation.

Caplow (1958) believes that occupational title has displaced other status-fixing attributes such as ancestry, religious office, political affiliation or personal character, and has become a meaningful indicator of individual income and educational attainment. An individual's occupational title indicates that they have made certain sacrifices to attain these highly valued positions in society. These sacrifices, according to functional theory, are later compensated for by the higher rewards attached to such societal positions.

However, although objective career success has been used, by many researchers including myself, to identify people in different positions of power, authority and wealth, the subjective evaluations of career success must not be ignored. Past research (e.g. Gattiker and Larwood, 1989; Howard and Bray, 1988) has suggested that subjective success to be positively, but, moderately, related to objective success.

IMPORTANCE OF SUBJECTIVE CONCEPTIONS OF CAREER SUCCESS

According to Bailyn (1989), the easiest option is to assume that external definitions coincide with internal ones. She suggests that it is instructive to note how readily one falls into the presumption that upwardly mobile careers are experienced as successful even when one's own definition specifically denies such a connection.

Nevertheless, some researchers have argued that it is imperative to give serious consideration to individuals' subjective conceptions of career success in order to gain an improved understanding of what they actually want from their careers and the impact this has on their career development (Parker and Arthur, 2000; Sturges, 1999). For example, Sturges' (1999) study shows how more managers expressed a concern with things like accomplishment, achievement and personal recognition than with hierarchical position and pay alone, as can be illustrated by the following quote:

> If I felt my job was important and I met my criteria for doing a good job
> ... and I could do that job well, then to me, that would be my definition

of career success ... it wouldn't necessarily mean being promoted or getting to the top of the tree. (Sturges, 1999, p.242)

Knowledge of how individuals define career success has been fundamental to the appreciation of the 'success' and 'failure' of a career, because, as Gunz (1989) states, a career that is perceived in 'objective' terms 'only scratches the surface' of what a career means to individuals. Further, as Sturges (1996) suggests, such knowledge about subjective career success will provide organisations with some indication of potential alternative foci for future career development and human resource management initiatives. As Gattiker and Larwood (1988) contend, success criteria can help human resource specialists achieve a fit between the employee's real career opportunities and needs.

Therefore, as has long been acknowledged, careers have two dimensions: internal and external. As Gunz (1989) suggests, the two facets of the career represent the processes of personal and organisational development for the individual. He argues that careers can be seen both as a means of personal development (sometimes called the 'subjective' career) and as a series of externally observable jobs (the 'objective' career).

Derr and Laurent (1989) see the two-dimensional concept of the career as a link between the individual and the social structure, which fuses the observable facts and the individuals' interpretation of their experience. They argue that the two dimensions are interactive and both are strongly influenced by organisational and national culture, as well as individual differences.

The requirement to become more familiar with the internal career perspective, which makes reference to an individual's own preferences for development in an occupation, has been emphasised by examinations such as that conducted by Korman (1980). His study determined that managers often feel alienated from their careers, despite their objective success as indicated by position and income. Another study confirmed that when an individual's career expectations are not satisfied and they feel a lack of affiliation with fellow colleagues, they might experience personal and social alienation (Korman, Wittig-Berman and Lang, 1981). Therefore, it is important to determine if people considered to have hierarchical success are satisfied with their own organisational advancement, because, as Gattiker and Larwood (1986) pointed out, there is a difference between how individuals perceive their accomplishments and how these are perceived by others.

Sturges (1996) discovered that the older managers and women in her study tended to view success more in terms of their own internal criteria of achievement and accomplishment rather than in terms of pay and hierarchical position. She suggests that this could be explained by the delayering of organisations, and the shift in psychological contact between employer and employee, which has caused individuals to rethink what success means in a new organisational context. If the perception is that hierarchical success is no longer available, or provides satisfaction, to certain individuals, they might resort to other, more attainable and potentially more valid models of success. This could be the case for the group of disabled people, some of whom may experience barriers to traditional career advancement.

A body of work suggests that individuals who are not hierarchically successful can still be very satisfied with their careers and thus feel successful (Eby, Butts and Lockwood 2003; Parker and Arthur, 2000). Parker and Arthur (2000) propose that there is a direct relationship between satisfaction and perceived career success, in that if an individual is satisfied in their career they are likely to believe they have achieved their success criteria. Thus, career satisfaction, in this sense, is believed to be derived from intrinsic and extrinsic aspects of their careers, including pay, advancement and developmental opportunities. This implies that for many people success cannot be explained purely in objective external terms, such as pay and position.

Although research has established that pay and promotion opportunities affect job and career attitudes (e.g. Gattiker and Larwood, 1988; Locke, 1976), for some career success may be evaluated in terms of their own goals, which may be influenced by a number of factors including the personal, social and physical. For example, as Greenberg and McCarthy (1990) noted, several studies have shown that women have lower expectations regarding pay and promotion than men. This suggests that female executives with a level of objective outcomes inferior to that of their male counterparts may achieve equal satisfaction (Dreher and Ash, 1990) or, concurrently, female executives with a level equal to that of their male counterparts may achieve greater satisfaction. In a survey of senior managers, Russo, Kelly and Deacon (1991) discovered that for men, the achievement of high rank and salary were significantly correlated with career satisfaction. However, this was not the case for women, who were described as having 'a differential sense of entitlement' and tended to perceive themselves as being on the same competence level as their fellow male colleagues, despite being inferior according to external measures. Keys (1985) discovered the reason for this was that women evaluated their success more in terms of how difficult it was to achieve, rather than the level of their salaries.

A comparable argument could be made with respect to disabled people, especially high-achievers, whose subjective rather than objective career success is more likely to equal that of non-disabled high-achievers. This may be due to attitudinal, physical and social discrimination blocking opportunities for disabled employees to progress in their career and thus achieve objective success alongside their non-disabled colleagues. Furthermore, as was suggested by

Miller (1991), expectations of upward mobility for employees with disabilities differ from expectations for non-disabled employees. He argues that society often expects disabled individuals to be satisfied just to be employed. However, as shown in this book, some disabled people do indeed achieve more than society expects in terms of career development and progression. Therefore although society's expectations of disabled people would inevitably have an influence on all disabled people, it is likely that disabled high-achievers are driven by stronger influences which allow them to rise above society's expectations and not be dragged down by them. This book will examine what motivates disabled high-flyers to achieve beyond societal expectations in a disabling society.

Further, given their experience of upward mobility and career success, it is likely that the disabled high-flyers illustrated in this book would perceive success to be more than just being satisfied to have a job. Such was the case with the disabled individuals in Baumann's (1997) study who were not content with working in low-skilled jobs, and perceived success as about being productive, independent and doing a worthwhile job recognised by the rest of society. These concepts need to be explored further. New research is required that incorporates 'expanded definitions of career success' (Powell and Mainiero, 1992) and uses both internal subjective criteria and external objective criteria of career success. This engenders the concept of a two-dimensional career (as explored above) which, according to Hall (1976), is crucial to understand fully the course of a person's work life.

Boundaryless careers

Career success by hierarchical advancement may be no longer available to many people. As Kanter (1989) points out, climbing the career ladder is being replaced by hopping from job to job. Career responsibility, she claims, is now in the hands of individuals who will need to acquire the current mix of 'portable' skills in order to enjoy a 'successful' career. Handy (1989) argues that the culmination of discontinuous change and new professionalism spells the end of a corporate career for most people.

Some believe that the traditional organisational career may be replaced by a boundaryless career, which moves across boundaries of separate employers and as such is independent of conventional organisational principles (Arthur, 1994; Mirvis and Hall, 1994). If a boundaryless career becomes reality, it will mean that for increasing numbers of the working population, it may not be possible to base career success on any kind of organisational success at all.

Furthermore, recent evidence suggests that employees are changing the way they conceptualise work in terms of the time and effort they spend on work-related activities. In the past, men were quite content to devote their lives to working their way up the company hierarchy while their wives looked after home and family. However, the changing organisation of society and expectations of its members means that non-work roles need not be secondary to work roles for men (Gerson, 1993).

The statement 'Professional status is the key to a long life' (*The Week*, 17 July 1999) is the focus of a research study which revealed that objective career success does have an impact on an individual's persona and psyche development. Peluchette (1993) suggests that subjective career success has implications for one's mental well-being and quality of life, implying that individuals who feel successful are likely to be happier and more motivated, which in turn can enhance their performance. This indicates that there could be significant inter-relationship between career success and life success. This is clearly evident when careers are seen as 'protean'. A protean career is a process that the individual, not the organisation, is managing (Hall, 1976). It acknowledges that work and non-work roles overlap and jointly shape a person's identity and sense of self. Further, a protean career enlarges the career space to enable people to seriously consider taking time off to spend with growing children or to care for ageing parents under the rubric of attaining psychological success. Already there are examples of people 'downshifting' in their careers to pursue hobbies or regain peace of mind (Hyatt, 1990), doing volunteer work to give back to the community and, of course, pursuing the option of working from home, from where house work can spill into paid work.

New ideas of measuring career success for disabled people

Although little, if any, research has been conducted on the subjective perceptions of career success for disabled people, one can argue that their experience of work-place inequity and restricted career advancement can be likened to that of women and other minorities striving to reach senior positions. For example, Davidson (1997) believes that one of the major career barriers faced by women and minorities is attitudinal prejudice such as 'Think manager – Think white male'. The women in her sample felt at a disadvantage compared to their white colleagues in terms of career prospects, recognition and feeling valued by their bosses. Similar prejudiced attitudes, such as the one given below by the manager of a major national company, have had causal effects on the advancement of disabled people in the work place:

> Society is embarrassed and frightened of those people who are 'different', those who have physical disabilities. It's this unease which makes the employment of a disabled person undesirable as their disruptive influence on a team at work can endanger the smooth running and the productivity of the organisation as a whole. (Graham, Jordan and Lamb, 1990, p.10)

Such attitudinal prejudice could be a possible reason why people with disabilities are likely to be disproportionately over-represented in manual, semi-skilled and unskilled employment and under-represented in managerial/professional occupations. For the small percentage who do achieve managerial or professional status there is evidence of a disequilibrium in earnings between themselves and their non-disabled colleagues (Doyle, 1995). Further, they are likely to experience repeated humiliating and debilitating access problems, and difficulty in meeting equipment needs that affected both their work and their relations with colleagues (Hendey and Pascall, 2001).

This does not suggest, however, that disabled people, given their differential psychosocial development, are unable to conform to the conventional idea of objective career success, which is measured in terms of hierarchical position and level of financial reward. Furthermore, it does not suggest that objective career success is unimportant to disabled people. It merely points out that the status and financial levels may be slightly less for this group compared to their non-disabled counterparts.

According to Priestley (1998), many disabled children and teenagers still attend segregated schools or respite care institutions, which exclude them from formulating friendships and social networks that may be useful in their future lives. Also, disabled people's socialisation and development may be interrupted by medical intervention, drug treatments and discrimination that can inhibit their future educational and occupational opportunities. For instance, it is only recently that universities and colleges are able to accommodate disabled students. Prior to the Special Educational Needs Disabilities Act (2001), potential disabled students were not always granted admission to the university or college of their choice on the grounds that their disabilities could not be catered for. They were deterred from pursuing their academic goals due to lack of appropriate support and accessibility for people with impairments on certain mainstream courses (Tinklin and Hall, 1998). Thus, people with disabilities are often restricted in terms of their choice of university and area of specialisation. Their choices are often dependent on disability-related issues which often do not conform to traditional measures of career success. For example, Swinyard and Bond (1980) and Warner and Abegglen (1955) suggest that a disproportionate number of successful executives are graduates from well-regarded universities. However, these universities may not have the facilities to accommodate people with disabilities. So, as a consequence of attending a more accessible but less well-regarded university, many disabled people do not fit the traditional model of a high-flyer. Furthermore, some researchers of career success (e.g. Swinyard and Bond, 1980; Useem and Karabel, 1986) suggest that certain types of education such as medicine, law, engineering and business are rewarded with higher degrees of objective success than others. However, an individual's disability may have a significant influence on the type of subject studied; thus, again, people with disabilities may be prevented from achieving high degrees of objective career success according to classical career development models.

Due to the fact that classical ideas of career development are based on the premise that a career entails a pattern of full-time continuous working (attaching little significance to social, personal or physical demands external to the work environment), it may be more difficult to apply them to disabled people. Lysaght *et al.* (1994) argue that the activity tolerance levels of people with severe physical disabilities have a negative impact on their success in managing a full-time competitive work schedule. The findings of their study suggest that disabled people may often be out of step with orderly models of progression typified by the careers traditionally expected of non-disabled successful males. This may be due to a need to incorporate the influence of personal factors when measuring their career success. For example, a disabled person who suffers from fatigue and loss of energy may produce work of a higher standard if they can work on a flexible basis with regular breaks, rather than if they need to work according to the working pattern invoked by the classical model of career success.

If conceptions of success were remodelled to include the notion of flexible working, this would counteract the fact that disabled people may not be able to work the hours considered average for non-disabled high-flyers. However, this may in itself affirm stereotypical attitudes of disabled people not being equal members of society's workforce. As Sutherland (1981) maintains, the more one conforms to the working patterns of mainstream economic society, the less significant one's disability becomes. Such barriers, obstacles and influences show that there is a serious need to recognise the importance of internal success.

DISABLED HIGH-FLYERS' CONCEPTIONS OF SUCCESS

The interviews with disabled high-flyers generated dense and intricate descriptions of what success meant to them in their own terms. Many of the descriptions were far removed from the conventional notion of what career success in organisation is – hierarchical rank and salary level. The following examples illustrate the range of ideas and definitions which emerged from the interviews:

> The achievement I feel depends on whether I feel I have had a good race or a bad race or I've done something the best that I can. For example, some of the races I have won are not my best races because I don't feel I did as well as I could have done. (Anna, athlete)

Success, now, means to know oneself and to be happy with oneself. I spent 15 years trying to do something which there was no way I was going to do because of society being the way it is, and as soon as I was free of that desire I found that a success. (Greg, actor)

Success, to me, means achieving what I set out to achieve for other people more than for myself. Success, for me, is seeing somebody able to use their house and built environment. (Adrian, architect)

Success is to find ourselves [X company], seven years down the road, being an international touring company in the main dance arena. (Amanda, artistic director of a dance company)

Despite the diversity of notions of success expressed in the interviews, it was possible to identify the use of internal criteria for success in all of the disabled high-flyers' descriptions. This is contrary to previous work on non-disabled professionals which adopts the view that an individual's career success is measured on the basis of relatively objective and visible career accomplishments, using the metrics of pay and ascendancy (Judge and Bretz, 1994; London and Stumpf, 1982). The literature reviewed above offers several reasons why disabled people may define their success more in terms of internal criteria, including the existence of physical and structural barriers in the mainstream work place, and society's low expectations of disabled people.

The kind of internal criteria for success the high-flyers used related in particular to feelings of personal satisfaction/happiness (being happy and satisfied with oneself, one's work and one's life in general); feelings of achievement (having succeeded in achieving one's personal goals); service (helping others by doing a good job); feelings of personal development (the expansion of one's personal capacity and experiences); and equality (being treated on equal terms to colleagues of the same stature). The use of such criteria will be discussed in more detail below.

Some of the disabled high-flyers expressed success as a two-dimensional construct according to external as well as internal criteria. They identified two external criteria for success as important to how they perceived success. These included career progression (achieving increasing respect, prestige and power by climbing the occupational ladder); and material wealth (earning enough money to be able to live a comfortable and healthy lifestyle; being able to afford the goods and services to do so).

There is a variation in the ways that the men and women with congenital or acquired disabilities describe what success means to them. For instance, the female high-achievers with acquired disabilities were more inclined to see their success in terms of personal happiness and being satisfied in whatever they were doing, rather than personal development and progressing up the career ladder.

Typical responses were, 'Success, for me, is being happy in what I'm doing', or 'Personal happiness is what I perceive as success.'

The high-flyers with congenital impairments were more concerned with personal development and obtaining societal equality compared to those with acquired disabilities. For example, Harry, a senior computer analyst who has a congenital impairment, perceives success as two-fold, that is, being seen as equal to his non-disabled colleagues and having a thirst for knowledge and perpetual progression:

> Being accepted within the normal bounds of industry, business and everyday life… Not to be left behind, acceptance by the population. Success to me is also about being satisfied by my in-house training, learning and taking courses which contribute to my personal and professional progression.

Similarly, Marty, a dancer, saw his work as a vehicle with which he could grow and become proficient in new arenas of competence. He welcomed change and challenge which, he felt, ignited hard work and inspiration, in turn breeding success:

> I am always trying to find new things for myself, just to see if I can do them. For example, the work we are doing at the moment, experimenting with voice and text. It's something new, and that inspires me and makes me try harder.

Table 3.1 shows how many of the 31 disabled high-flyers described success in terms of each of the seven criteria identified.

Table 3.1 Criteria for success

Respondent group	Internal Criteria					External Criteria	
	Achieving personal goals	Personal happiness/ satisfaction	Service	Equality	Personal development	Career progress	Material wealth
M/A[1]	6	5	3	0	1	2	2
M/C[2]	7	4	4	4	3	4	2
F/A[3]	2	3	1	1	0	0	0
F/C[4]	5	5	3	1	2	1	0
Total	**20**	**17**	**11**	**6**	**6**	**7**	**4**

[1]Males with acquired disabilities = 8   [3]Females with acquired disabilities = 3

[2]Males with congenital disabilities = 11   [4]Females with congenital disabilities = 9

Internal criteria for success

Three-quarters of the high-flyers perceived success in terms of *achieving personal goals*. This was important to men and women with congenital and acquired impairments. They presented extensive evidence of their achievements in their interviews, but they considered their achievements as successful only when they believed they had worked to the best of their ability to meet their achieved goals. According to Sunny, an established actor, success is about 'achieving the goals you set out'. One of Sunny's biggest goals, from childhood, was to become an actor but he was repeatedly rejected from drama schools. He thought this was because of his congenital physical disability, and the fact it was seen as a problem for drama schools to cope with. So he went to university and got a good degree in Philosophy, Psychology and Sociology. But Sunny was still determined to become an actor, so he started his own theatre company and achieved the goal he set out to achieve.

Like Sunny, Rachel, a Member of Parliament, saw her success as being about 'doing what I set out to do'. This belief has enabled her to overcome barriers to reach her goals. For example, Rachel's first ambition was to become a teacher. However, her doctor maintained that pursuing a teaching profession would be completely impossible for a person with a disability like herself. This only made Rachel more determined, so she attained qualifications to teach English, history and modern studies and went on to pursue a successful teaching profession, starting as a teacher of English and history in a secondary school, and moving up to vice principal and then principal. She did what she set out to do.

Timmy, who at the time of interviewing had worked as the minister of a Baptist Church for five years, saw success as being good at his job and 'doing what I'm meant to do to the best of my ability'. Similarly many women believed their sense of achievement came from them working as hard as they could to do the best they could. Anna, a full-time professional athlete, pointed out:

> The achievement I feel depends on whether I feel I have had a good race or a bad race or I've done something the best that I can. For example, some of the races I have won are not my best races because I don't feel I did as well as I could have done.

Anna's description of success is also linked to the idea of getting a sense of personal achievement from work. This is what success means to Amil, a computer programmer and analyst who had to work twice as hard to get promoted as his non-disabled colleagues but who now manages his own team, leads meetings and makes managerial decisions: 'when you have finished a project, when you know you have done it well, and when you see it working.'

The second group of success criteria was related to *personal happiness and satisfaction*. Just over half of the disabled high-flyers conceived success to mean being happy and satisfied with their current life situations. One of them was Roger, a university professor who became disabled in early adulthood while completing his undergraduate degree. Roger's idea of success is bound up with being happy by living a full life and having the ability to satisfy his life goals and responsibilities.

Greg, currently an actor in theatre and television, spent 15 years as a drummer in a rock and roll band: 'There was a maximum barrier between the audience and the disability.' He explains how his definition of success changed with time and experience:

> Success, now, means to know oneself and to be happy with oneself. I spent 15 years trying to do something which there was no way I was going to do because of society being the way it is, and as soon as I was free of that desire I found that a success.

Over half of the women with congenital disabilities and all three of the women with acquired disabilities identified personal happiness/satisfaction as fundamental to their current success. Lara trained as a sociologist but, soon after, become pulled towards disability arts, realising that was where her heart lay: 'I'm successful in that generally I'm happy. I'm happy, I'm doing something that I believe in and get paid for it.'

Amanda has always been passionate about dance, both as a non-disabled and disabled person. First, dance was her hobby, then her education and now a successful career. As the Artistic Director of a leading international dance company, Amanda believes: 'Success means having satisfaction in what I'm doing.'

Another group of internal criteria was identified as *service*. This was described in terms of helping others do a good job, or being of service to others by doing a good job. Just under a third of the high-flyers defined their success in terms of serving others. This included the feeling that what one did was worthwhile, that it was purposeful and helped others. Needless to say, these included the Church Minister, Timmy, who determines success as 'being a service to others'.

Ed, a TV critic and freelance author, has worked on disability-related matters for many years. However, he has often been the victim of disability discrimination and, throughout his life, has had to struggle to overcome prejudice, get accepted in mainstream society and meet his life goals. Such a battle can be exhausting, but made Ed stronger and more determined to help other disabled people to combat disabling barriers and be part of the majority. He believes that his success will come only after he has made a difference to society:

> I want to make a change to help the old. I want to help to make a change
> for the better. My aim in life is to help our community as much as I can.

Adrian, formerly a lawyer, had to adjust to a different life after falling 20 feet,
breaking his back and becoming a wheelchair user. After months of rehabilitation and the realisation that he could not physically access the courts to practise
law, he trained as an architect. Now, as a senior architect in his own practice,
serving the needs of other disabled people, his feeling of success comes from
helping another person to live comfortably in an enabling environment:

> Success, to me, means achieving what I set out to achieve for other peo-
> ple more than for myself. Success, for me, is seeing somebody able to
> use their house and built environment.

Similarly Ali, a barrister in Sudan, felt successful by being of service to his
country. He says he needs to 'feel I do make a certain contribution to the welfare
of my country'.

Mary, who trained and worked as a solicitor for a number of years before
retiring and becoming a disability consultant, believes that it is important to
have a purposeful role in society. To her, success was about 'feeling that you are
actually doing something that is useful and not wasting your energies on the
desert air'.

Although the other high-flyers did not identify service as a primary component of their success and felt the other criteria were a better reflection of their
own perceptions of success, they did feel it was important to work hard and be
committed. For instance, Amanda felt her position as Artistic Director of a dance
company called for her to do a good job for the company to be successful.

Only a small number of the disabled high-flyers measured success in terms
of *equality*. The majority of these were men with congenital disabilities who considered themselves successful if they were treated on an equal level to their
non-disabled counterparts, be they colleagues, peers or siblings. So for Harry,
the senior computer analyst, success was defined as 'being accepted within the
normal bounds of industry, business and everyday life. Not to be left behind.
Acceptance by the population, by the community'.

Bob, a financial planning advisor, expressed a similar concern and saw his
success in terms of achievement. He felt it to be important 'to achieve the same
goals as my friends and colleagues achieve and not to fall behind, but not necessarily to be any better than they are'.

The high-flyers with acquired disabilities did not include equality in their
definitions of success. This could be because they had already experienced
non-disabled status and, for most, this status remained. As Sutherland (1981)
maintains, individuals who acquired disabilities in adult life have much more
power than those with congenital disabilities in terms of factors such as money,

legal status, position in the social structure and experiences in dealing with encounters with other people. This makes it easier to reject attempts made to coerce them into conforming to a stereotypical role of disabled person with second-class expectations.

However, closely related to individual equality is the desire, expressed by one of the women, to improve and develop the organisation/company to compete equally in a mainstream arena. For instance, Amanda felt that true success was about [X company] being included and competing within mainstream society: 'We're an integrated company so we didn't want to belong to any camp, we want to be in mainstream.'

Although the men with acquired disabilities did not believe that being successful meant being considered as equal to non-disabled counterparts, one of them stated that it was important not to allow issues surrounding his disability to compromise his life choices:

> Success means I am not sensitive or ashamed of my disability. Occasionally people talk over me, the 'does he take sugar' treatment, but it doesn't upset me. I just feel 'if they only realised'. (Roger, university professor)

The final criteria that emerged relates to *personal development*. Only a small number of the professionals perceived this to be important to their conceptions of career success. The majority of these had childhood disabilities. Harry, who was also concerned with being seen as equal to his non-disabled colleagues, referred to success as a thirst for knowledge and perpetual progression which is, he perceives, 'satisfied by my in-house training, learning and taking courses which contribute to my personal and professional progression'.

Marty, a dancer, saw his work as a vehicle through which he could grow and become proficient in new arenas of competence. He welcomed change and challenge which, he felt, ignited hard work and inspiration, in turn breeding success:

> I am always trying to find new things for myself, just to see if I can do them. For example, the work we are doing at the moment, experimenting with voice and text. It's something new, and that inspires me and makes me try harder.

Ali, who also described *service* as a component part of his definition of success, was the only professional with an acquired impairment to perceive success in terms of developing personal capacities and experiences. He considers perpetual personal development to be crucial to feed the human body and mind, and for people to survive in an ever-changing world: 'If a person feels he has attained his required goals and desired destinations then he has to die.'

Personal development was only mentioned by two women with childhood disabilities, in relation to definitions of success. Rachel, the MP who also described success in terms of *achieving personal goals* and *service*, stressed: 'If I can do something today that I couldn't do yesterday, then I'm better off. Success is actually about taking the next step forward.'

Anna, the wheelchair athlete, believes that each achievement is coupled with new opportunities to learn and develop, and success is about taking advantage of these opportunities:

> ...playing in [X city] as an athlete has changed things. Because I did well in [X city] it changed the way I was treated and what is asked of me is much nicer as a result of that. I was then suddenly asked to be involved in lots of things like working for the sports council in [Y country] and some military panels and being invited to places as an athlete.

External criteria for success

Although internal criteria, such as achieving personal goals, personal happiness/satisfaction and personal development were important to the disabled high-flyers' definition of success, a few of their descriptions did include external criteria. Just under half mentioned being concerned with objective success and identified two criteria: *career progression* and *material wealth*.

Seven of the high-achievers, mostly men, were concerned with *career progression*. They perceived climbing the career ladder and achieving prestigious positions in the occupational hierarchy as significant to their conception of success. For example, Harry, whose occupational status of senior computer analyst demonstrates his thirst for advancement, contends:

> I have done this job for a number of years, about eight or nine years, more or less doing the same job but the responsibilities have got stronger and harder. My career has progressed in that it certainly hasn't gone backwards.

Sam who, at the time, worked as a sports development officer for disabled people expressed a similar view. His description of success includes 'getting into a career where you can go from strength to strength, where you can progress'.

Clint had a non-disabled middle-class childhood, growing up in a family where one was expected to go to university and graduate, achieve an acceptable standard of living and have a respectable lifestyle. He started working for an international bank immediately after university, at the age of 21, and has been there ever since, slowly climbing up the company career ladder. At the age of 28, Clint had a debilitating accident resulting in a severe spinal cord injury. As a consequence he lost the use of his legs and became reliant on a wheelchair to get from A to B. After a recovery and rehabilitation period, Clint returned to work at the international bank as a disabled person, and has been promoted four times since. At the time of interview he was working as a trade finance advisor for the bank, advising multinationals and corporates. He also is the transactional advisor for other branches of the company in the UK and overseas. Such a story suggests career progression is central to his definition of success: 'In the early years every time I thought about moving they made me an offer of promotion I couldn't refuse.'

Only one woman in the group measured success in terms of career progression. Corin's status of university lecturer is indicative of her preoccupation with career advancement as she spent years studying and achieving qualifications to reach her current status. Her view of success can be described as significantly objective in that it is concerned with status:

> The first time I really thought 'yes, I've made it' was when I got appointed to this job because (1) lectureships are hard to come by, (2) being appointed internally is very difficult, (3) being given a permanent post is outright unheard of! After that I thought people must view what I do as important. It has given me a relatively high status and it is what I'm meant to be doing, therefore I think I am successful.

However, although Amanda did not define her personal success in terms of hierarchical advancement, she was concerned with building her company up to make it a universal success. It was only then that she would have achieved a personal sense of success, as her statement reveals: 'Success is to find ourselves [X company], seven years down the road, being an international touring company in the main dance arena.'

Only a few of the high-achievers described their success in terms of *material wealth*, and they were men. Greg, also concerned with career progression, commented:

> Success, for me, with my middle-class upbringing and thus middle-class aspirations in terms of material wealth, means material wealth equivalent to someone like a junior doctor.

Clint supported the 'work to live' ethos, believing that as well as earning a respectable income and status, success is about being able to enjoy and benefit from these achievements in other aspects of his life. He considers success as 'being able to stop working in the next couple of years with enough money to enjoy myself while I'm still fit enough'. None of the women mentioned material wealth when defining their meaning of success.

The findings indicate that the gender of the disabled high-flyers had an influence on their conceptualisation of success. This is consistent with the work of Sturges (1999) and Russo *et al.* (1991), which suggests that non-disabled men were more likely than women to measure success in terms of salary and position in the occupational hierarchy. By comparing the literature on non-disabled male high-flyers with what this study has discovered about disabled male high-flyers, it can be seen that the two groups have a differential sense of entitlement, in that more disabled men define success in terms of internal criteria. This could be explained by the fact that society holds different expectations for upward mobility for employees with and without disabilities.

CONCLUSIONS

This chapter clearly shows that career success is a concept far more complex than many writers on careers have suggested (e.g. Melamed, 1995; O'Reilly and Chatman, 1994). It cannot simply be represented in the external terms of hierarchical position and level of pay because this is not how disabled high-flyers see it; in reality, they use far wider criteria to define their own career success. This conclusion reflects the work of Sturges (1996), who has examined what success means to managers and discovered that the majority of her sample defined success in terms of internal criteria, although a small number of managers did view success more closely to the conventional notions of what it means. This chapter shows that career success, for disabled high-flyers, is a concept that involves two large dimensions: *internal* and *external*, each of which are composed of smaller themes.

CHAPTER 4

Childhood

Childhood shows the man as the morning shows the day.
John Milton, Paradise Lost

INTRODUCTION

The importance of childhood events in influencing adult behaviour has long been recognised in philosophical and psychological literature. Developmental psychologists tend to view young children as often being moulded by the complex social world in which they live and grow into adults. Although many social factors and groups affect the process of socialisation, the family is frequently regarded as the most influential agency in the socialisation of the child. As postulated by Hetherington and Morris:

> From the moment of birth when the child is wrapped in a pink or blue blanket, swaddled and placed on a cradleboard, or nestled in a mobile-fastooned bassinet, indulged by a tender mother or left to cry it out by a mother who fears spoiling the child, socialisation has begun. (1978, p.3)

Close attention is paid to an individual's early years, perceived by many as their most formative years, to identify the origins of later attitudes, behaviour, success or failure.

Such a contention is not recent but has recurred in a large body of writings ever since Plato (428–348 BC), who stated in *The Republic*:

> The first step, as you know, is always what matters most, particularly when we are dealing with those who are young and tender. That is the time when they are taking shape and when any impression we choose to make leaves a permanent mark. (cited in Cox and Cooper 1988, p.8)

Cooper and Hingley (1985) maintain that, for the group of high-flyers, the 'change makers', in their study, there was a definite connection between past childhood experiences and present occupational achievement. This was investigated by an earlier theorist, Roe (1956), in her studies of the concept of need and the importance of early childhood experiences in shaping occupational interests. For example, in her report, she suggested that person-oriented occupations are selected more by children with secure attachments in their childhood. However, having tested this hypothesis, Trice *et al.* (1995) reject the view, claiming that there is no evidence of family structure determining occupational preferences. As Gottfredson (1981) discovered, many things determine the formation of occupational preferences including sex, age, race and region of residence. Moreover, she suggests that from an early age a person develops different conceptions about themselves in terms of who they are and are not, who they expect to be and who they would like to be. An individual's self-concept has a major impact on their future orientations, and therefore their occupational preferences can be argued to be significant to, and highly compatible with, their sense of self. Other important predictors of vocational aspirations are socio-economic background and intelligence.

SOCIAL CLASS, PARENTAL OCCUPATION AND INFLUENCE

Influence of parental occupation

The vast discourse on the impact of fathers' occupational status on their sons' futures demonstrates that social origins do, undeniably, lay down the foundation for a child's life. According to Blau and Duncan (1967), a man's social origins exert a considerable influence on his chances of occupational success. They contend that a father's occupational status not only influences his son's career achievements by affecting his education and first job, but it also has a delayed effect on achievements that persist when differences in schooling and early career experience are statistically controlled.

Pronounced differences in social class and ability level are found among high school students, especially among boys. Research by Sewell and Shah (1968) indicated that within all ability groups, the higher social class youngsters had the higher aspirations. Further, as evidence from Eysenck and Cookson (1970) revealed, high-achieving children are encountered more frequently in more affluent families where parental occupations are of a significantly high status, and the practised culture values hard work and encourages the achievement of high-flying goals. On investigating the family backgrounds of primary school children, the researchers found positive correlations between high occupational status of parents and children's academic success in school. A similar finding has been demonstrated by Cox and Cooper (1988), in their study of male high-flyers, a significant number of whom reported that their achievement-oriented parents were significant to their own successful future orientations. Moreover, as Katovsky, Crandall and Good (1967) believe, parenting styles practised by achievement-oriented parents serve to instil the child with the belief that their own behaviour, not external factors, will determine the reinforcements they receive. Therefore parental encouragement is important to the enhancement of self-esteem and the individual's successful mastery of challenges.

Furthermore, as has been established by a large body of literature, children aspire to the careers of their parents at rates significantly above chance (Holland, 1962; Werts and Watley, 1972). According to Trice *et al.*'s (1995) thesis, this could be encouraged by children being concurrently exposed to situations and talk related to parental work. Their analysis argues that the family is the first link a child has with the occupational system. Professionals and executives, for example, attempt to instil in their sons the behaviours and mannerisms appropriate to their own status. Consistent with this is the work of R. V. Clements (1958), who found that the chances of young people from higher social class origins attaining a high occupational status is considerably greater than those of lower social origins.

Influence of social class

The parallel between the emergence of awareness of class symbols and the emergence of class differences in aspirations were found in more qualitative studies of vocational development. For example, Ginzberg, Atelrad and Herma (1951) discovered that all of the boys from the higher social class took it for granted that they were going to college. Conversely, none of their lower-class counterparts did, either saying they were not sure or were definitely not going. Gottfredson (1981) believes that the existence of such different choices among children in society is largely a consequence of societal stratification. Therefore, in most cases, youngsters will take the group that they are a member of as their reference group. For example, a lower-class child is more likely to orient to the lower class and adopt its standards for success, and a middle-class child will orient to the middle class with its more demanding standards. Evidence suggests that youngsters use such social class references when evaluating their occupational futures. Gottfredson (1981) contends that as youngsters incorporate considerations of social class into their self-concepts, they reject occupational alternatives that seem inconsistent with the new elements of self. In particular, they reject options that are of unacceptably low prestige in their social reference group.

D. Norburn (1986) discovered, in his comparison of British and American corporate leaders, that the UK manager comes from a 'professional', 'non-business' background, with 'parents who have already achieved that echelon of social status'. Similarly, when investigating the significant antecedents of female high-flyers, White *et al.* (1992) discovered that 75 per cent of the successful women in their study had middle-class origins compared to 38 per cent of the general population. This finding is consistent with other studies of female managers, which have shown that they have predominately middle-class origins (Hennig and Jardim, 1978; White, 1989). Other evidence emphasising the importance of social background on career choice comes from Simpson's (1984) study of female lawyers. The findings revealed that all of the lawyers had parents who instilled them with middle-class values such as high achievement needs and the importance of education. Thus, as Himmelweit, Hasley and Oppenheim (1952) conclude, occupational aspirations and a sense of social mobility depend on the social class to which one orients.

The significance of social class background and parental occupation is deemed important to the career decisions and aspirations of disabled people. The way and extent to which it influences the career success of the disabled high-flyers in my study are revealed below. In addition, the issue of gender socialisation and the influence it has on the professional and personal development of the high-flyers is discussed.

Social class background of the disabled child

There is a body of work (e.g. Priestley, 1998; Shakespeare and Watson, 1998) in which disabled children are characterised by narratives of dependence, vulnerability and exclusion, and described as a homogeneous grouping with few rights and choices to enable them to achieve universal standardised developmental targets (Morris, 1997). However, to accept such a theory would be to deny the fact that all children, regardless of their physicality, are social actors with the capacity to develop multiple identities shaped by a wide range of social influences such as race, gender and social class.

There is ample evidence to suggest that the socio-economic situation of a non-disabled child has a significant influence on his/her future achievement orientation and occupational preference. However, as Jahoda, Markova and Cattermole (1988) discovered, disabled children's aspirations about future employment seemed to reflect those of non-disabled children. Their 'future selves' seemed to be shaped less by disability status than by other social influences. Similarly, upon reviewing comments made by disabled teenagers in his study, Norwich (1997) maintains that their hopes and fears seemed to be more a reflection of their socio-economic background than their status of being disabled. As Ginzberg (1952) contends, children of ages 11 to 14 are more likely to aspire to occupations in accordance with their interests, with the only constraints being father's occupation or parental suggestions. Thus socio-economic situation plays more of a pivotal role in the early years of the life of a disabled child than does disability itself.

Even if external factors prevent disabled individuals from maintaining their social class origins due to intragenerational mobility, particularly downward mobility, their social class origins have already influenced the individual's self-concept and character formation during the early stages of their development. For example, class origins can affect one's educational and occupational opportunities, achievement values and moral judgements. As has been emphasised by Kluckhohn (Kluckhohn and Strodtbeck, 1961), the 'core culture' of the middle classes not only stresses the importance of accomplishment and doing well but also other values facilitating the development of achievement needs.

Empirical comparisons of middle-class and lower-class groups have usually found stronger needs for achievement in the former. Evidence from a nationwide survey of achievement motivation cited by Veroff *et al.* (1960) reported that the percentage of men with above-median achievement scores on a projective test was greater the higher their educational and occupational levels. The correlation between education and achievement was exemplified in Pfeiffer's (1991) study of the socio-economic situations of disabled people. His qualitative investigation indicated that the social class structure which enables white males to have access to things such as education, jobs and higher income still rules in the disability community. His report suggested how better-educated disabled persons were more likely to participate in full-time employment and more likely than poorly educated disabled people to have a professional or managerial occupation. Furthermore, Sutherland (1981) believed that a middle-class background could serve to reduce the negativity associated with disability. Such a thesis may be explained by the fact that disabled people nurtured within middle-class environments are exposed to values and practices of working hard and doing well. Furthermore, as was explained by Priestley (1998), they have greater access to services and facilities, and higher levels of surveillance than their working-class counterparts. This, in turn, permits occupational participation and induces acceptance by non-disabled people, which, according to Sutherland (1981), becomes easier the more one conforms to the norm of the societal majority.

PARENTAL EXPECTATIONS AND THE DEVELOPMENT OF THE DISABLED CHILD

Thomas (1998) argues that while parents and the wider family grouping can provide the disabled child with emotional security, promote a sense of self-worth, assist in opening up opportunities and encourage social inclusion rather than exclusion, they can also do the opposite. The narrative of one disabled woman in Thomas's (1998) work shows how, although parental ambition and encouragement to pursue 'normal' activities can be an asset to a child's future orientation, it can also be disempowering. For example, the disabled woman recalls being nurtured in a highly competitive family where her parents expected her to succeed as a non-disabled person. Her family's inability to acknowledge and engage with her physical difference and the wider disablist social reaction to this did not help her accept herself.

On the other hand, disability and impairment can add new twists to relationships with parents and can become a vehicle for the expression of emotional abuse and the erection of barriers. As Priestley (1998) contends, disabled children are likely to be deprived of growing up and experiencing the natural affinities in terms of gender, sexuality, culture and class. Furthermore, they may be excluded from the important patterns of social processes and childhood socialisation by differential mechanisms of surveillance and segregation. Some authors have raised the serious point that some disabled children are prevented from developing social skills and self-confidence because their lives are controlled by adults (Alderson and Goodey, 1998; Morris, 1997; Norwich, 1997). Therefore, as postulated by Middleton (1999), a disabled child is likely to experience neither a normal childhood, nor adolescence, and is likely to be conditioned into an adulthood of dependency.

It can be argued that societal stereotypes of disabled people being passive and dependent have had extensive influence on parental expectations of their disabled children. Any preconceived expectations parents may have had of their disabled children tended to be measured according to the child's level of impairment, and influenced by the implications of bringing up a disabled child in a predominately non-disabled world. As the structure of society is based on the non-disabled majority, parents are unaware of what is physically achievable for people with disabilities and therefore are unlikely to push them in any particular career direction. However, it could be argued that while parents may have no premeditated goals for their disabled child to aspire towards, the encouragement and support they do provide does indeed facilitate the generation of the child's full potential. This is supported by Wood (1973), who asserts that where parents are warm, loving, respectful to their child as a valued individual and able to enhance her/his self-esteem, the child has the best opportunity to develop their personality to the full. Furthermore, the provision of such a nurturing environment permits the cultivation of individual potential. Consistent with this is White et al.'s (1992) study which reported that a high proportion of successful women in their sample had supportive, autonomy-granting parents who had no rigid expectations of them other than for them to be happy. Mussen, Conger and Kegan (1979) assert that children who receive a lot of parental affection and attention, and have their needs gratified quickly, feel secure and are more likely to explore and move towards independence. Evidence reveals that such treatment is most likely for only or first-born non-disabled children (Mussen *et al.*, 1979; White *et al.*, 1992). However, this kind of parental treatment may also be prevalent in the socialisation of disabled children who often make care demands that go well beyond what is required of parents of young non-disabled children (Baldwin and Glendinning, 1982; Glendinning, 1983; Sloper and Turner, 1992). The volume of work that needs to be undertaken directly with the child, on both a routine and non-routine basis, tends to be greater.

PARENTAL INFLUENCE ON THE CHILDHOOD SOCIALISATION OF DISABLED HIGH-FLYERS

Parental influence and expectations were identified as an important element of the disabled high-flyers' childhood socialisation, and how they perceived and arrived at their goals of success. Childhood socialisation is, as a great body of discourse suggests, critical to a child's transition to adulthood in terms of their behaviour, their life choices, their strengths and weaknesses.

Analysis of the interviews revealed a variety of parent–child relationships, although, in most cases, they facilitated the cultivation of potential and encouraged the achievement of personal goals. Furthermore, it highlighted the extent to which gender and disability influenced the childhood socialisation of these respondents.

Some researchers argue that high parental expectations are fundamental to a child's success. The popular image of the 'ambitious parent', moulding and encouraging their child to get a good education and a respectable job in a particular field, is seen as the norm for non-disabled male high-flyers in other studies (e.g. Cox and Cooper, 1988). It would seem to be at least partially true for some of the men in this study, especially those who acquired their disability in adulthood and therefore had the experience of a non-disabled childhood.

Parental ambition was not prevalent in the formulae of career success for the disabled high-flyers with congenital disabilities. As they were all disabled during or immediately after birth, disability inevitably became a major factor in their childhood socialisation, especially influencing what was expected of them. However, while there was no evidence of parents setting premeditated goals concerning the future occupation of their disabled children, there was evidence of contrasting levels of parental expectations.

Many parents had low expectations of their disabled children. This was suggested by several of the high-flyers with congenital disabilities, who expressed comments like:

> If you are a disabled person, particularly born disabled, parents, society and the medical profession don't really expect you to achieve that much. They have pretty low expectations.

This further implies that, in a stratified society disabled people are automatically ascribed with a low status as they are perceived as socially and physically incapable of contributing to the development of society's economy. Most of the people in the study were born between 1940 and 1970. This was an era when disability politics had not been established and the whole concept of disability was not clearly understood by the lay person. Therefore parents automatically valued the opinion of the medical profession who conceived disabled people to be passive, dependent and incapable of pursuing an independent autonomous lifestyle (Oliver, 1990). This was apparent in Tom's case. Born in Liverpool with spina bifida, an impairment which damages the spine, Tom spent a lot of his childhood in hospital. He was not expected to live for long, and even if he did he was expected to be dependent on others for the rest of his life. He remembers:

> My mother didn't really have any prior expectations of me, because she had received so much advice and medical prognosis about me always being dependent on someone or dying at birth.

This was similar to Lara's perceptions of her disabled childhood. Lara was the only child of very supportive parents who gave her a lot of attention and encouraged her to read and achieve academically. However, they were unsure how her disability would affect her and her future, whether she would live to adulthood or indeed to the following year. She believes:

> Because of attitudes towards disabled people, and attitudes towards people with my impairment generated by the medical establishment, I think my parents had been given quite low expectations in terms of how long I would live.

However, parents of several of the high-flyers with childhood disabilities had relatively high expectations of them. They placed a high value on achievement and encouraged the attainment of high-flying goals, particularly in academic pursuits. Five of the 11 men claimed that, although their parents recognised the constraints of their disability, it was not perceived as a barrier to opportunity as they were still ambitious for their children to succeed. Bob, brought up into a middle-class culture (a culture that placed a strong emphasis on achievement), was expected to achieve at the same levels as his siblings and peers. The fact that he was in a wheelchair as a result of polio did not influence what was expected of him:

> I was expected to do and to achieve what my brothers and sisters did and what all my friends were achieving. I was very rarely allowed to get away with the excuse 'I can't walk, I can't do it.' In nearly everything I

did I had to achieve the same as everybody else and, I think, that was vital to my later success in university and my career.

Similarly, Christian was nurtured within a supportive environment with parents who encouraged him to strive for, and achieve, high goals. He affirms the existence of relatively high parental expectations, during his childhood, by his comment:

> My parents are both teachers and never stated their exact expectations of me. However, what they did say was, 'Why is your report bad?' 'Why aren't you working harder?' 'Don't you think you can do better?'

Such familial behaviour was not limited to the men. Five out of the nine women born with a disability felt that although they were not directed by prescribed expectations, they were still encouraged to aim high. Katey, the middle of three sisters, was born into a very achievement-oriented family. All of them were expected to do well, and Katey's physical disability, restricting her growth, did not seem to affect this:

> It was never any good, in my family, to be as good as other people, we were supposed to be better. How success was defined to me is probably how I define it to myself now.

Another woman, Maria, who works as a speech and language therapist, felt that her parents pushed her slightly harder than her non-disabled siblings to ensure her achievements were on par with them and satisfied the family's underlying middle-class principles. She points out:

> My parents expected me to get on with things. Mum has said that maybe I was treated slightly harder than my brother and sister to make me get there and achieve.

Half of the high-flyers with a congenital disability had at least one parent who occupied a high-status profession. Furthermore, they had been nurtured within a culture that stressed the importance of accomplishment and doing well. Thus, high achievers, high aspirations and strong need for achievement were predominant. It can be suggested that certain observable cues and abstract social class symbols (e.g. education, parents' jobs) within the family unit were recognised by the disabled people during their childhood, and inevitably influenced their occupational preferences and their lifestyle. For instance Kay, Mary's younger sister, identified her birth family's financial wealth as a great advantage for the two disabled sisters who needed specialist facilities and equipment in order to have a healthy lifestyle:

> In the 1960s, when I was little, I would have been completely stuck in and become socially isolated if I hadn't grown up in a fairly wealthy family. Wealth has enabled me to do all sorts of things like the way I set up my household; to get the care support that I needed that made it possible for me to get out to work on time and get home on time.

In contrast, just over a quarter of the successful people with congenital disabilities had parents who did not have significant amounts of wealth or did not occupy a high-status position in society's stratification system. They recalled that although their parents had no rigid expectations of the children in terms of achieving, they did expect the children to do what made them happy and supported their choices. As Rachel stated:

> I came from a very traditional working-class family with very loving parents who always said 'just do your best'. They were always happy to support and be supportive.

So for these high-flyers, parental expectations were neither low nor achievement-orientated, but simply for them to gain happiness.

Eleven of the disabled high-flyers in the study acquired their impairment, either through illness or accident, in their early adult life. For this reason parental expectations were not influenced by childhood disability. Unlike several of the men and women with congenital disabilities, none of the people with an acquired impairment recalled their parents having low expectations of them. Most of the men were nurtured within a middle-class or Asian culture where education was prized and the achievement of high standards was emphasised. Such was the case for Adrian, the only son and eldest child of a Lieutenant Navy Commander:

> My father was a Lieutenant Commander in the Royal Navy. He was ambitious and successful. My father and his brothers were extremely well educated. By the age of five I was doing trigonometry!

Similarly, Ali, who was born and brought up in a large but close-knit Muslim family in Sudan, stated:

> My father's connection with Government officials taught him education was very important so all my family, all children, from the first sister to the last, are educated.

Again, the parents who were ambitious for their children to be great achievers themselves worked in high-status occupations. Such was also indicated by the case of Roger, a university professor whose parents both graduated from Oxford University and whose father was a medical doctor in tropical medicine.

Out of the three females with acquired disabilities, not one recalled being exposed to the ambitious or achievement-oriented styles of parenting. Rather, their upbringing was described as primarily working-class and their parents as supportive and loving, permitting them to do anything that would generate happiness. As one woman claimed:

> My parents never pushed me to become anything particular. Their philosophy was to do what's right for you, what you want to do and what makes you happy.

The difference in the perceptions of both male and female respondents with acquired disabilities in terms of what their parents expected of them, suggests that gender had a significant influence on parental expectations of the non-disabled children. Gender socialisation will be discussed further, and in relation to disabled childhoods, later in the chapter.

CHILDHOOD EXPERIENCES

The truth of Carlyle's words, 'the history of a man's childhood is the description of his parents and his environment' (cited in Cooper and Hingley, 1985, p.4), has been revealed in a body of work (e.g. Cox and Cooper, 1988; White *et al.* 1992) which delved into the early childhood experiences of groups of high-flying professionals. They explained how significant experiences during the early years of a child's life have deep and lasting effects upon his/her personality development. For instance, Cox and Cooper (1988) discovered that experiencing the loss of a parent, during a child's formative years, engendered added strengths such as survivability and self-sufficiency, which served them well in their future careers. Therefore, as Thomas (1998) maintains, narratives concerning significant experiences and people in one's childhood help to give structure and meaning to one's life.

A common theme of many existing discourses (e.g. Cooper and Hingley, 1985; White *et al.* 1992) is the effect of deprivation in childhood, particularly separation from one or both parents. The male high-flyers in Cox and Cooper's (1988) study believed that traumas of orphanic existence, through death of parent(s) or being sent to boarding school at an early age, were significant to their future orientations. These experiences could be seen as generating a general sense of independence and self-sufficiency. The connection between early trauma and future success can be explained by Cooper and Hingley's (1985, p.24) reasoning:

> ...as the physical wound produces a healthy scar tissue often stronger than normal to protect the damaged area, so the personality may protect itself by defending vulnerable aspects of the psyche in similar ways.

Several of the successful professionals interviewed by Cooper and Hingley (1985) reported feelings of strength through adversity. This illustrates the assumptions, put forward by several writers, that the overcoming of early adversity contributes to later success. For example, Tony Blair, Britain's most recent Prime Minister, experienced an early sense of insecurity, at the age of ten, when his father became very ill. Similarly, Anita Roddick, founder of the Body Shop, believes that most entrepreneurs have understood a sense of loss. She claims: 'They've been pushed out of childhood and, rather than entering adulthood, they become providers.'

In an interview with Martyn Lewis (1998, p.835), Roddick identified two childhood experiences which she considered to be influential to her present achievement motivation. One was the death of her father, the second was the prejudice that she encountered from mainstream society during her immigrant upbringing, instilling her with the notion that outsiders have to try harder than people who are part of the mainstream.

Childhood experiences of disabled people

David Blunkett, former Home Secretary (UK), believes childhood trauma can either drive you forward or pull you under. It drove him forward, as he explains:

> I had to go to boarding school when I was four … because that was the way in which schooling for blind children was organised, on a residential basis. There was the trauma of finding yourself in a dormitory with other children for the first time... I had to deal with my dad's death when I was 12. (cited in Lewis, 1998, p.130)

Residential segregated education was not uncommon for disabled children prior to the emergence of the disabled people's movement. According to Saunders (1994) and Abbot, Morris and Ward (2001), parents believed that a residential school setting was an optimum learning environment for their disabled children. It was thought that residential placements also offered disabled children emotional and social support, which local schools failed to do (Abbot et al., 2001). However, the negative effects of uprooting a child have been documented by many, including Shakespeare and Watson (1998), who argue that segregated education may result in isolation, as it may mean losing regular contact with non-disabled peers and family, because it involves attending a school well outside the local community.

Feelings of isolation among disabled children may also be caused by regular time out for medical or therapeutic interventions (Shakespeare and Watson, 1998). Thomas (1998), who investigated the childhood experiences of 68 disabled women, found that long periods of hospitalisation, at a time when parents were kept out of the wards except for brief visits, left some women with lasting fears of separation and a strong sense of insecurity. An early account of disabled children by David Thomas (1978) focuses on the problem of their isolation. He maintains that the cultural experiences of disabled children differ from those of others in their age group because of prolonged periods of hospitalisation, separate forms of schooling, institutionalisation, restriction of mobility and overprotection.

Moreover, the regulatory structure of the residential institutions can either be beneficial or detrimental to the disabled child's self-concept. Barnes (1991) argues that segregated schools are a fundamental part of the discrimination process. He believes that not only do they create and perpetuate artificial barriers between disabled children and their non-disabled peers, but they also serve to reinforce the traditional medical model of disability and generally fail to provide the children with the necessary skills to lead an autonomous lifestyle in adulthood.

History reveals that childhood experiences resulting from impairment engender certain personality traits that may have a significant impact on one's adult life. William Hay, born in 1754, describes himself as 'bent in my mother's womb' (cited in Barnes, 1991, p.14). He believed that the socio-psychological difficulties he experienced because of his impairment had caused him to be bashful, uneasy and unsure of himself. However, such experiences can also induce perseverance, stubbornness and problem-solving skills that will be valuable for successful future career orientations. This supports what has been discussed previously in this chapter about childhood trauma inducing strength and other survival skills, and its importance for successful adulthood.

CHILDHOOD EXPERIENCES OF DISABLED HIGH-FLYERS

A few of the men recalled their 'orphanic existence' – separation from parents during childhood – as significant to their achievements in adulthood. Sam, sent to a residential school at an early age, felt it was the school, not his parents, that had the greatest influence on his personality and character formation. It provided him with the opportunity and facilities to realise and demonstrate his full potential. He points out:

> Being sent away to school obviously gave me the opportunity to learn, to obtain qualifications and to gain real life experiences. If I hadn't gone to that Scope school, I would be in some poxy little day centre and would have been treated like a five-year-old for the rest of my life.

This suggests that the orphanic experience, if it involved alternative supports, could promote a general feeling of independence and self-reliance. The positive correlation between the development of competence and self-confidence and the separation of maternal bonding, as Hoffman (1972) argues, is thus essential in order to cope with an environment independently.

Three men who acquired their disabilities in early adulthood also experienced this sense of childhood deprivation. Nick recalls the effects of being brought up in a matriarchal society, culminating in being separated from his father by the war:

> From nil to six I was in a one-parent family purely because my father was off fighting in the war. I'd had a very good relationship with all sorts of females – my mother, my grandmother, my aunts. I was the one nephew and grandchild, so I was really, really petted.

Adrian had to develop an early sense of responsibility and moved into an adult role from a young age:

> My father was very ill so a lot was put on the shoulders of my mother to bring up the family, and on my shoulders, as the eldest child, to look after my sisters.

Other tales of childhood deprivation expressed include the death of a parent, a traumatic hardship that was experienced by a few of the male respondents. Tom, the vicar, identified the death of his father as a significant determinant to his current occupation: 'My father died when I was eight, while I was in hospital. This influenced my spiritual being…'

Unlike the non-disabled high-flyers in other studies and those with acquired disabilities in this study, many of the high-flyers with childhood disabilities here spent a substantial part of their childhood being recipients of substantial medical intervention and negative prognosis. They recalled frequent periods of hospitalisation and '…staring death in the face', which suggests that, for these individuals who also had adult support during childhood, early traumas could induce the emergence of added strengths of self-sufficiency, independence and 'survivability' which were beneficial to their future orientations.

However, all of the high-flyers who experienced childhood trauma, whether disabled as children or not, developed a sense of strength through adversity. They coped successfully with early traumatic events that set a pattern for successfully coping with future life events. According to Cooper and Hingley (1985, p.24), early adverse experiences could be argued to instigate an early sense of mastery, independence and self-sufficiency because the wound of adverse experiences is said to lead to the creation of a healthy scar tissue which is stronger than normal and protects the damaged area. This line of reasoning was supported by several of the disabled professionals. For example, Christian, who was nurtured by his family to realise his potential, demonstrated his determination by his comment:

I had a tracheotomy which prevented me speaking for four months. During that time my self-esteem was pulled down by doctors who made me feel like nothing. I think my drive to succeed stemmed, firstly, from my determination to defeat them and prove them wrong.

Many of them identified positive experiences in their childhood which, they felt, influenced their occupational choice. Bob's decision to go into finance was greatly influenced by his father and grandfather, both of whom were bankers. He recalls:

> As a child I was always interested in work, business, how things were made. As my father was a banker he had a lot of contacts with business people who ran factories. Every week we (my brothers and I) were pestering him to arrange a trip to one of the factories.

Similarly, Rachel, who was brought up in a supportive working-class family, remembers a childhood experience that seemed to have a strong influence on her beliefs and thus her choice to become a candidate for the Labour Party:

> When I was about nine, I remember going into this flat; there were bare floorboards and hardly any furniture. I was aware of deprivation, of real poverty. That was a very important political thing for me in as much as I realised this wasn't right, we shouldn't have people living in these conditions. I realised that we should have social equality, that people have responsibilities for each other.

The connection between childhood events and current occupation was also indicated in Katey's story of why she became a freelance journalist:

> I remember going to the *Sunday Telegraph* when I was eight years old and seeing big rolls of paper being loaded onto presses and seeing my dad's name being printed a million times with the knowledge that it was going to go out all over Britain.

Although Cane is now an established theatre director, as a child he wanted to be a chicken farmer and follow his father's footsteps. So, after taking some O levels, he left the all-boys grammar school, much to the disappointed of his parents, to pursue his ambition. But when Cane was in his teens something happened which changed his mind about being a chicken farmer. He suddenly developed a keen interest in performing arts:

> When I was 13 or 14 I remember walking along the canal with a friend, on a school night, and meeting these two really attractive girls who invited us to this thing called Youth Theatre on Sundays. I only went to

seek their affection as I had no interest or knowledge of drama, but somewhere along the line I got interested in drama.

Two women who have successful careers in the arts mentioned that their familial environment had a significant impact on their choice of occupation. Their reports suggest that as children, they were frequently exposed to positive experiences and attitudes associated with their current vocation. Amanda reflects:

> My mother actually used to be a dancer when she was younger. She and her sister used to do cabaret, doing tap, and they used to perform at tea dances and other places. My aunt, my mum's sister, was in the entertainment team during the war; she was a dancer. One of my brothers, although he was in the Air Force, has always had a band and played guitar. My sister also trained as an actress years ago.

Similarly Judith remembers the influence her childhood environment had on her occupational choice: '...My family were involved in the arts as well so they had an inevitable influence.'

So, as has been demonstrated above, many of the disabled high-flyers identified childhood events that they believed had an impact on their personal and professional development later in life. Some issues discussed centred on overcoming hardships – for instance, death of a parent, leaving home at an early age, frequent periods of hospitalisation. Others were about single events which occurred during the individual's childhood but were considered to have had an influence on their future occupational choice.

Several of the high-flyers, with and without childhood disabilities, experienced some kind of deprivation and trauma as children. Although some of these experiences were disability-related, some were not. However, whatever caused such adverse experiences, they made the high-flyers stronger, more aware of potential barriers and able to improve techniques of coping with future life events successfully. As Cox and Cooper (1988) have suggested, it is not the events an individual encounters that are important to their development, but how he or she responds to them.

GENDER SOCIALISATION

Cottone and Cottone (1992) have suggested that women with disabilities comprise a double minority, in that they are 'dis-abled' partly due to a defined disability, and partly because they live in a larger culture that devalues the contributions of women.

Being a female and having a disability both have consequences for the individual. In society, with its many agents of socialisation, each of these descriptions engenders preconceived notions, expectations and stereotypes. In both instances, according to literature reviewed by several researchers (e.g. Horner, 1972; the National Information Center for Children and Youth with Disabilities, 1990), it is the negative stereotypes that hold girls back or unnecessarily channel them along certain occupational paths.

Much statistical evidence demonstrates the occupational disparity, in terms of status and income, between males and females with disabilities. For example, the National Longitudinal Transition Study (Wagner and Shaver, 1989) revealed that males with disabilities out of school for two years were most likely to work as semi-skilled or unskilled labourers or in service occupations. It found that women were more commonly employed in service or clerical jobs. In addition, it was discovered that being male, older, white and from a higher socio-economic background were factors that had significant influence on the high probability of competitive employment.

Hazasi et al.'s (1989) longitudinal study of students who attended segregated school suggested that, in the first year after school, males were more likely than females to be employed, to be employed full-time, and to remain employed full-time during the next two or three years. In addition, all of the female students with disabilities were employed in unskilled jobs, a discovery that was consistent across different studies, in a variety of areas, with a diversity of employment opportunities.

Gender differences not only exist in employment, but in many walks of life. However, much research shows that the seeds of future independence, self-sufficiency and productive employment are planted at home, with messages given by parents or guardians, consciously or unconsciously, from the earliest moments of children's lives. Hoffman (1972) suggests that boys and girls enter the world with different constitutional make-ups. Evidence shows that this difference is reinforced by the way society treats, speaks to, and teaches children acceptable patterns of behaviour and social roles, in accordance with their gender. Typically, society expects and encourages boys to be sturdy, and to become self-supporting in anticipation of the day when they have to support a family. They are nurtured to show more task involvement and more confidence. Conversely, girls are perceived as more passive and more reliant on others, which could be connected to Hoffman's (1972) theory that girls are subject to more overprotection than boys, and thus prone to become more dependent on others, especially parents. Such protection, Hoffman asserts, may be detrimental to the child's exploratory attempts because they will doubt their own competence, be unwilling to face stress and have inadequate motivation for autonomous achievement. For instance, if a child receives help too quickly, he/she will be unable to develop a tolerance for frustration and thus be more likely to withdraw from the difficult task rather than tackle it and tolerate the temporary frustration. Crandall and

Rabson (1960) point out that this withdrawal behaviour is more apparent in female children.

Females are also more likely to be motivated by the desire for love and approval from parents, teachers and peers (Crandall, 1963, 1964) and not encouraged to strive for mastery in occupational pursuits (Hoffman, 1972). Further, as the future 'nurturers' of society, females are rewarded for their sensitivity to the needs of others and their ability to co-operate rather than aggressively pursue their own interests.

However, traditional stereotypes of males and females may be somewhat detrimental to girls with disabilities. Disabled children are assumed, by many, to be more dependent than non-disabled children. Boys with disabilities can often escape the disability stereotype of helplessness or dependence by aspiring to traditional male characteristics of competence, autonomy and work. However, these are not traditional characteristics for females who are expected to fulfil housewife/mother roles. Yet such roles, regardless of their importance, are even less likely to be adopted by disabled women (Bowe, 1983). This may be, as Russo (1988) suggests, in part due to the societal myth that disabled women are asexual, and incapable of leading socially and sexually fulfilling lives. Drawing from her personal development she recalls that during her youth it was assumed that her disability would prevent her from finding a partner or having children.

Lang (1982) postulates that girls with disabilities are likely to confront two stereotypes: the 'passive, dependent' female and the 'helpless, dependent' person with a disability. This could place the individual in a situation resulting in 'rolelessness' (Fine and Asch, 1988), producing low self-esteem and a lack of self-confidence.

However, as indicated in Baumann's (1997) study, such a stereotype sometimes generates a strong desire for disabled women to be productive and independent, and also a need to fulfil a purposeful role in society by having a career. Several of the women in the study wanted to leave a legacy through their work and, interestingly, these women had no expectations of having a family, a belief stemming from their early socialisation. Baumann believes that the lack of gender socialisation in childhood and the limited choices available to disabled women could make them more dedicated towards a career. Further, she suggests that being born with a physical disability and the stereotypes that come with it had a significant influence on the women's career aspirations in terms of driving them to work harder and occupy a higher status to divert attention away from their physical limitations.

GENDER SOCIALISATION OF DISABLED HIGH-FLYERS

Not one of the high-flyers with congenital disabilities mentioned anything to suggest that their gender had any influence on their parents' expectations of them. All of them, both male and female, believed disability was in fact a primary attribute of their childhood and thus significantly influenced others' behaviour towards, and expectations of, them. Jude, who studied IT and taught it in a college of further education for several years before becoming a vicar, said that her parents '…were told not to expect anything. They never tried to hold me back, they never said "you can't do that or you can't do this"'.

Similarly, Corin, a university lecturer in applied computer science, was brought up to be the best she could in whatever she chose to do. Although she was encouraged to achieve academically, her parents' expectations of her were never guided by her gender, which is evident by the fact that she chose to study and teach computer sciences: 'The possibility of computing came up, and that's what they encouraged me to do.'

The two sisters, Mary and Kay, spoke about how their disability had a substantial effect on what their parents expected of them compared to what was expected of their two non-disabled brothers:

> Not quite sure whether they [parents] had high expectations of us girls, but they did for the boys because they're 'normal'. For us girls, I think they just took things as they came and didn't hold us back. They expected us to do as well as we could.

The narratives reveal that a third of the women with congenital disabilities were greatly inspired by their fathers. Both Kay and Mary mentioned the positive influence that their father had on their career development and success in careers that would have been considered gender atypical during the late 1970s and 1980s. Kay, who spent her former years developing a career in IT, thought of her father as her mentor:

> I think my dad is my only real mentor. He was a management consultant towards the end of his career from the age of about 52. And I learned a lot from him. I actually model myself, quite a bit, on him.

This was also the case for Katey. Her father was a great inspiration to her, and from childhood she was ambitious to one day be a journalist, like he was:

> My dad's career in journalism was what set me towards what I wanted to do. I learned from him, by going down to his London office and seeing how he worked.

However, for the high-flyers with acquired disabilities and non-disabled childhoods, there was a noticeable gender-related difference in what they perceived their parents expected of them. As has been mentioned above, while the men believed their parents were ambitious for them to achieve high goals in terms of education and employment, the women considered their parents' only expectation of them was to do what made them happy.

CONCLUSION

Although the discussion in the preceding review demonstrates that early childhood socialisation does have a significant influence on the transition to adult success, it must be remembered that family and childhood experiences alone do not determine individual vocational development. Astin (1984) points out that if socialisation alone determined work expectations then there would be little change; once set, expectations would remain stable.

It can be seen, however, that early childhood does have an influence on later attitudes and behaviours. Indeed, as John Milton suggested: 'The childhood shows the man as the morning shows the day' (cited in Cooper and Hingley, 1985, p.4).

Although this discussion has centred around disabled high-achievers, it should be remembered that other, less successful, disabled people may have similar background events in childhood. In some cases they obviously do. Many disabled children experience separation from their parents, but they do not all grow up to be successful in their career, or indeed have a career. Many disabled children seem to spend the majority of their early years under medical surveillance. While these are, obviously, very significant events, what is important is not the event itself, but how the individual responds to it. The support the individual receives is also important for them to successfully cope with adverse situations. The ways in which the high-flyers in this book responded and coped with these difficult childhood events set a pattern for successfully handling other events throughout life.

CHAPTER 5

Education

It's what you learn after you think you know it all that
matters.

Unknown

INTRODUCTION

It is widely recognised that a primary function of education is to ingrain
individuals with the skills and abilities, both social and academic, deemed
appropriate to serve a purposeful role in society's developing economy and live
an autonomous lifestyle. Giddens (1997) argues that education is an essential
agent of socialisation, which is required for a society to survive. Further, by
bringing generations of young people up to accept dominant norms and values,
education plays an important role in the maintenance of social conformity, both
in formal and also less obvious ways. Minuchin and Shapiro (1983) argue that it
is the school that provides the child with their first social arena within which
they are taught to realise the consequences of social and academic competence,
competition and power development. While in educational institutions,
students experience several ecological transitions which entail progressive or
more drastic movements into more complex contexts. The mastery of these
transitions will have a positive impact on the student's move from school to
work in the future.

EDUCATION AND ECONOMIC PARTICIPATION

Towards the end of the twentieth century the relationship between education
and the economy arguably assumed even greater significance than it had before.
As suggested by the Warnock Report (1978), education prepares individuals to
become economically participative members of society by teaching them the
formal and informal skills necessary to pursue a valuable position in the labour
force. The attraction is that investments in education are viewed as profitable for

both the individual and society (Marginson, 1994). Furthermore, Brown and Lauder (1996) argue that the quality of the nation's education and training system holds the key to future economic prosperity. So, as Tomlinson (1995) suggests, the major goal of schools is to produce students who have collected a large number of qualifications, skills and competences as a passport to their possible future.

The allocation of occupational status has been shown to be strongly correlated with education. Hall (1969) contends that particular amounts and, in many cases, particular kinds of education are prerequisites for entrance into the occupational system. Burton R. Clark (1964) argues that men become part of the potential labour force by qualifying for the work required and, increasingly, capability is defined by formal schooling. He believes that while advanced education offers competence, little schooling defines occupational incompetence and thus occupational achievement is prefigured by education. Therefore the education system can be seen as a major factor in placement of people within the whole social system.

The nature of the relationship between the educational and occupational systems is one of mutual dependence. The occupational system essentially relies upon the educational system for its supply of personnel, while the output of the educational system is consumed by the occupational system. Furthermore, education has presented itself to be a prerequisite for upward mobility. For instance, two-thirds of the managers in Davidson's (1997) study had gained degrees at undergraduate and postgraduate level. A similar point was also demonstrated in the *Wall Street Journal* (1987) which reported high levels of education among American managers. The statistics show that 6 per cent had graduated from high school, 40 per cent were university graduates, 35 per cent had qualified with Masters degrees and 13 per cent had doctorates.

However, exceptional educational achievements do not guarantee exceptional working conditions. Evidence headlined 'No job security for academics' (*Guardian*, 9 December 1999) warned that the reality is that individuals with vocations such as professors, lecturers and researchers are victims of 'miserable exploitation'. According to research which analysed the working conditions of 200 sections of the workforce, nearly a quarter of those in university posts had only 'temporary' employment, on short-term or fixed-term contracts, for example.

Education and economic participation for disabled individuals

According to the Fish Report (ILEA, 1985), the aims of education for all children and young people include achievement of personal goals and the learning of the skills required to be autonomous in their lifestyle while successfully contributing to the developing economy. In an ideal world such goals may be possible, but in present day society the optimism that underlies the philosophy of education is somewhat frayed by the lack of facilities available to society's culturally diverse population, thus having a detrimental influence on educational attainment and future career advancement.

So, despite the overall aim of education to encourage all members of society to work together to create and realise desirable futures, disabled children have not been given the same educational opportunities as their non-disabled peers. It has been suggested that, whether disabled children attended segregated or mainstream education, they are twice as unlikely as their non-disabled peers to attain formal qualifications (DRC, 2000). As a group, disabled children are not conceptualised as future economically contributing citizens, and expectations about them progressing up career ladders beyond achieving non-dependent status were rare (Middleton, 1999). Dobson and Middleton (1998) point out that raising a disabled child costs three times as much as a non-disabled child. As disabled children often require additional facilities and support to function successfully, they are considered to be disruptive and difficult to educate. Furthermore, their presence is perceived as harmful to the educational progression of non-disabled students and the school's success in achieving specific targets (Barnes, 1991; Lloyd-Smith and Tarr, 2000). In the regime of the 'education market' (Ball, Bowe and Gerwitz, 1994) where the pursuing policy is to attract the most able pupils who are perceived to contribute the most to the wealth of the nation, the disabled child/young person, perceived to have low value, is considered 'damaged goods' (John, 1996). Consequently, the disabled child will often be placed in a segregated institution, conceived as a helpful variant to mainstream schooling, and cajoled to achieve – in terms of eradicating their impairment as the price for acceptance. Tomlinson (1982) argued that the aim of special education was to enable disabled children to fit unobtrusively into adult society, not to facilitate them to achieve academically or secure employment. In this sense, independence implies no more than achieving an economic balance with society, not making a contribution to it, and therefore can be defined as low-level ambition.

However, despite this institutional discrimination against disabled people in education, whether mainstream or segregated, there are several disabled adults in the UK, such as David Blunkett and Stephen Hawking, who have broken through the barriers and whose occupational success has been significantly facilitated by education. This chapter takes a look at how, and the extent to which, the disabled high-flyers felt education influenced and determined success in their lives. It tells stories of how these people broke through the barriers of discrimination to achieve their success in education and other aspects of life.

EDUCATIONAL EXPERIENCES OF THE DISABLED HIGH-FLYERS

Education is important to the success of a society's future. While it may not, on every occasion, directly determine an individual's exact vocational direction, the literacy and social skills it provides are viewed as necessary conditions for economic development and thus have significant impact on individuals' positions within the labour market. Such was the case with the disabled high-flyers.

All of the high-flyers had GCSEs or O levels, the majority of them had undergraduate degrees and a few had achieved postgraduate qualifications. In several cases, there was an obvious connection between the subjects the high-flyers previously studied and their current occupational status, suggesting that education has been imperative to their present lifestyle.

The following accounts of the individuals' educational experiences highlight the extent to which educational careers differed for the high-flyers with congenital disabilities and those who acquired their impairment later in life. It was noted that the latter group became disabled during their post-college years and did not really encounter the potential discrimination and prejudice that children with congenital disabilities may have been exposed to. In addition, the stories reveal how gender had an impact on the educational experiences of the high-flyers.

For the majority of the disabled high-flyers, education was considered to be the source by which they could learn the basic norms and values of the society in which they lived in order to function safely and harmoniously. They identified education as a primary ingredient in their social, psychological and cultural development.

Type of school

Seven out of the 20 professionals with congenital disabilities attended purely segregated educational institutions prior to university. Tom was one of them. After passing his 11+ examination he went to a boarding school in Hampshire for physically disabled students: 'This is when I discovered I had a brain.' He felt that the special school enabled him to develop and compete academically and in sport with other like-minded disabled people:

> I had the choice of going to a mainstream school or a special school. I chose the special school because I thought if I went to a mainstream school I would be discriminated against. I think it would have been the case, particularly in the early 1970s.

Corin went to a segregated school in South Africa, studying with disabled children who had low expectations and little familial support and encouragement. She was resented for her protective and supportive home background and the fact that she aimed to go to university. She was, academically, on a par with her non-disabled friends but, in South Africa at that time, there was no integration of disabled children into mainstream schools:

> My parents tried frantically to get me into a regular primary school at the age of ten, but no one would accept me for various reasons. For example, one of the excuses was that my typewriter would make too much noise and disturb the other children, and I would frighten them.

Another eight of these high-flyers were integrated into the mainstream educational system for the whole of their educational career. However, a small proportion (25 per cent) of those with congenital disabilities experienced a combination of segregated and mainstream education. Nine of the 20 high-flyers with congenital disabilities (45 per cent) attended residential school and/or college for part or all of their compulsory education. For example, Jude attended a segregated residential college after being at a mainstream day school for several years:

> I went through the mainstream educational system until I was 14. Then I had some time out because I was beginning to feel I could not cope. Then I went to a day school for disabled children. Then I went to a mainstream FE college for a year but it became difficult to cope, and that is when I was offered a place at [X] college [a residential college for people with disabilities] where I stayed for three years.

As previously mentioned, 11 of the 31 high-flyers acquired their disabilities, through accident or illness, during their adult years, and thus had a purely mainstream educational career from nursery school right through to university. This was the case for Clint, who, after a short period of time at public school, went to grammar school where he achieved substantial qualifications, in terms of O levels and A levels, to guarantee him a place at university where he did a BA (Hons) degree in international economics: 'I went to public school but got kicked out, so went to grammar school then university.'

The experiences of attending public school also concerned Nick:

> My childhood experiences were purely of the sporting and academic nature and really very little else. The one thing that a boys' public school teaches you is that you are a leader by definition.

Level of education

Several of the high-flyers, especially those with acquired impairments, believed education was important, if not vital, to their current occupational status. This can be likened to research by Carr-Saunders and Wilson (1944), suggesting that the major criterion for professional status is the presence of an intellectual technique, acquired by special training, which performs a service for society and is unavailable to the lay person. For example, Ali, now a barrister, believed: '…without education I can't be a lawyer, without education I can't join the legal profession. So all my life is indebted to my education.'

Ali's father, a local authority official, believed it was important to get a good education in order to get a respectable job. Ali had a good schooling and aspired to become a physician. But at the age of 17 he had an accident that left him severely injured and unable to walk:

> In a third world country you have two occupational choices: either be a doctor or a soldier. I knew I could not be a soldier. But my brother told me that my disability will deprive me of being a doctor so the best thing to do was to join the legal profession.

So Ali took an extra year to get the qualifications he needed to study law at university.

Kenny, a management accountant, was expected to do well in life, and was sent to a private boarding school where expectations and standards were high. He perceives his education has informed his whole career:

> I did an economics degree which put me in a good position to do an accountancy qualification, so my whole career was initiated by my education.

A large proportion of the disabled high-flyers had attained a high level of education.

All of them had GSCEs or O levels. Twenty-six of them were university graduates. Five out of the six individuals who did not have a university degree were professional artists who underwent vocational training to be successful in their occupation.

Fifteen of the 26 university graduates were men while 11 were women; 16 had congenital disabilities and 10 had acquired their disabilities. Only 8 of the 16 high-flyers with congenital disabilities perceived their education as being an essential prerequisite to their occupational choice and success. Tom, one of the vicars, recognised that it was the theology training that he gained 18 years after his initial schooling that proved to be the key to his current status. Harry, a computer analyst, had the ambition of becoming a computer programmer, so he decided to do a degree in computer science which, he believed, provided him with the knowledge base and qualifications to do so. He claims, 'the degree was relatively interesting, something I could do and there were good job openings available.' Similarly, Mary, who pursued a career in law and became qualified as a solicitor as a result of doing a degree and a number of professional qualifications, claims:

> There was no point being educated just for the sake of being educated, I had to be educated for a purpose. So doing law was a purpose. The way my education panned out led inexorably to me going into the law.

For Corin, every stage of her educational career was critical for her to progress and achieve her current position of university lecturer. She admits '...getting my PhD was one of my biggest positive landmarks.'

Some of the high-flyers with congenital impairments did not identify education as being overtly significant to their career success. For example, Sunny, now an established actor and director, points out how his university education had no influence whatsoever on his current career success:

> I went to college and did business studies, which has nothing to do with acting, and then I did a degree in psychology, philosophy and sociology, which has nothing to do with acting.

This point is echoed by Kay, a disability strategy manager and formally a software programmer in the IT industry:

> I did a degree in language which was kind of linguistics. It's a bit like a philosophy degree so it didn't prepare me for anything in working terms.

So, although several of the successful individuals followed education-related career patterns, others pursued careers in fields completely unrelated to their previous education. Those with congenital disabilities were less likely to follow education-related career patterns or achieve a university degree than those with acquired disabilities. However, many of them perceived education to still be significant to their occupational and social life situation in different ways. As Katey, a freelance journalist, contends:

> In a conventional sense, I haven't done what I have because of my education. But the fact that I was educated and the level of education I have has enabled me to do as much as I've done. The fact I did English as a degree and subjects in English and history has given me an articulateness, sense of structure, sense of plot, addiction to grammatical correctness and use of language. My interest in history and folklore, stemming initially from my education, has been a great influence on the novels I have written.

Similarly, Jude, a vicar, regarded her educational career to be a critical precursor of her employability and economic security:

> The opportunity to go to a university in the East Midlands and study information technology was a great opportunity at that time. I know that whatever I do I won't be unemployed. This actually gives me a lot of confidence because there is security. This all resulted from my education.

She considers her degree in theology to be the critical key which facilitated her with knowledge and training she required to meet her calling and to become a successful vicar.

Overall, nine high-flyers had a postgraduate qualification. A number of them perceived it to be significant to their career development and success. For Roger, a university professor, his PhD in cosmology enabled him to pursue a career in academia, a career that could not be hindered by his deteriorating impairment: 'Had I chosen almost any other career options I was considering, such as the civil service, I wouldn't have been able to continue.'

Corin felt that she needed a PhD to meet her desired career goal (which was to teach) and achieve a respectable status which would overshadow her disability:

> I did a straight computing degree and I couldn't get a job after that. No one would look at someone who was disabled, especially in South Africa which is way behind... I needed some more background because I wasn't getting much teaching out there, so I came here to do a PhD... After that I thought people must view what I do as important and I won't have to keep having to prove myself.

Several respondents underwent professional and business training to facilitate their career progression. The importance of professional qualifications was confirmed by Harry, a computer science graduate working for an international information technology company:

> I also have some on-the-job training to keep up with new developments. I've just been working for a professional qualification recognised by the industry which would qualify me for the role of certified Microsoft Systems Engineer. This is an industry-recognised qualification based on all the Microsoft packages that are available and will give me the opportunity to move within the company and within the industry.

On a similar note, Kay felt the acquisition of an MBA would provide her with more career scope and speed up her career progression. As she asserts:

> I took an MBA, because I got to the point where I thought I wasn't making the sort of progress that I really ought to be making. So I sponsored

myself through an MBA in order to demonstrate to myself, as much as to everybody else, that I was a competent and able manager.

Tables 5.1 and 5.2 show the proportion of qualifications attained by male and female high-flyers with congenital and acquired disabilities.

Table 5.1 Percentage of qualifications among respondents with congenital disabilities

Type of qualification	Male (N = 11)	Female (N = 9)	Total % (N = 20)
Postgraduate degree	9	44	25
Undergraduate degree or equivalent	63	100	80
Professional qualification	27	22	25
A levels or equivalent	90	100	95
GCSE, O level or equivalent	100	100	100

Table 5.2 Percentage of qualifications among respondents with acquired disabilities

Type of qualification	Male (N = 8)	Female (N = 3)	Total % (N=11)
Postgraduate degree	38	0	27
Undergraduate degree or equivalent	100	67	91
Professional qualification	13	67	27
A levels or equivalent	100	67	91
GCSE, O level or equivalent	100	100	100

The data demonstrates that a larger proportion of the females in the sample have undergraduate degrees than the males.

As mentioned above, the majority of men without undergraduate degrees worked in the arts and trained via more vocational means. However, this was not always the reason behind their decision for not going to university. Some had no real drive to go to university, expressing comments like: 'I had no intention of going to university ever' or 'I didn't want to be educated. I had had enough once

I left school.' However, Jonathan did want to go to university near his home in the capital, but there was no access for wheelchair users, so he started a musical career as the lead singer and songwriter of his own band.

The high-flyers who did not attend university were mostly men who had a congenital disability and were exposed to low expectations during their childhood. Moreover, their social class backgrounds did not emphasise the need for achievement in educational pursuits.

Subject of education

A number of the high-flyers, most with acquired disabilities, said they chose their education with a career in mind. Eleven of all 19 males opted for degrees, at either undergraduate or postgraduate status, which they believed was paramount to their career development and in the same field. Ali was one of these men:

> In 1980 I joined [X] University, where I spent four years. By 1984 I qualified with an LLB second class. The next year I registered for a postgraduate degree but my supervisor disappeared to join the Forces. Now I am doing an LLM in environmental law. Getting the required qualifications from a recognised, prestigious university and passing the bar examination was a major turning point in my career development.

Only 4 of these 11 males were disabled from childhood. Bob was one of these men. He considered his degree to be the key to a career in accountancy:

> I went on to university and got a BSc in economics and accounting at [X] University. Then I went on to do my professional training and I am now a qualified chartered accountant and financial planner.

A possible reason why there were fewer high-flyers with congenital disabilities who followed careers related to their education could be that non-disabled students have more control over their choice of academic subjects, and thus their future career, than their disabled counterparts. This could be either as a consequence of the disabled person's actual impairment or how others react to it. Furthermore, the limited choice available to people with congenital disabilities could be due to the restrictions imposed on the disability community by institutions in mainstream society including schools, colleges and universities. It could be suggested that because the high-flyers with acquired disabilities experienced a non-disabled childhood, were exposed to high parental expectations and went to mainstream school, they had a wide range of educational and career options. Although many of these individuals became disabled in early adulthood, several had already graduated from university and become established in their careers. Others were fortunate enough to continue with their original career development plan, even after the acquisition of their impairment. For example, Amil, who acquired his impairment just prior to starting university, followed a conventional career path, perceiving his choice of education to be the key to his occupational future. Further, as he chose to pursue a career in computing, the acquisition of his impairment had no detrimental impact on his academic achievements or career success: 'When I went to [X] University I did a degree in computing because I knew that was the sort of career I wanted to go into.'

Two-thirds (six out of nine) of the women with congenital disabilities obtained educational qualifications that they believed opened doors to their current occupations (e.g. degrees in law or computing). Mary, who qualified with a degree in law, which enabled her to work as a solicitor for many years, firmly believed 'the way my education panned out led inexorably to me going into the law.' This was also the case for Maria, a speech and language therapist, who selected an undergraduate degree that would provide an opening to the career of her preference: 'My degree was in speech and language therapy so I really use the basics of that every day.'

Amanda, an artistic director and dancer, was the only woman with an acquired disability who achieved academic qualifications that were direct pre-requisites to her current career. She left school at 16 and went straight to dance college where she spent three years training to become a professional dancer. From there she joined a dance theatre. Her education and training were so specialised that she was concerned that her professional horizons are very narrow and she would not be able to do anything unrelated to the field of dance.

SEGREGATED EDUCATION

Prior to the introduction of segregated or special education, children with physical and learning difficulties often found themselves at the lower end of the elementary school structure due to lack of facilities and awareness of support requirements, which prevented them from achieving and demonstrating their full potential.

As a result of the 1944 Education Act in the United Kingdom, the 11+ examination was introduced, which used a procedure whereby selection by ability sanctioned selection by disability (Barnes, 1991). In addition, as the National Curriculum was designed for the majority, children with disabilities who required different or extra facilities and support were placed at a great disadvantage as their individual needs could not be met in a mainstream environment. Hence, Local Education Authorities were instructed to make separate provisions for children with an impairment of the 'body or mind' (Barnes, 1991), a haven for general education's cast-offs (Kauffman, 1999). This instigated the establishment of segregated education, initially set up by charitable organisations to serve individual differences in learning styles and capacity, which were less understood than they are today.

In the United Kingdom, segregated or special schools were the most common form of provision, with 58 per cent of students with disabilities in England attending special schools (Norwich, 1994). By 1971, there were 1019 special schools in England and Wales (Jowett, Hegarty and Moses, 1988) and 482 new ones opened during 1971–72 (Department of Education and Science (DES), 1978). In 2003, there were 1160. Currently, in the UK, 94,000 young disabled people attend special schools and of those 2000 also attend mainstream school part-time (Department for Education and Skills (DfES), 2004).

However, the cost of special education per child is too high for most countries. Governments are recognising the need to develop a more affordable system which will provide quality education for all children. Furthermore, legislation is clearly moving towards an increasing emphasis on inclusion. The SEN and Disability Act (Department for Education and Employment, 2001), which amends the Disability Discrimination Act (1995), delivers a strengthened right to a mainstream education for disabled children unless this is incompatible with the parents' wishes or the provision of efficient education for other children. Consequently, those working in special education are seeing the need to make links with mainstream in order to move towards more inclusive practices. This is one of the main aims proposed in the recent White Paper, *Removing Barriers to Achievement* (DfES, 2004). The strategy aims ultimately to reduce the number of special schools and encourage more mainstream schools to adopt fully inclusive practices. Furthermore, by curtailing the number of residential schools and reallocating resources to local provisions and service, disabled children and young people can be educated closer to their homes and families.

Even with the worldwide trend towards inclusion and the increasing participation of disabled children in mainstream schools, special education still has an important role and, for some students, is still the best option. For example, students who require more time, assistance and special equipment to achieve academic goals are at more of an advantage in special education. However, others need to be put in situations in which they have opportunities to succeed and develop self-esteem and confidence.

Advantages of segregated education

There has been much debate over recent years concerning the so-called provision of segregated/special education for individuals with disabilities. Underlying the debate are two clear ideological views. One takes an altruistic perspective, implying that there are several advantages of segregated education, related not only to practical and economic factors, but also to the perceived effects on both students with disabilities and non-disabled students of an inclusive education (Jenkinson, 1997). Further, Middleton (1999) argues that special education is marketed to parents as a safe option for their disabled child, who would otherwise be vulnerable in the 'hurley-burley' of mainstream education. Similarly, Barnes (1991) asserts that one of the principal functions of segregated education is to protect disabled children from the 'rough and tumble' of the 'normal' environment. According to one parent:

> My child has high needs and is vulnerable to other children. He would be unable to function in mainstream education. It would not be a positive experience for my child or for other children. The special school is the only appropriate situation for him. (Jenkinson, 1997, p.92)

It was assumed that economies in the provision of special instructional methods, aids and equipment could be more easily achieved if students with a specific disability such as hearing impairment or physical disability were congregated in a limited number of settings rather than dispersed over many schools. Similarly, Jenkinson (1997) maintains that specialist teachers could be concentrated in a single school, enhancing the development of professional expertise in a specialised area.

A further economy is achieved by centralising ancillary services such as speech therapy, physiotherapy and specialist teaching to one location rather than being dispersed over schools in a wide area or requiring the student's withdrawal from classes to attend a specialist centre. Moreover, paramedical staff can work in close collaboration with an educational team in a special school. Multi-professional perspectives or the combination of different expertise can be helpful to develop individual education programmes designed to maximise individual students' educational potential. Pearse (1996) suggests that the existence of a multi-professional team under one roof ensures consistency, and quick adaptation and response to ongoing and changing needs. For instance, while therapists possess the talent and capability to teach students how they can perform certain skills to the best of their individual ability, teachers contribute to the knowledge concerning the functional use of these skills in selected activities (Campbell, 1987).

Some research claims that segregated educational institutions offer the best options for disabled children. For example, Jenkinson (1997) maintains that with small classes and high teacher–pupil ratios, special schools permit intensive one-to-one attention and instruction which can be pitched at a level appropriate to each child's needs rather than at the traditional age-grade level that caters for the majority of students. Further, they are perceived as more supportive, both physically and socially, and less threatening to students with disabilities, encouraging their feeling of security and enhancing their self-esteem by avoiding continual comparison of their achievements with other, more physically competent, students. According to Pearse (1996), segregated institutions are an integral ingredient of the social and psychological independence of disabled children. Moreover, being nurtured in an environment free from the intervention of mainstream barriers permits the children to explore and develop a sense of self. In their study, *Life as a Disabled Child*, Watson *et al.* (1999) discovered that there was much more autonomy in a segregated setting than in a mainstream setting. This was due to children of special schools having the freedom to associate with others in child-defined spaces, albeit within the usual parameters of the school environment.

Cook, Swain and French (2001) suggest that disabled students are likely to build positive social relationships more easily in segregated establishments where they not only share common goals and interests, but values, aspirations and ways of conceptualising the world. There are many accounts by disabled adults who testify to the importance of the friendships they made with other young people in special schools (French and Swain, 2000). Sullivan, speaking of her experiences of school, recalls:

> ...For the first time I began to make friends with other children, to have fun... Every weekend when my mother, brother and sister came to visit me I had so much to tell them about school, about my friends and the nurses I lived with. (1992, p.173)

In mainstream school, where a disabled child requires support, Watson *et al.* (1999) suggest that successful social integration with peers may be impeded. They found that for some young disabled people, the physical proximity of the helper could work against social processes of acceptance among other children in the class. On a consistent train of thought, Allan (1996) suggests that all aspects of the child's interpersonal relationships can be brought under the vigilance of the staff, as disabled children are more comprehensively observed than their non-disabled peers:

> All children are the object of scrutiny within schools, but for pupils with special educational needs, the gaze reaches further. They are observed, not only at work in the classroom, but also at break times. The way in which they interact with mainstream peers or integrate socially is often viewed as equally important, if not more so, than their attainment in mainstream curriculum goals. (p.222)

Criticisms of segregated education

Alderson and Goodey (1998) argue that reports suggesting that students have higher self-esteem or do better at special schools are meaningless if self-esteem depends on being in an unreal, protected world, or if the school is unable to cultivate their full potential and facilitate their achievement progression. Therefore, they argue, many special school students will continue, as adults, to be unable to live the full life envisaged by the United Nations Convention (1989) which sees all children as contributing citizens, and affirms faith in the dignity and worth of the human person.

Similarly, Barnes (1991) argues that being in a protective, segregated environment until one's late teens (as has been the norm for many disabled children), and being denied the experiences considered essential for the transition from childhood to adulthood, shields disabled individuals from the realities of society. This will only serve to reinforce the commonly held conception that individuals with impairments are eternal children. Dr John Mary and the British Council of Organizations of Disabled People (1986) believe the special education system is one of the main channels for disseminating non-disabled perceptions of the world and ensuring that disabled school leavers are socially isolated. This isolation results in disabled people passively accepting social discrimination, lacking the skills necessary to successfully pursue the tasks of adulthood and not understanding about the main social issues of our time. Therefore, as well as reinforcing the myth that disabled people are 'eternal children', segregated education ensures disabled school leavers lack the skills for overcoming the myth (BCODP, 1986). This is supported by Jenkinson (1997) and Fuchs and Fuchs (1998) who believe that the lack of appropriate behavioural role models, the lack of feedback from non-disabled peers, and the removal from the common culture of childhood and adolescence contribute to later isolation in the community.

So by producing socially and educationally disabled individuals, the special education system perpetuates and legitimatises discrimination practices in all other areas of social life, particularly employment (Barnes, 1991). This is consistent with Dunn (1968), who asserts that it is the actual segregated placement itself that is responsible for individuals with disabilities being labelled with negative terminology and excluded from mainstream society. He contends that diagnostic procedures based on the administration of standardised tests tend to categorise the student under a particular label, with damaging effects both on teacher expectations and the student's own self-concept.

A further major criticism of segregated education is that in developing an isolated curriculum that focuses disproportionately on specific educational needs, it prevents students from learning a wide range of subjects offered in mainstream schools and perceived to be important to successful economic participation. Furthermore, Jenkinson (1997) offers the opinion that the small number of staff in special schools, coupled with their significantly limited, if not deficient, curricula expertise, undeniably serves to restrict the range and content of the curriculum. She anticipates the lack of training and experience of most special school teachers in the secondary curriculum to be an increasing handicap as students with disabilities move into adolescence.

An article entitled 'Special School Shame' (*Disability Now,* January 1997) reported on a study, conducted by the Alliance for Inclusive Education, which evidenced that special schools are less likely than mainstream schools to enter their students for public examinations. According to the sample statistics, only 6 of the 85 special schools in the study (7 per cent) proceeded to compete in nationally recognised exams. The general line of reasoning was based on the assumption that children in special schools were unable to learn as well as their peers in regular education. As GCSE qualifications are the benchmark of ability to enter further education, the evidence proposes special schools to be a barrier to equality as they persist with their unjustified presumption, and fail to permit their students to follow an educational path parallel to their non-disabled counterparts.

INCLUSIVE EDUCATION

The International Year of Disabled People in 1981 influenced the community to think more deeply about the way in which services should be provided to people with disabilities. The United Nations Declaration made during that year included the right to receive an education that would facilitate students with disabilities fully to develop their academic and social potential. As Barnes (1991) has argued, inclusion plays an imperative role in the fight towards the elimination of discrimination and of disabled people being accepted as citizens of the social majority. Furthermore, he suggests that being educated in mainstream institutions is positively correlated with the successful transition of individuals with disabilities into employment and wider society.

However, being placed in mainstream school does not necessarily equate to experiencing total inclusion. Inclusive education means more than simply placing a young disabled person in mainstream school and providing extra support. Inclusion demands major changes within society to enable everybody to participate, interact and make choices as they wish. Young disabled people are less likely than their non-disabled counterparts to pursue academic subjects of their choice due to restrictions imposed by the physical environment. (2003) maintains, even now, that mainstream schools are not fully accessible as those responsible for developing inclusion still often think of accessibility as ramps and rails. In her study of disabled secondary school students throughout the UK, Burgess found that their curriculum choices were severely curtailed. 36 per cent of young disabled people she talked to could not study subjects of their choice due to lack of access to the curriculum and the disabling environment, including attitudes of teachers. One student in her study commented:

> Teachers underestimate what I can do. I do loads of sport outside school, like basketball, tennis, archery and cricket, and I can swim. Teachers never want to hear about what I can do, but always assume I won't have done it before. (Burgess, 2003, p.15)

Discriminatory attitudes among teaching staff in the mainstream sector have also been confirmed by UK education inspectors. For example, a survey by the UK Government's Department of Education and Science (DES), published in 1989, noted that the attitudes of some staff were 'patronising', while others were reluctant to work with disabled pupils. These attitudes, it was found, were likely to be reflected in the attitudes and behaviour of non-disabled students towards their disabled peers. The effects of such attitudinal discrimination among peers may be fatal. As Haring (1991) argues, peer acceptance is a primary outcome of schooling, with important consequences for the quality of life of students with disabilities. Existing discourse reveals that low childhood peer acceptance induces loneliness, truancy, psychopathology and suicide (Parker and Asher, 1987), as it deprives children of opportunities to learn normal, adaptive modes of social conduct and social cognition as well as undermining their academic progress. Thus, Saborine (1985) proposes the educational philosophy of developing the 'whole child', and the egalitarian intent of recent UK special education legislation appear to entail an emphasis on the social outcomes of students with disabilities.

Thus, the ultimate goal of education is not only to mould the student into a 'responsible contributor' to society, as maintained by proponents of inclusive education (e.g. Giddens, 1997), but should also be to encourage conversation and social interaction between disabled and non-disabled peers in a co-operative group situation. Fuchs and Fuchs (1998) believe that, within that context, educators should help change non-disabled children's stereotypical thinking about disabilities and help children with disabilities develop social skills, which, in turn, will enable them to interact more effectively within increasingly broad professional and personal networks. Without positive social learning experiences and opportunities to fully develop their self-concept, children with disabilities will neither be prepared, as adults, to play a valuable role in the economic life of society, nor have the ability to perform essential tasks required to live an independent and dignified lifestyle.

The deficiencies of segregated and mainstream education can be eliminated and their benefits combined by partial integration and a curriculum developed so all students can participate. A flexible interpretation of content ensures that a wide range of functional skills may be included, such as health and physical education (which includes hydrotherapy and physiotherapy), road safety, sex education and personal hygiene, together with leisure activities such as camps and riding for the disabled. Mathematics may include skills with money and time. Work experience and legal rights may be taught as an integral part of the studies of society and environment. English may incorporate argumentative communication or receptive language skills. Similarly, other key areas include activities that are appropriate at all levels of ability.

Partial integration, increasingly perceived as combining the 'best of both worlds' (Jenkinson, 1997), permits the disabled student to have access to a special curriculum and small classes in a special school, while also having the opportunity to socialise and participate with non-disabled peers in activities and classes that are not available in the special school. Therefore, those disabled students who are able, are encouraged to pursue subjects not available in the special school's limited curriculum, and achieve the prerequisites regarded essential for successful vocational participation and career development. However, these students can still retain access to facilities and resources from the special school that may be lacking in the mainstream school.

The idea of partial integration is further discussed below, as the disabled high-flyers present their perceptions of the benefits and drawbacks of segregated/special and mainstream education and how, if at all, the type of institutions attended influenced their transition to adulthood, particularly employment.

DISABLED HIGH-FLYERS' EXPERIENCES OF SEGREGATED AND MAINSTREAM EDUCATION

The majority of high-flyers in this book were educated in an era when children with disabilities were placed into predominately segregated educational institutions, which were considered to give them the intensive tuition they needed, and therefore 'a better start in life' (Simpson, 1990). However, according to their stories, segregated education was not favoured by all disabled people nor by their parents. Some believed it to be a fundamental part of the discrimination process, creating and perpetuating artificial barriers between disabled children and their non-disabled peers. As mentioned earlier in the chapter, 12 of the 20 professionals with congenital disabilities experienced mainstream education, either on a part-time or full-time basis. Eight of them were integrated throughout their educational career, and the remaining four had participated in a combination of segregated and mainstream institutions.

A few of the individuals went to residential educational institutions, either segregated or mainstream. However, residential schooling was perceived as a different type of schooling from day schooling and thus is discussed separately from the other two types of education. Although some of the issues uncovered were specific to residential education, there were a few overlaps.

Analysis of the interviews highlighted several issues that are perceived as benefits and drawbacks of either mainstream or segregated/special education. The high-flyers identified the benefits of segregated education to be related to: academically and socially supportive environment; role models; and physical access. They perceived the drawbacks of such education as being in terms of: the curriculum and teaching standards; and being isolated from their local and non-disabled community.

Several of the individuals who were educated in establishments specifically for students with disabilities saw this education as paramount to their career success. Jude had been through the mainstream and segregated education system, but considered her years at a further education college for people with physical disabilities to be a major positive influence on her career success:

> I went to a mainstream FE college for a year but it became difficult to cope, and that is when I was offered a place at [X college] where I stayed for three years. Going to [X college] was a big determinant. Without that push, the rest of my achievements wouldn't have happened.

Sam left his home in South Wales at the young age of five to go to a residential school for children with cerebral palsy. He left there at 16 years old, with nine GCSEs, and went straight to a segregated residential college where he got three A levels. He believed it was his experience in segregated education that has moulded him into the person he has become:

> It made me stronger more independent, competent and worldly wise. If I hadn't gone there I would be a completely different person. It also provided me the facilities and support I needed, in terms of physiotherapy, speech therapy, so I could maintain a healthy life.

Following this line of reasoning, segregated education was thought to facilitate the cultivation of the children's personality without the interruption of non-disabled barriers. As Sam comments: 'I was never exposed to the consequences of having a disability, because disability at school was never an issue.'

This was pointed out by Jude who considered the experience of being in a supportive barrier-free environment to be critical to her initial character formation: 'the segregated school enabled my personality and character to flourish because I wasn't the "different" person out of the 800 people in my school.'

One of the unfortunate realities faced by disabled children integrated in mainstream school is being constantly reminded of their disability or, as Sunny put it, 'they are pointed at as "different" in mainstream schools'. This, in itself, could inhibit the establishment of social relationships, as was the case for Sam during his time at university:

> The barriers to form any kind of relationship seemed enormous. Nobody really had time for me and it suddenly made me realise who I was and what I was.

This encounter, and others like it in Sam's adulthood, did present him with challenges. However, the fact that most of his pre-adult years were spent in what he perceived as a supportive, encouraging and responsive environment where his individual cognitive and physical needs were met, means he had developed the ability to master and manipulate obstacles out of his way and did not feel intimidated by them. Therefore, in this respect, segregated education indeed had a positive influence on future success.

Another advantage of segregated education, according to Tom, was that it provided role models to the younger generation of disabled people:

> Segregated education does give disabled people role models. Sadly, within a mainstream school there tends to be half a dozen disabled students in a population of 600–700. Where do you get positive role models? The message conveyed in mainstream schools is that the way to succeed is to be non-disabled because all your peers are not disabled. In segregated school you have disabled peers you can talk to about your disability, challenges and obstacles. When I was at school there were people who challenged me academically and people who were really good at wheelchair sport. So I had different role models for academia and how to use my wheelchair.

This was echoed by another respondent, Mary, a retired solicitor and ex-student of both mainstream and segregated school, who felt disabled role models were important to the lives of young disabled people in terms of their outlook on life and their drive to achieve:

> I think that if you meet people who are 'worse' than you, medically speaking, it really does encourage you to be able to think you can do it too. I'm absolutely convinced that role models are important, and if disabled people aren't seen in prominent roles and doing normal things then other disabled people lose out.

In this sense, therefore, segregated schools and colleges permit disabled young people to build relationships with each other, support, understand and encourage one another, and be able to empathise and learn from each other in terms of how to use their individual potential to succeed.

Several of the high-flyers praised the physical architecture of special schools and colleges, maintaining that it permitted an enabling environment that was crucial to their developing independence. Furthermore, it offered them the freedom, as children, to explore their environment independent of non-disabled influences. Mary identified physical access to be the primary reason she left mainstream school to attend a school for disabled people:

> The reason why I moved to segregated school was because the sixth form was upstairs and I couldn't continue at my mainstream school. At my mainstream school, if I wanted to do music, and sometimes French as well, we had to go to a classroom further up the hill. For me, this meant going through the caretaker's house. This wasn't easy.

The inaccessible environment of mainstream school was demonstrated by Bob's experience. He had to work twice as hard to overcome the access barriers and prove his academic abilities to staff and fellow peers. He recalls:

> I had to go from home to an environment which is not very easy to function in if you are in a wheelchair, because boarding schools are mainly in old Victorian properties, not designed for wheelchairs.

Although many of the disabled professionals favoured educational segregation, their accounts of their personal experiences confirmed that there are definitely significant drawbacks to the special education system. Several respondents commented on the limited curriculum and the low standard of teaching in special schools. Mary pointed out:

> The maths teaching in my special school was so abominable. Although I was ahead and did maths O level early, I felt I would fail my maths A level. The teacher couldn't even answer the questions, let alone teach me what the right answers were!

Mary's sister, Kay, expressed an equal disappointment at the standard of teaching in the school they went to, and both sisters implied that their own potential to progress into prestigious high-status employment of their choice was suppressed by the school's low quality of education and limited curriculum:

> The teachers appeared, in retrospect, to have been cast-offs; the curriculum was really, really narrow. When I started there I repeated work, for about the first two years, that I had already done twice and it was hopeless. When I came to choose O levels there was a choice of about five that could be done within the school and a couple that could be done next door, at the grammar school.

The limited choice of subjects available in special schools was an influence on the high-flyers' future choices. Their reports imply that their original career aspirations did not always correspond to what their schooling permitted them to achieve. This was the case for Mary:

> I wanted to become a graphologist so I took up the relevant subjects at my mainstream school, but when we moved I realised I wasn't going to become a graphologist, because there wasn't any related subject at my segregated school.

The standard of education and the expectations special schools had of disabled children during the 1940s–1970s were exceedingly poor, as indicated by Sunny, whose primary, secondary and further education was segregated and residential:

> With segregated education, they have a particular attitude about you as a disabled person. They don't expect anything of you. The education you receive is different and poor quality. I left school at 16 with 2 CSEs which was the most that was offered. Just me and one other guy from that school took them.

A further negative aspect of segregated schools/colleges, highlighted by the disabled high-flyers, was that their schools were some distance from their homes, and so the children had to be transported out of their local community, away from local children who attended a school in the local area. This meant they had few friends among local non-disabled peers. Furthermore, as children, the high-flyers experienced long travelling times, sometimes of up to two hours a day, which meant that they missed out on participating in after-school activities with non-disabled children from their local area. This also has negative implications with regard to children's ability to learn either in the classroom or when they return home for homework. Both Marty and Harry lived in large cities and had to travel to the opposite side of the city every day to their schools.

This problem is worse for children who are boarders. They will experience the negative effects of being uprooted and distanced from their family and childhood home environment. As Sunny points out:

> Special schools took children from all over the country and you were separated from your home, so when you left school your friends were from all over the place. In this estate, for example, kids go to the local school so when they leave school they still have their friends.

The social aspect of being away at boarding school was quite negative for Lara, who confesses that, 'I probably enjoyed the social experience less, being away from home, being ill, being bullied.' Harry also did not like the fact that he had to go to a further education college in a different city from his home and was not integrating with the non-disabled community:

> The college was residential which meant I was living away from home, although I did come home quite frequently. But I perceived the college as quite an isolating environment, with purely disabled students there.

Similarly, Ed's experience of residential education was not very positive:

> My secondary school was also residential for kids with cerebral palsy. From the age of 11 to 18 you were forced to be on your own. Some people may like that, but I certainly didn't, not because it was segregated but because it forced you away from home at a very early age. I don't approve of that for anyone, disabled or not.

As mentioned before, being away from home at boarding school proved to be quite a socially isolating experience for Lara, who recalls feeling isolated '…because of being ill which meant I couldn't go to school as I had to spend the whole day in bed and on my own'.

A few of the high-flyers, especially those who experienced residential education, maintained that segregated education had made a crucial contribution to their social and cognitive development. For Sam, who has a congenital disability, boarding school not only cultivated his academic potential but also, as he reflects:

> It took me away from my little house in South Wales, where there were certainly no job opportunities for me and I would have been treated like a five-year-old for the rest of my life. Being away at school obviously gave me access to a wider range of people from a variety of different backgrounds and the opportunity to gain real life experiences. This contributed to the whole learning experience.

As stated previously, 12 of the 20 high-flyers with congenital disabilities attended mainstream establishments, either for part or the whole of their educational career. Only one of these attended boarding school. Like segregated education, being integrated into mainstream schools and colleges engenders both positive and negative experiences for the disabled individual.

Several of the men and women who attended mainstream schools, both private and public, day and residential, conceptualised it as a significant driving force to achieve the standards required to compete in a predominately non-disabled employment market. On reflection of his experience at a private mainstream boarding school, Bob claimed:

It gave me bags of confidence to know that I could achieve things and, from an educational point of view, it gave me all the exam success that you could ever hope for. I was lucky that I was always in an environment where the expectations to achieve were so much higher than in most other schools. And everyone came out with good grades, good exams and a very, very broad breadth of educational achievement, and that was always well looked on by the next school, the university, employers.

This was not dissimilar to the experience of Anna, a successful athlete, who found that her good mainstream comprehensive schooling instilled her with the drive and perseverance to achieve, and not to fear failure. It also influenced her ambition to become a professional athlete:

We were encouraged to do as much as we were able to, whatever level you were at, and that was fine. That encouraged me and taught me, from a young age, that it was OK to work and try to do something well, it didn't matter if you failed but it was more important to actually try to do it. Being in that school environment taught me to be really ambitious, to be able to set goals so actually I started thinking about competing for Britain from when I was about 12 years old.

The different expectations of mainstream and segregated institutions were indicated by Greg's experience and awareness of how disability was perceived in the late 1960s/early 1970s. He was sent to a mainstream private school for boys where, he maintains:

I was taught to expect a lot more than many other disabled people, partly because of the school I went to and slightly because of the social surroundings around my impairment. I was in quite a posh school. I wasn't asked to sew blankets, as were special school equivalents, although they are different now to what they were then. But for my generation at school, mid to late 1970s, like Sunny, the expectations were 'be lucky if you get an O level, mate'. Pathetic! Although it is hard to be in a mainstream school, it's worth it.

However, Katey, who is now a freelance journalist, pointed out that although mainstream environments are known to offer a more diverse curriculum and encourage high levels of achievement, they also must have the right ingredients to cultivate and support the academic potential of disabled individuals:

Whenever I'm in a smaller pond, I tend to rise to the top of it. Whenever I went into a big area I just sank! I went to a big university very briefly but didn't do very well because I didn't manage in self-catering accommodation in the middle of a big city. But [a Midlands] school, [a Midlands] convent and [a Midlands] university were three places where I could do very well without being patronised because it was a small enough place for my abilities to be recognised.

It has been argued that inclusive education permits the establishment of social relationships between disabled and non-disabled peers, as awareness and understanding of disability is said to engender an increasing acceptance of it. Bob believes his time in mainstream education taught him some critical lessons of how to become accepted and valued in mainstream society:

> I was expected to do what everybody else did. If I didn't I would feel left out, so I just got on and did it. The other boys could see that I could achieve what they could achieve and there was nothing special about me. At that age, they quickly realised that you can put up with the rough and tumble and the teasing and the physical fights, and that I was just like the other boys except in a wheelchair.

Jonathan's comment below demonstrates that inclusion is important to the reduction of discrimination and the maintenance of positive relationships between disabled and non-disabled peers:

> I remember being in the cloakroom once and a kid started calling me names so I kicked him very hard several times until he was on the floor in tears. He then became my best friend! I realised that my able-bodied friends were no more special than I was. Mainstream education is good for disabled people to learn that non-disabled people aren't better than them.

Katey's experience shows how inclusion is a two-way learning process and, with the right people and the right attitudes, can be very positive:

> I started off in a mixed school, both sexes, where people could say what they like and I wasn't protected. But it ended up that I made a good circle of friends and they would black the eye of anyone who was rude to or about me.

The varied mainstream education experienced by Maria, a speech and language therapist, taught her some valuable lessons about cultural diversity, flexibility and being aware of individual potential. She believed that this invariably influenced her current perspective on life, both professionally and socially:

> I kept going to new schools so I had to get used to meeting different people, making friends in different places and not being fixed with the same people all my life. I think that was a very healthy experience

which I think has set me up for the moves I have had to make in my adult life, i.e. jobs, house etc.

Bob, a financial planner, and several other of the disabled high-flyers perceived the lessons taught through their integrated education, both formal and informal, to be critical to their successful participation in mainstream economic society:

I think it's that attitude that's been so important later on and that's why I'm a very great believer in integrated education. It's only in that, that the individual can feel they're important, they have a role in normal society and believe they can achieve what everyone else can achieve.

Jonathan, a television presenter, who favoured mainstream education and societal equality, asserted a similar view, pointing out: 'Disabled people need to be taught the same as their non-disabled counterparts in order to compete with them in today's economic society.'

As mentioned above, several of the respondents were educated in mainstream institutions where few, if any, adaptations were made. They admitted feeling frustrated and disadvantaged by the inaccessible accommodation. Sam, a sports development officer, explained how engaging in simple social activities could be a major undertaking:

Ordering a pint of beer from the student union bar was a battle in itself. There was first the physical access problem of getting into the bar, then getting past all the people, then getting myself heard at the bar...

While Harry preferred his time at a mainstream comprehensive to segregated education, he admits that it was a physically challenging experience:

My 12–16 years schooling was at the local comprehensive. Two main buildings, 200 yards apart, with three floors on one, four on the other and no lift. We had to change classrooms a number of times a day. Boy, was I fit or what!

He was initially denied the option of pursuing a certain degree at a university of his choice due to potential access problems:

We had to fight to get a place on the computer science course at [a Midlands] University. Initially the guy I had spoken to, on the phone, turned me down, not through lack of grades but because I was disabled. So we had to go up there and show them I could walk around and there really wasn't a problem.

Physical access is an issue in all aspects of society and can cause unnecessary restrictions to the career development of some disabled people. Two of the actors, both with a congenital disability, were rejected from drama school in the 1970s and denied the opportunity to be trained in the conventional way. As Greg, an actor and singer, explains: 'For my generation drama school was a no. In my day, you just assumed their courses wouldn't be accessible and accepted it.'

Jonathan, a singer as well as a television presenter, believed that his career development had been restrained by the inaccessible physical accommodation of education:

> The only thing about education that has influenced my career is that I didn't go to university. As I have gone through my life I have found that this has gone against me in a lot of situations. When it was my time to go to university I had only one option, which was in the north of England because it was the only accessible university. I wanted to go to university in London, but nowhere was accessible.

CONCLUSION

Education played an important role in the career success of all 31 high-flyers in this book. Most were university graduates. Several, especially those who acquired their impairment in adulthood and went to mainstream schools, pursued degrees which would lead them directly into employment with a similar focus. Those high-flyers who had opted for degrees with no direct link to their current occupation nonetheless identified their years within the education system to have been critical to their social, cognitive and professional development. It gave them an opportunity to develop relationships, to learn how to become articulate in spoken and written language, and to obtain qualifications that would open doors to professional opportunities.

It is clear that although all of the disabled high-achievers faced some kind of adversity in education, mainstream or segregated, they all believed their education was beneficial to their individual development and in some respects helped them be successful in their occupation. It can be suggested that although the disabled high-achievers' educational lives were perceived to be scattered with challenging and traumatic experiences, what was important was not the event itself, but how the individual responded to it. If achievement depends on a balance between support and challenge, then this book supports the general point that segregated education provided support, while mainstream education was stronger on challenge. It can be argued that disabled children need to be increasingly exposed to the culture and expectations of mainstream education, while maintaining the appropriate support and services available in segregated schools. Bearing in mind that all the 31 disabled people were high-achievers, it seems that they found ways to benefit from the support while not lowering their sights, and to benefit from the challenge without being crushed by it.

CHAPTER 6

Individual Personality and Motivation: Their Roles in Career Success

Behaviour is a mirror in which everyone shows his image.

Goethe

INTRODUCTION

It is common practice for human behaviour to be explained with reference to a clear profile of underlying personality traits (Costa and McCrae, 1994; Goldberg, 1990). Traits, according to Dweck (1999), are one way to describe people's behaviour. As Ajzen (1988) suggests, when people are caught lying or cheating, they are considered dishonest. When people perform poorly, they are said to lack ability or motivation. When they help a person in need they are called altruistic and compassionate, and when they discriminate against members of a minority group they are termed prejudiced. However, as personality traits are latent characteristics, they fail to explain human behaviour that can only be inferred from external observable cues (Ajzen, 1988). For example, the fact that an individual approves or disapproves of abortion, or likes or dislikes the Prime Minister, can become known from their covert or overt responses to themselves or others.

Personality is seen to have a dual impact, both on occupational and on life success. Hendey (1999) argues that if a person starts off on the right path, achievement is likely which, in turn, leads to an increase in self-confidence and the attainment of further knowledge and skills which hold the key to success.

Personality traits have multiple implications for individuals' lives in that they have an influence on people's occupational choice, and on whether they achieve success or failure in their job (Bee, 1996). Research has indicated that certain traits are typical of certain kinds of people. For instance, work relating to career success and high-flyers (e.g. Cox and Cooper, 1988; White *et al.*, 1992) shows that high-achieving individuals scored higher than average on intelligence, assertiveness, emotional stability and self-sufficiency. Furthermore, as demonstrated by Cox and Cooper (1988), the high-flyers, in their study, tended to have high levels of determination, indicated by their ability to set very clear objectives, for themselves and organisations, and to follow them through to see them achieved. This is not a recent finding, having been expressed in much earlier literature. For example, in 1926, Cox found that the two most important characteristics of high-flyers, including great leaders, intellectuals and artists, were their persistence and drive. In yet another early investigation, Tead, in his 1935 book *The Art of Leadership*, reported that the traits of the effective leader were:

> ...nervousness and physical energy, a sense of purpose and direction, enthusiasm, friendliness, integrity, technical mastery, decisiveness, intelligence, teaching skills and faith. (cited in Cooper and Hingley, 1985, p.118)

Writings from Stogdill (1974), the American psychologist and author of *Handbook of Leadership*, suggest that the effective leader can be seen as exhibiting a persistence in pursuit of goals, venturesomeness, originality in problem solving and a drive to exercise initiative in social situations. Similarly, Close (1983), in his article 'Dogmatism and managerial achievement', reveals that successful managers demonstrate greater intelligence, have higher aspirations, and more desire for responsibility than both the general population and less successful managers. Further, he found top managers to be more dogmatic than their junior contemporaries. Spillane (1985), in *Achieving Peak Performance*, suggests that effective managers show decisiveness, self-assurance, intelligence, independence and risk-taking. Upon investigating the reasons for success of the executives in their study, McCall and Lombardo (1983) noted they were outgoing, well liked, charming and technically brilliant.

The high-flyers in Cox and Cooper's (1988) study demonstrated a very high internal *locus of control*. This means that they worked from internal reference points and their actions were mainly influenced by their own internal beliefs and values, not by external factors such as luck, fate or significant others. Similarly, the successful women in White *et al.*'s (1992) study demonstrated a belief that their success was a product of their own hard work, perseverance and drive to achieve, thus maintaining an internal locus of control and a high *need for achievement*, which, they argue, are prime precursors of success.

In view of the likelihood that disabled high-flyers also show similar traits to their non-disabled counterparts, this study explores the personal accounts of the disabled adults in relation to the three major areas of personality and motivation, and how they contribute to the career success of disabled adults. The three areas conceived to be significant by previous research and this work are as follows:

Need for achievement – Since the respondents in the study were all high achievers, it seemed appropriate to explore achievement motivation and its driving mechanisms. The degree of difficulty of tasks the individual feels capable of attempting and how long behaviour is sustained in the face of obstacles and aversive experiences will be examined.

Work centrality – is concerned with the degree of importance work has in an individual's life. Work centrality is measured by hours worked, involvement and commitment, and the extent to which work is part of the individuals' identity.

Locus of control – this area is concerned with the individual's perception of who controls the rewards he/she receives; essentially whether the rewards are believed to be contingent upon an individual's own behaviour or controlled by forces outside themselves. This focus is also concerned with the familial origins of locus of control, that is, the differential child-rearing practices that engender internal or external locus of control, particularly in disabled children. This is followed by a discussion, heavily influenced by Heider's (1958) attribution theory, looking at the four causal attributions of success and failure.

In this chapter I will discuss the three factors above and the findings in relation to each.

NEED FOR ACHIEVEMENT

Given today's intensely competitive business climate worldwide, it is important to understand how individuals' need for achievement may be acquired and changed, and the extent to which this serves to influence their occupational success or failure. This is not a new concept, as has been evidenced by Vernon (1997) who considered the ways in which people consciously strive to attain some criteria of excellence, discovering that the achievement of such criteria leads to feelings of well-being and great satisfaction. Further, it motivated them to strive to the next level of their career. Conversely, an individual is likely to lower their standard of achievement in the instance of failure, thereby inducing feelings of frustration and humiliation. Raynor (1974) argues that immediate success is known to guarantee the opportunity for subsequent career striving, while immediate failure is known to guarantee future career failure through loss of opportunity to continue in that career path.

The formalisation of the achievement-motivation construct is derived primarily from the work of Henry Murray (1938), who was a central influence in achievement motivation research and the development of achievement theory. He based his theory of behaviour on the concept of 'need', believing that the environment can provide the necessary support for the expression of a need or it can contain barriers that impede goal-directed behaviour. Further, he developed an extensive taxonomy of needs, derived from psychological deficits, which represent enduring personality characteristics. One of these needs was the need for achievement (nAch) which Murray describes as:

> the desire or tendency to do things as rapidly and/or as well as possible. [It also includes the desire] to accomplish something difficult. To master, manipulate and organise physical objects, human beings or ideas. To do this as rapidly and as independently as possible. To overcome obstacles and attain a high standard. To excel one's self. To rival and surpass others. To increase self-regard by the successful exercise of talent. (cited in Weiner, 1972, p.172)

McClelland and his associates (1951, 1955) were greatly influenced by the work of Murray (1938) when explaining the different ways that individuals perceive situations and are motivated to strive for a particular success goal. They defined the need for achievement as behaviour directed toward competition with a standard of excellence, where performance in such situations can be evaluated as successful or unsuccessful (McClelland *et al.* 1953). Their theory characterised high-need achievers by their single-minded preoccupation with task accomplishment, believing this to be essential to entrepreneurial success. Moreover, McClelland concluded from his research that the need for achievement is established during childhood and largely influenced by child-rearing practices and other parental influences. His work suggests that children who have been nurtured by parents with relatively strict expectations about right and wrong behaviour, who provide clear feedback on the effectiveness of the children's performance and help their children accept a personal responsibility for their actions, tend to have a fairly high need for achievement.

Achievement behaviour is not just the motivation to achieve. As Atkinson (1964) suggests, it is also the motivation to avoid failure. Together these two motivational tendencies determine whether an individual will ultimately approach or avoid an achievement task. High-need achievers have a tendency to pursue achievement tasks for which there is a reasonable probability of success. According to McClelland (1961), these individuals have a tendency to choose to pursue difficult, challenging tasks that offer opportunities to demonstrate their competence and will avoid tasks that seem too easy. Individuals with a high need for achievement also tend to fear failure (Atkinson, 1964) and thus avoid tasks conceived as being too difficult. As Farmer (1985) points out, high-need achievers are also characterised by their inclination to persist in the face of adversity and, as Murray (1938) claimed, their desire to excel and surpass others. Such self-motivational drive was rated as strong for 94 per cent of the successful women in Boardman, Hartington and Horowitz's (1987) study. Similarly, just under 75 per cent of the women in White *et al.*'s (1992) study demonstrated a high need for achievement by expressing a strong need to do a good job and be the best in their field. It is feasible, as argued by Murray (1938), that individual achievement in the work arena may be engendered by the need to expand one's career 'sub-identity' in order to detract from other sub-identities. Hall (1976) suggests that sub-identity growth may be experienced by an individual acquiring competence relevant to their career role, which is comprised of the expectancies people hold for individuals in that career. Sub-identities may include gender, race, religious orientation or disability. The use of work to counteract disability prejudice has been argued by Sutherland (1981), who believes that if people occupy a status that is socially prestigious and economically rewarding and possess a university degree, they have a stronger possibility of counteracting prejudice stemming from their disability. The concept of diagnostic overshadowing has been used in writings by Hahn (1988) to describe when an individual is being characterised by their disability as opposed to their abilities or, as Wright (1960) argued, when the disability is perceived as the most important attribute of the individual, obscuring all other attributes. However, the acquisition of a respectable high-status position in society's economic structure has been found to dilute any discrimination engendered by disability. As Sutherland (1981) argues, acceptance becomes easier the more one conforms to the norm of the societal majority. This was certainly the case for several disabled high-flyers who were motivated to achieve a professional status to divert attention away from their disability.

DISABLED HIGH-FLYERS' PATTERNS OF MOTIVATION

A possible explanation for the low proportion of disabled people in powerful, prestigious positions in the labour market may be their motivations to work. As discussed in previous chapters, it can be argued that societal stereotypes of disabled people as being passive and dependent have had extensive influence on their own aspirations and their underemployment.

However, the prejudice of negative expectations society holds of disabled people may, in itself, be an incentive to strive towards career success. The interpersonal competition of trying to gain the approval of others or avoiding social segregation can be argued to be significant causes of motivation (Raynor, 1974). It is possible that some disabled people choose to work in order to divert attention away from their disability and be identified by the contribution they make to society. As Sutherland (1981) maintains, the more one conforms to the functioning and maintenance of economic society, the less significant their disability becomes. Furthermore, career striving, according to Raynor (1974), represents a major means of obtaining self-esteem. It facilitates the development of the self and its function in society and becomes a source of motivation, encouraging the attainment of various goals that define who a person is.

Interviews with the disabled high-flyers generated seven patterns of motivation. The majority were intrinsic, although money, an external source of motivation, was identified as very important for most of them. The interviews highlighted many differences and similarities, in terms of motivations, caused by gender or diversity.

The seven patterns of motivation identified by the disabled high-flyers were related in particular to *achievement* (the targets and objectives that have already been met or achieved, and the success of these achievements which generates the desire to achieve future goals); *ambition* (personal drive to achieve some future objective, either personally or as part of the overall success of a organisation or company); *purposefulness/moral satisfaction* (giving someone a sense of purpose and opportunity to contribute to the welfare of society); *determination* (not giving up easily; persevering, even through adversity, to meet personal and professional objectives); *feedback and recognition* (concrete results providing external evidence of achievement, and getting recognition of others for doing a good job); *interest and enjoyment* (enjoying the job and having a keen interest in it); and *money* (financial or material payment). The following examples illustrate some of these different motivations identified to be important to the disabled high-flyers:

> The research I do aims to help to enable, probably, the most severely disabled people communicate their wants, feelings and desires, so when I see people using something I have developed, or teachers and clinicians implementing ideas I have taught them, even my students becoming enthusiastic about programming, it's satisfying (Corin, university lecturer – *purposefulness/moral satisfaction*)

> I haven't reached my desired goals. I've written a novel but it hasn't been published. I'd like to have my novels published and I would like someone to ask me to write more of them. (Katey, freelance journalist – *ambition*)

> I need to be recognised and need to be admired, by others. (Katey, freelance journalist – *feedback and recognition*)

> You have to enjoy and be interested in what you are doing. It's no good working day in, day out in a full-time job if you hate it and it bores you. (Amil, computer programmer – *interest and enjoyment*)

> Now I have my mortgage and my car, I have to say money motivates me to work. (Greg, actor – *money*)

Table 6.1 shows how many of the disabled high-achievers perceived themselves to be driven by each of the seven motivations. Several mentioned being driven by more than one. Further, one must be aware that, although money was not identified as a principal motivator for a large proportion of respondents, most considered money to be important.

Table 6.1 Patterns of motivation

Respondent Group	Motivations						
	Achievement	Purpose-fulness & moral satisfaction	Ambition	Deter-mination	Interest & enjoyment	Feedback & recognition	Money
M/A[1]	8	7	7	5	4	3	7
M/C[2]	10	10	9	10	8	4	5
F/A[3]	3	3	3	3	3	2	2
F/C[4]	9	8	9	6	5	4	2
Total	**30**	**28**	**28**	**24**	**20**	**12**	**16**

[1] Males with acquired disabilities = 8   [3] Females with acquired disabilities = 3

[2] Males with congenital disabilities = 11   [4] Females with congenital disabilities = 9

The key motivation for the disabled high-flyers was undoubtedly *achievement*. Almost universally, when asked what drove them in their professional and personal lives, a typical answer was, 'I'm totally driven by my need to achieve.' Although they all knew that they had not achieved everything they wanted to achieve and were ambitious to keep goal posts moving, they also believed they had already successfully achieved many of their targets. As Bob commented:

> I've achieved what I wanted to achieve and I have got the qualifications I wanted to get, I got the job I would have hoped to have achieved at this stage and station of my life.

Similarly Mary spent many years studying and training before she achieved her previous ambition to be a sole practitioner in her own law practice:

> I did a BA in law at [X] University, then I went to law college for six months because I took all the heads of exams all at once. Then I went into articles for two years with one firm of solicitors. After qualifying I was a partner in that firm. I then left and set up my own firm, becoming a sole practitioner for about three or four months until my partner joined me.

After becoming a disabled person and working for several years in a role offering careers advice and guidance to young disabled people, Nick believed he had achieved some of the major goals he set for himself during his time in this career:

> I've been successful in terms of my criteria, which is that I have sup-ported people, mostly young people, some older people, to come to choices which they can then execute for themselves.

For a number of the high-flyers, achievement was indicated by the mere nature of their careers which involved long periods of training and hard work culminating in perpetual success with no financial incentives. For Roger, a professor of physics, achievement motivation was imperative for the acquisition of knowledge and proficiency in such a specialised discipline as physics and astronomy. His career inherently calls for the ability to master and manipulate, show evidence of good achievement over time and persist in the face of difficulties.

The high-flyers' motivation was perceived as almost entirely intrinsic. From the narratives it can be inferred that, for some, need for achievement was facili-tated by the disequilibrium between the disabled minority and non-disabled majority, the need to prove their self-worth and to disprove traditional stereo-types of disabled people being passive and dependent. As Marty, a dancer, was determined to achieve, especially because he was not expected to: 'I think peo-ple always expect me not to do well so, therefore, I have to do it that bit better!'

This point was echoed by Greg who believed, 'We, disabled people, have to try a bit harder in order to achieve the equivalent to our able-bodied counter-parts.' Ali, a barrister in Sudan who acquired his impairment in early adulthood, strongly supported the idea of disabled people being economically independent:

> I feel it is very important for disabled people to work and not rely on the Government or relatives. By working they achieve some autonomous goals and prove to society that disabled people can do as well as their fellow non-disabled people.

The disabled peoples' need for achievement was also demonstrated by their tendency to persist in the face of adversity. The existence of such a psychological tendency is illustrated by Sunny's story of being an actor with a congenital disability who took 12 years to achieve his childhood ambition because:

> I wrote to drama schools up and down the country and every one told me to get lost, 'you're a cripple, you're in a wheelchair.' I didn't get to become an actor until I was 27.

The stories revealed that the need for perpetual achievement was instilled into several of the respondents with acquired disabilities during the childhood socialisation process, inclusive of its religious beliefs, culture traditions and/or social class values. Two men, Amil and Ali, were nurtured within non-Western cultures which impressed the value of achievement and doing well in everything they did. Amil pointed out, 'Even when I was younger there was this need to do well, to achieve things for myself.' Many of the other men and women were filled with stringent beliefs about being able 'to do things to the utmost of your ability'; an attitude which was either manifested in childhood by familial values or engendered as a consequence of becoming physically impaired.

Ambition was reported, in the stories of several of the high-flyers, as another strong motivational force. They had a need to focus on future intentions and possessed an inner drive to master and manipulate their environment, stimulated by challenge and the need for change. Typical comments made by 'ambitious' high-flyers included: 'I shall always want to move forward' or 'My goal posts shift all the time. I achieve one thing and then want the next league up.' For a university lecturer, ambition was inferred by the nature of her career which required a long period of hierarchical training with progressive academic successes to reach the end goal. It can be argued that her successful past achievements drive her perpetual ambitions to achieve further. Similarly, another woman asserts, 'I am constantly striving to achieve the next target', thus indicating her strongly ambitious nature and her preoccupation with perpetual learning and personal progression.

The accounts from the other disabled women revealed that they all had a future vision and were ambitious to reach it. For example, Amanda was ambitious for her dance company to keep growing in terms of the work they do and the kind of audiences that sees it:

> We're making good work now and I want to do the best we can do. I want it to be challenging to us; I want it to challenge the audience; I want it to be exciting and fun and dark and all those things. That's the kind of achievement I seek – to have people come and enjoy that work.

Judith also demonstrated a concern for long-term goals by her career development. She started working for her current employer as a part-time trainee and climbed the career ladder to her current position. As she affirms: '…it has gone from a three-month contract to a one-year contract to a two-year contract and now it is a fixed-term post.'

It can be inferred, by the life stories told by the respondents with acquired disabilities themselves, that they have a perpetual thirst for knowledge and are constantly striving to further their skills and capacities. Furthermore, they are considered to be proficient and committed to several avenues of expertise which is again demonstrative of their ambitious drive. Most hold no fewer than three respectable positions in society that may or may not be connected to their principal occupational role. For example, Adrian, an architect by profession, is a joint senior partner in three practices. Another example of personal ambition is voiced by Ali (a barrister) who is ambitious to continue learning new skills and gain knowledge, and is eager to become proficient in several avenues, not just his professional career. He believes that he has been given a life to use it productively, to continue to learn and develop, not to be idle and do nothing, and therefore he is ambitious to do so. For example, he speaks of how he spends his spare time:

> The work I do as a translator and lecturer is done in my spare time. Also, as a volunteer of a political society I have to attend meetings twice a week, from 6pm to 10pm. Last year I succeeded in winning a scholarship to a Masters in Environmental Law, which will, hopefully, continue into a PhD.

Ali, like many of the other men in this group, conceives future orientation as fundamental to the development of the self-concept and 'if a person feels he has attained his required goals and desired destinations then he has to die'.

The high-flyers' aspirations and ambitions were not heavily influenced by the need to conform to traditional gender stereotypes. This was particularly true of the women with congenital disabilities, some of whom, when interviewed for this research, occupied gender atypical careers. However, three of the women with congenital disabilities were in fact wives and, in one case, a mother, despite not being encouraged to aspire to such roles as disabled children.

Another motivational factor found to be important to the career success of the disabled high-flyers was *purposefulness and moral satisfaction*. Most of those interviewed perceived themselves to be motivated to engage in the act of working because it provided them with a purposeful role in society. Pauline, who developed a disability during her final year at university and found it difficult to get a job for some time after that, considered it to be very important: '...having known a time when I thought that I couldn't work, work now is so important. I hated the feeling of not having any role in society!'

This was also critical to Kay, who felt that disabled people need to prove that they are not passive and dependent as is construed by traditional stereotypes, but in fact are capable of making a purposeful contribution to the development of society:

> ...for disabled people, particularly those who have been disabled since early childhood or birth, there is an element of discrimination and that drives you to constantly justify your existence, to prove that you are worth keeping on the planet.

However, the significance of marriage became evident for three women in the sample who, prior to their marriage, saw their work as an imperative means of feeling valuable and proving their worth to society. But this emphasis on work became somewhat diluted when taking on other roles such as wife or mother. This is expressed by Katey, the freelance journalist: 'Getting married was a major turning point because it gave me permission to stop having to prove myself at work.'

Kay, as mentioned above, also described her work as important to her in terms of proving her worth as a disabled person, but felt her need to constantly achieve in the work arena became less strong since she married:

> Since I met my partner my need for achievement has been much less because he gives me my reason for being, so the stuff I said about my career being the reason for my being has been tempered for the past five years.

Many of the disabled high-achievers perceived work as providing them with the opportunity to make a positive contribution to the happiness and well-being of their fellow citizens, from which they derived moral satisfaction. This was perceived to be more important than financial gain. As Nick declares:

> I think if you don't serve people, you no longer exist. If you serve your-self all the time, sooner or later, you'll be only appreciated for the money you have.

Adrian maintains that his work permits him to guarantee the happiness and comfort of others. Occupying such powerful statuses provides opportunities to exercise original ideas and play an active part in inducing change, which several high-flyers found to be an incentive to work hard and do a good job. This suggests that they are motivated, in part, by the moral satisfaction engendered by their occupational role. Kenny, a chartered accountant declares:

> Doing a good job for my clients is what really motivates me. You feel very conscious all the time that what you do for them has a significant impact on their future.

This is also true for Corin, a university lecturer who believes she is driven by the moral satisfaction derived from her work, '…helping to enable, probably, the most severely disabled people communicate their wants, feelings and desires'. Mary, who felt she has been the victim of disability discrimination on several occasions in her life, believes that her empathy towards other disabled people motivates her to want to change things, '…because I know things can be better'.

The above are all manifestations of a general determination to succeed, which was considered to be paramount to the success of several of the high-flyers, regardless of their gender. Almost universally, determination was noted as beneficial to their professional and personal progression. Typical comments were: 'hard work and determination are the determinants of my success' and 'I'm a fighter.' Many of the disabled people used adjectives such as 'stubborn' and 'bloody-minded' when describing their path of progression. Several showed no evidence of giving up easily in the face of difficulties, demonstrating an internal locus of control. Determination was also considered essential for the high-achievers to survive prejudice against them as disabled people and progress successfully in the non-disabled world. Rachel tells the story of how her determination helped her to become who she is today:

> I wanted to be a teacher, and when I applied to go to college to qualify as a primary school teacher that was the first time somebody had said, 'no, you can't do it'. The doctor at the college said 'no'. I had a genetic condition that was gradually getting worse but I didn't think there was anything wrong with me. But he said 'no' so I was determined I was going to be a teacher... I went off to university and got my degree, then I applied back to do a postgraduate at college, during which time the same doctor was still telling me that he wasn't very happy letting me qualify. In Scotland it's different, we have a general teaching council and all teachers must be registered with them before they can teach. The doctor stipulated that I had to have two years absolutely free of any kind of absence at all before he would let me register with the general teaching council. So I got through a year of teaching college and I also had an extra year at university and I didn't have any absences at all luckily, I didn't have the flu or anything. I started teaching in 1978 so I was successful that I got into teaching.

Determination was also considered to be vital to the recipe for success of the individuals who acquired their impairment in early adulthood, they had to reorientate their lifestyles and learn about a different culture as a disabled person, and how to combat the struggles they encountered as a result. For Amil, a computer programmer/analyst, determination was perceived to be an essential enabler '...to pursue something and find ways of getting around it if it's difficult'. Adrian believed his determination was a latent personality trait triggered by the acquisition of his disability. His determination has enabled him to persevere against obstacles and relearn skills to live a full and healthy lifestyle as a disabled person. Further, it facilitated his successful career by providing him with the drive to achieve new skills, persisting through adversity to do so. He believes that becoming disabled has forced him to learn to drive and travel on an aeroplane:

...my disability caused me to learn to drive a car to get from A to B... I probably would not have flown if I hadn't become disabled. Since my accident I have flown to most parts of Europe to lecture.

It can be argued, from the evidence given in this and previous chapters, that determination may well be a characteristic derived from individuals' early situations (e.g. separation from parents), which required them to take responsibility for themselves at quite an early stage in their lives. The respondents with congenital disabilities were, as has been highlighted in Chapter 4 and Chapter 5, victims of discrimination and prejudice during their childhood, and needed quite a bit of determination to persevere against it without breaking down and giving up.

Twelve of the disabled high-achievers valued external evidence of achievement. This was not necessarily in monetary terms, but more *feedback and recognition* – to be seen by others as doing a good job or getting some concrete results from the work. For example, Corin explains that it is important for her to '...get feedback from fellow colleagues and people who admire my work'. Similarly Adrian also considered feedback, especially from clients, to be fundamental to his improvement and success as an architect.

Recognition was particularly important to the artists in the sample, whose success and progression on stage and screen was largely dependent on who saw them perform. Furthermore, this was also important to the future inclusion of disabled people in the arts. Greg considered recognition to be important, not only for self-satisfaction and professional advancement, but also as a motivator to others, as he believes, '...it's good for younger disabled people to have comfortable safe role models'. A similar point was made by Amanda who directs a dance company which does a lot of outreach work with young people in schools:

> Through our work, we do inspire people, not just disabled people, but dance critics. Obviously we do get bad reviews as well and some people don't like our work at all, and that's absolutely fine. But at least it provokes a response.

A few men and women perceived recognition to be important for their personal development and career success. Katey felt that she needed to be recognised and admired by others in order to feel was successful. However, Maria who was always expected to achieve and meet the high expectations of her parents, was more concerned with parental recognition.

Many of the respondents expressed a keen interest in their job. Their narratives indicated that *enjoyment and interest* was seen as an asset to their current situation and helped them sustain their enthusiasm to do a good job and persevere through the difficult times. Several maintained it was their interest in their job that kept them committed and motivated. As Pauline pointed out, 'I can be the most lazy person if I don't actually like what I'm doing.' Those with vocational careers, like the artists and vicars, were motivated to do a good job because they enjoyed the work it involved. The vicars in the sample expressed an interest for the work they do with comments like, 'I believe I am doing something I am gifted to do, I am called to do. I also enjoy doing it, which really helps' and 'I love life. I love living. I love people.'

Kenny, a trained management accountant, believes, 'It's very important to enjoy the work that you do because you're doing it for most of the week.'

A similar response was delivered by Amil who proposed 'enjoyable work' as being work that is '…stimulating and challenging to keep me interested and allow me to actually learn something from it'.

The women devoted a substantial amount of their energy to their work. Many believed it was the leading interest in their lives and perceived it as crucial to their lives, not only for subsistence and relative maintenance of life, but also to create wider social ties. Lara who, at the time, was the associate director of a leading theatre company of disabled people believes that, for her, the work she does has been crucial on many levels:

> How I earn my living is something that is very important on an economic, social and political level. I'm mixing professionally and mostly personally with people of a like mind, people that I would choose to spend time outside of work with.

By the same nature, Corin, a university lecturer, perceives her work to be the key interest in her life and this motivates her to become very involved in it and work long hours, 'I'm very passionate about the research I do, therefore most of my time is spent thinking about work.'

So, as suggested above, many of the high-flyers felt they needed to enjoy their job in order to dedicate their time and effort to producing good quality work.

While most of the high-flyers who were interviewed, particularly those with children, mentioned that money was indeed necessary for a decent level of subsistence and a respectable lifestyle, they all maintained that this was quite secondary to other motivations. For instance, one vicar declares, 'My salary is not phenomenal, and although it is important to allow me to live, I wouldn't say money is a major motivator.'

For Greg, money was not an essential prerequisite to his work, but was considered important to satisfy his definition of success: 'I don't want to be a millionaire but I do want to have a house with some land, because I want to do my organic gardening.'

Roger, a university professor, believes:

> Without the stimulation and earning power of a career, I probably wouldn't be still alive today. It enables me to earn enough money to support my family.

Amil needs a job that is challenging and stimulating, but considers the financial rewards acquired from it as important. He maintains that even though he is not primarily driven by money, '...it's always nice to earn a good amount of dosh!'

Therefore, despite the old saying, 'money can't buy happiness', it can be exchanged for many commodities that are necessary for survival and comfort. This was confirmed by two of the women with acquired impairments, Pauline and Judith, who made comments like, '...now I have my mortgage and my car, I have to say money motivates me to work, although it didn't use to'.

However, out of all of the 31 high-flyers in this book, Jonathan actually did identify money as very important to him to achieve the standard of living he wants:

> ...I am 32 now and want my own house, a decent car, to be able to travel the world etc. All this needs money. I think this is the best job in the world because you get loads of money for just being yourself.

Money was not considered to be important to all of the high-flyers in their current professional lives, even though it may have been in previous periods of their lives. For example, Timmy recalled that, as a child, he was socialised to define success in terms of external factors of money and status. He was constantly reminded of the value of achievement and importance of exceeding others. He, therefore, became very driven. Thus this could have had a significant influence on his first career choice as he affirms:

> My first degree was in economics. I used to think of a career in terms of business. I was always taught to be better than others, in exams, in jobs, earning more money etc.

However, Timmy soon realised that money was not enough to drive him to achieve success. He recognised that he was principally motivated by doing a good job and being of service to others, both of which are criteria of his current occupation of church minister:

> I have become more humble in my years, recognising that I am here to do whatever I'm called to do. And now I determine success as being a service to others.

The motivations of the disabled high-flyers spring from them being ambitious and determined people with a reasonably high need for achievement, who find their work interesting, enjoyable and a worthwhile activity. It is also evident that a couple of the patterns of motivation identified are the same as the identified success criteria reported in Chapter 3, i.e. achievement and material wealth. Therefore it can be argued that there is a strong connection between what motivates these disabled people and how they perceive success.

WORK CENTRALITY

High-need achievers, evidence indicates (e.g. Harpaz and Fu, 2002; MOW International Research Team, 1987), tend to spend a significant amount of time and energy in work-related activities, and thus are said to be high in work centrality. This is one of the three primary components of achievement motivation, conceptualised by Farmer (1985), and refers to the extent to which an individual sees involvement in a career as central to his/her adult life. The work of Dublin (1956) and Barker (1968) proposes a decision orientation component of work centrality which begins with the premise that an individual's life experiences are segmented into different sub-spheres, and that people differ in their preferences for particular life spheres. Therefore when the work sphere occupies a central or most preferred position in an individual's life, they are said to be high in career centrality.

A further indication of the degree of individual career centrality is involvement or commitment. Involvement includes behavioural elements such as the amount of time spent participating in work activities. The MOW International Research Team (1987) contends that the time one spends in training or preparation for work is indicative of how fundamental work is to their life. Furthermore, as Judge et al. (1995) suggest, working overtime, evenings or weekends is a fair indicator of high work centrality. The high-flyers in Cox and Cooper's (1988) study were significantly involved and dedicated to their work. The majority of the sample worked above and beyond the statutory 37-hour working week. They often took work home at weekends and/or evenings. Individuals are also more inclined to become significantly devoted to their job if they believe in its worth and thus get a sense of moral purpose. As Vroom (1964) postulates, many work roles provide their occupants with an opportunity to contribute to the happiness and well-being of their fellow men.

Substantial commitment to work is also indicative of high career centrality. This, as was put forward by the MOW International Research Team (1987) and Harpaz and Fu (2002), is partially free of short-run experiences, thus being more concerned with future orientations and meeting long-term goals. This is consistent with the work of Dublin, Hedley and Taveggia (1976) who found that workers with high levels of work centrality particularly valued the chances for advancement and promotion. Furthermore, their research showed such workers to particularly value job responsibility, only successfully achievable with sufficient involvement and commitment.

In recent years the act of working has been seen as vital, not only for financial survival, but also as a means of attaining personal satisfaction and earning a respectable position in society (Charles and James, 2003; Harpaz and Fu, 2002). Furthermore, work has been proposed to facilitate the growth of one's psychological well-being which is crucial for a perpetually healthy autonomous lifestyle. Aiken, Ferman and Sheppard (1968) argue that when a person experiences unemployment, career perspectives are destroyed and the various spheres of life become fragmented. Similarly, upon reviewing the thrust of empirical research concerning a large number of cross-sectional longitudinal studies, Warr (1985) concludes that many facets of the psyche, such as self-esteem, anxiety, distress, depression and happiness are impaired by unemployment.

Work has been seen by many as a means of securing a purposeful position in society. Many workers in a study conducted by Charles and James (2003) indicated that working gives them a feeling of being tied into the larger society, of having something to do and having a purpose in life. Furthermore, it can be argued that one's occupational position serves as a means of identification and will engender certain types of behaviour from fellow citizens. As Friedmann and Havighurst (1954) have discussed, the job is a label which marks the person inside and outside of their paid employment. They maintain that job status is an important determinant to an individual's position in his/her family and community. As Hall (1969) maintains, knowledge of what a person does provides a handy indicator of where the person fits vis-à-vis oneself. In addition, occupational identification is perceived as a powerful indicator of one's place in the stratification system and provides a strong indication of their educational background and income. So, occupation has been noted to be a primary means of identification, for the self and society, where some behaviours are prescribed rather than voluntarily chosen.

Although, as can be seen above, a significant body of literature exists that demonstrates the positive correlation between high achievers and career centrality, its focus is largely on the non-disabled population. Therefore, this book strives to fill the gap in the literature and investigate if the same is true for disabled high-flyers. It explores the level of importance disabled high-flyers perceive work has in their lives, and questions whether they use their work as a means of identification and a way of proving their worth to society. It may be argued that work gives people a sense of purpose, and for disabled people who are stereotyped as passive and dependent, it provides an opportunity to override their disability status. Furthermore, by fulfilling a purposeful position in society, disabled people will serve to reduce negative attitudes and discrimination. Therefore, this chapter explores the extent to which disability has an effect on work centrality and whether the high-flyers see their work as a means of reducing diagnostic overshadowing.

WORK CENTRALITY OF DISABLED HIGH-FLYERS

All of the high-flyers displayed a high career centrality, defined by MOW International Research Team (1987) as a 'general belief about the value of working in one's life'. Examination of the cognitive and behavioural orientation, in relation to their work, revealed that work presently, or had previously, occupied a central position in their life. Three attributes were identified from the interview data, and also proposed by previous research (e.g. Dublin, 1956; MOW International Research Team, 1987; White et al., 1992), to demonstrate an individual's level of career centrality. These were *hours worked* (the number of hours one spends participating in work-related activities); *identification with work* (the extent to which work is central to one's self-image); and *involvement and/or commitment to working* (commitment to work demonstrated by a focus on future goals, not short-run experiences, and the amount of physical and emotional energy spent working). The following quotes, from the disabled high-flyers, illustrate the three attributes defined above:

> The average is supposed to be 54 hours but it's usually between 60 and 90. (Jude, vicar)

> The standing I have within the professional community I work in has given me a relatively high status. I feel I am respected in society. (Corin, university lecturer)

> Although teaching is a 9 to 4 job it never was for me, I always took work home and I've always worked beyond the expected hours and all of that is part of being an MP. (Rachel, MP)

The evidence below suggests that all of the respondents were high in career centrality, and were characterised by either one or more of the attributes.

Many of the disabled high-flyers felt they worked above and beyond their statutory working hours or, as one man put it, '...more than those listed in the job description!' The general belief was that 'you work the hours your job requires'.

Many of the successful people affirmed that they would rarely work fewer than 40 hours a week, and were likely to take work home with them in the evenings. In addition, several worked weekends. Tom calculated the time he spent working amounted to:

> A minimum of 12 hours a day, 6 days a week. Wednesday is my day off as you get one day off a week. Roughly that works out as 72 hours a week.

Likewise Nick, now retired, recalls that the hours that he was paid to work did not equal the hours he actually worked in his role as a careers advisor:

> I was paid for 37, but altogether I probably worked between 45 to 50 hours because the targets and goals which were set for me were horrendous. I had to do what I was paid for in the 37 paid hours, and the rest of the time, I did what I knew had to be done.

Several women felt this too. Mary, a retired solicitor who, at the time of interview, was a disability consultant, claimed:

> I work full-time and more! For example, yesterday was Sunday and I was reading a draft guidance on the NHS disability things and was getting very hot under the collar! And Saturday I was reading the first draft of the first half of my research report. I sort of try not to work at the weekends but it's impossible.

It is clear, from the high-flyers' stories, that 'number of hours worked' was not always a satisfactory indicator of their work centrality. Data from their interviews compared with existing literature revealed two possible explanations for this. Firstly, the artists felt that due to the nature of their profession, their work pattern varied from week to week. However, this is largely dependent on the fact that erratic freelance employment is typical in the arts industry. This was expressed by Sunny:

> As an actor, it's generally freelance. So the work isn't continuous, it goes in spurts. For example, I was working in Scotland for two months. When I was working in City of Joy, in Calcutta, it was for ten weeks. Sometimes nothing happens for weeks. So the hours vary. If you work in film, you could be working 16–18 hours a day. When I work in theatre, an average day is eight hours during rehearsals but as the show gets closer the hours increase. While the show's open, you may only be working three to four hours a day.

Amanda, who sees her work as central to her life and important to her psychological well-being, delivers a similar point about the number of hours she works:

> It does depend on what we are doing. A working day, for us, is 10am to 6pm. That's on a rehearsal day. When we are performing, work starts at 12pm and we then go through the day until the end of the show, which is about 10 in the evening, with breaks in between. We may be doing workshops or residencies. Residencies usually last a week or two weeks. Workshop days are 10am to 4pm.

The other possible reason why 'hours worked' may not be a suitable indicator of career centrality was supplied by Pauline who sees her work as important to her life, but due to fatigue stemming from her impairment, is unable to work more than 37 hours a week:

> Although it is possible to work 37 hours a week, I do get physically tired, and if the job involves travelling a long distance to get there and back it may be questionable as to whether I can cope.

It can be deduced from the findings that although all of the professionals rated their work as highly important to their lives, not all of them could demonstrate this by the extra hours they worked, either due to the nature of their career or their physical stamina. However, several men and women with acquired or congenital disabilities worked overtime including weekends. Therefore the differences in the number of hours the respondents claimed they worked was not necessarily always an indicator of work centrality.

A large number of the high-flyers felt their work was instrumental to their identity. Several believed it gave them value and importance. Often the successful individuals saw their work as a means of expressing their self-worth to others and earning a respectable position in society. Several believed that, on many occasions, their disability seemed to be the primary attribute by which they were identified. Thus they perceived their occupational status to be crucial to the reduction of diagnostic overshadowing, in that it served to override their disability identity which equated to a low status identity. For instance, Roger felt that his occupational title of 'professor' provides a handy indicator of his position within the social stratification system. Moreover, it influences how he is treated, and responded to, by other people inside and outside his working environment. Roger maintains that since earning his occupational status, his disability status has become less prominent.

A similar contention was put forward by Ali who sees work as a means of gaining equity in society and demonstrating individual potential. He believes that by holding a respectable, purposeful position in the developing economy disabled people will be identified by their occupational role as opposed to their disability:

> It is very important for disabled people to work and achieve some autonomous goals and prove to society that disabled people can do as well as their fellow non-disabled people. Once you succeed in competing with and beyond others, you divert people's concentration from disability to other factors concerning your life.

Many of the women perceived their work to be central to their self-image. They saw their work as a means of satisfying an obligation in terms of personal responsibility or internalised norms of duty, and having a purposeful role in society. These successful women believed that their work permitted them to make a positive contribution to the development of society, which they saw as significant to their psychological well-being, as well as economic growth. Corin, a university lecturer, believed, '...getting this job gave me confidence that people weren't paying lip-service for what I was doing'.

The correlation between work and personal self-esteem was demonstrated by Katey's situation: 'On a working day I am more assertive and decisive than on a day when I'm not working.' She believes that the more she contributes to society, the more her abilities are recognised and valued, thus making her feel she is respected by others and motivating her to do more work. However, unlike men, women are said to be interpersonal in their orientations. Maria, a speech and language therapist, believes that although her work has been central to her identity for a number of years, it has become more peripheral since she undertook a mothering role: 'Work is probably less important now than it was two years ago, since I had the children. But financially, it's probably more important.'

Most of the disabled high-flyers were significantly committed to their work. The amount of time they spent in training or preparing for work is indicative of how fundamental work is to their lives. Furthermore, it demonstrates the future intentional element of their work centrality. For instance, Corin attained several qualifications and years of training to hold the occupational status of a university lecturer:

> After doing an MSc in biomedical engineering I came to [a Scottish university] to start my PhD in 1989 which took three years. In 1992 I was appointed as a research assistant to carry on with my PhD research. Since then I have had several short-term contracts, until last year when I got a permanent lectureship.

On a similar note, two of the men with acquired disabilities held occupational titles of 'barrister' and 'professor' which implied that they had spent many years in training, in preparation for work, and planning for a more advanced work situation. This suggests that work-related activities make up a substantial part of their lives.

For many of the disabled high-flyers, work was the most preferred life sphere among multiple life spheres, thus implying the extent of mental and physical energy spent on activities related to their job. Their commitment was not only displayed by behavioural elements such as the amount of time spent participating in work activities, but the personal value they attached to it and their concern for long-term planning and future orientation. They tended to place great value on progression and career advancement as well as learning new skills and achieving new goals. As Clint put it: 'since my accident in 1981, I've been promoted four times. I've worked in London, Southampton and London again.'

Many high-flyers were committed to their work as it concerned contributing to the welfare of others, as was mentioned before when identifying their patterns of motivation. The 'dedication to a cause' theme was affirmed by Christian who worked as a parliamentary officer of two charities with the principal aim of empowering disabled people and working towards a cure. He wants 'results that are feasible and visible, that are making a difference'. Similarly, Tom maintained that his work as a vicar was imperative to the growth of his inner self, both on a professional and personal level. He conceptualised his work as a means by which he could put his ideas into action and become an inspiration to others.

Two of the women with acquired disabilities demonstrated their commitment to their work by the strong passion they felt towards their chosen profession for which they underwent many years of training. For example, as noted in Chapter 5, Amanda started learning to dance at the age of three, went to dance college at the age of 16 and has been in the dance profession ever since. She claims:

> ...all I ever wanted to do was dance, before I was disabled. I wanted to be successful in dance... I trained with [a South England] Dance School and then joined [a South England] Dance Theatre for nearly three years until I had my accident.

A similar contention was expressed by Judith, who maintains that a significant prerequisite when applying for a job was:

> It's got to be in the arts because I don't know how to work in any other sector. I thought about it sometimes but then resorted to the fact that my work has got to be in the arts.

Her commitment was further indicated by her tendency to persist in the face of obstacles to achieve her work goals successfully: 'if you don't get it the first time, you will come back and keep trying.'

It can be argued, on the basis of the evidence above, that all of the disabled high-flyers, regardless of their gender or disability, perceived their work to occupy a central or most preferred position in their lives. Some demonstrated this by working long hours, like the high-flyers in Cox and Cooper's (1988) study, while others showed a strong commitment to their work by their long-range planning and futuristic vision. Most of the disabled people perceived their work as very important to their self-image and how others behave towards them. Even the women who occupied other life roles like wife and mother described their work as crucial to their psychological well-being, although their personal life roles had reduced their need to use work to confirm their worth as disabled people in a non-disabled society.

LOCUS OF CONTROL

An event regarded by some persons as a reward or reinforcement may be differently perceived and reacted to by others. Rotter's (1966) work suggests that one of the determinants of this reaction is the degree to which the individual perceives that the reward follows from, or is contingent upon, their own behaviour or attributes, versus the degree to which they feel the reward is controlled by extrinsic factors. Those who believe that they exercise some kind of control over their destiny are described as having an *internal* locus of control. Conversely, when a reinforcement is perceived by an individual as the result of luck, fate, chance or under the control of significant others, they are said to have an *external* locus of control.

Individual differences in the tendency to perceive events as internally or externally controlled can be represented as a continuum known as the *internal-external control scale* (I-E scale). This scale was deemed most suitable because, as Rotter (1966) argues, behaviour in complex situations is usually not a matter of making absolute judgements such as 'I agree' or 'I disagree', but a relative matter of deciding on something as a preference to the alternative. People's positions on the I-E scale will determine the extent to which they perceive success or failure as being contingent upon their own behaviour.

Locus of control and career success

Andrisani and Nestel (1976) contend that the psychological construct, locus of control, has received much attention in connection with research on employment success. Upon an examination of the literature, they identified strong evidence to suggest that an internal locus of control reflects a propensity to influence one's environment, which they believe is a mark of initiative and confidence. Weiner's (1972) theory is concerned with the relationship between I-E scores and achievement striving. He believes that individuals who perceive that outcomes are under personal control may be expected to engage in more achievement-related activities than those who believe that outcomes are a consequence of external factors.

Andrisani and Nestel (1976) and Garfield (1986) argue that successful individuals have a primarily internal locus of control, thus holding the belief that success results from hard work and that failure is the individual's responsibility. For instance, Garfield (1986) points out that such people have a self-confidence which generates an internal authority to act, based on their own expertise and knowledge that if something goes awry they will know what to do. Internals (i.e. individuals with an internal locus of control) count on their capabilities and trust their own effectiveness.

Lefcourt (1982) suggests that locus of control plays a mediating role in determining whether a person becomes involved in the pursuit of an achievement. For example, Gurin *et al.* (1969) find that internality in the personal sense predicts school grades, educational aspiration and confidence in school. Moreover, as DeCharms (1984) asserts, individuals with an internal locus of control have a strong feeling of personal causation and are likely to attribute changes in the environment to personal behaviour. This is a powerful motivational force directing future behaviour. Lefcourt argued that the process of planning and working for deferred gratification would seem tolerable if the individual believed that they had the ability to determine the results of their efforts. It can be argued that the feeling of personal causation is crucial for individuals who are preoccupied with achieving large successes which, although offering much larger extrinsic rewards in the long term, operate in a delayed incentive system involving a long period of deprivation with only small extrinsic rewards. These individuals are referred to as *intrinsically motivated* individuals as they seek to maximise their satisfaction through behaviours that serve to enhance feelings of competence and self-determination. Such behaviours include seeking responsibility, excitement, learning and challenge derived from the task itself.

However, when individuals do not possess such a feeling of personal causation, they are more likely to let themselves be influenced by external factors (DeCharms, 1984) and find the path from the initiation to the completion of their plans fraught with unpredictability and uncertainty (White *et al.*, 1992). They are, therefore, more likely to opt for the certainty of immediate gratification, and less likely to engage in activities that lead to feelings of competence and self-determination. This logic is consistent with the tenets of expectancy-valence theory advanced by Porter and Lawler (1968), which states that the expectancy that effort will lead to success is crucial in generating motivation to work. Lewin (1951) comments that success generates success in that a person is more likely to set a new higher level aspiration following a successfully attained goal. In addition, as Bandura (1982) states, repeated success and failure avoidance is the most powerful means of creating a strong, resilient sense of self-efficacy which, he argues, will reduce the negative impact of occasional failure.

Although there is limited evidence to suggest that locus of control has a significant influence on success at work, a body of existing research supports the notion that an internal locus of control is a precursor of success. Andrisani and Nestel (1976) discovered, in their large-scale longitudinal study, that, over a two-year period, 'internals' achieved a more pronounced advancement in their annual earnings and job satisfaction than their counterparts who demonstrated an external locus of control. They prepared a further report, based on cross-sectional data, which suggested that internals are more likely to occupy high-status professions, earn more money and tend to experience greater levels of satisfaction with their work than 'externals'. Similarly, Waddel's (1983) comparative study of a group of female entrepreneurs and a group of female managers and secretaries evidenced that the women in higher-status occupations (i.e. the entrepreneurs) tended to have an internal locus of control. The positive correlation between internal locus of control and occupational success was also supported by White et al. (1992) who found that a significant proportion of successful women in their sample had a personal sense of internality. They attributed their success to hard work and good performance, as opposed to chance factors such as luck or fate.

Attributions of success and failure

In accordance with attribution theory (Heider, 1958), there are many possible reasons why a particular success or failure might occur, and therefore there are many causal attributions which can be made. Although the causes of success and failure may be assigned to many different sources, it is postulated that four frequently cited causal elements generalise to all achievement outcomes: *ability, effort, luck* and *task difficulty* (Weiner et al. 1971). These four causal elements differ from one another along two dimensions, as shown in Table 6.2: locus of control (internal or external) and stability (stable or unstable). Along the locus of control dimension, the first two attributes, ability and effort, are causes originating within, or internal to the individual. Weiner et al. (1971) classify them as internal determinants of action, and Heider (1958) refers to them as 'personal forces'. However, the remaining causal elements, namely task difficulty and luck, are classified as external determinants of success and failure; that is, they are causes within the environment and external to the individual.

The second dimension along which ability, effort, luck and task difficulty may be ordered is stability. Frieze (1975) contends that although ability and task difficulty may be relatively invariant, effort and luck could be highly changeable. For example, exertion may increase or decrease from moment to moment or from one task to another, just as luck may be good at one time and poor at another.

If success at a particular type of activity was due to high ability or simplicity of the activity, one would anticipate continued success at the same task. Similarly, if a failure was due to stable causes, continued failure would be anticipated. Conversely, as Frieze (1975) argues, unstable causes lead to expectations of change. So if bad luck is perceived as the primary cause of failure, future success would be anticipated as luck changes. Lack of effort would be variable and therefore seen as less negative than lack of ability.

Table 6.2 Classification of attributions of success and failure

Stability	Locus of control	
	Internal	*External*
Stable	Ability	Task difficulty
Unstable	Effort	Luck

As detailed in Chapter 3, significant evidence (e.g. Bar-Tal and Frieze, 1973; Kukla, 1972) has been uncovered to suggest that high-achievers tend to attribute their success and failure primarily to internal causes. Kukla (1972) demonstrated that highly achievement-motivated men tended to attribute their success both to high ability and effort, while they perceived their failures as due to lack of effort. The attribution of failure to lack of effort would lead to greater subsequent trying, thus indicating the internality and motivating effects of high-achieving males (Atkinson, 1964; Weiner, 1972). Conversely, it is argued that low achievement-motivated males are less likely to attribute their successes to internal causes, but are more likely to attribute their failure to lack of ability (Weiner and Potepan, 1970). Such patterns suggest that highly achievement-motivated individuals believe their own performance behaviour determines achievement outcomes, therefore feel compelled to work harder to ensure that these outcomes meet their original aspirations. On the other hand, those who consider luck or significant others to play a prominent part in their life development feel less pride in success and are discouraged by failure.

Previous work has indicated that the concept of expectation has wide-spread implications for understanding individual differences in achievement-related behaviour. Colwill (1984) asserts that a key variable in explaining one's own success is whether or not one is expected to succeed. For example, when people are randomly assigned to high and low expectancy groups, the high expectancy group tends to perform better than the low expectancy group (Tyler, 1958). Rosenthal and Jacobson (1968) demonstrated in their study that teacher expectations influenced student performance in a situation where teachers were given randomly assigned high or low status expectations about their students. Furthermore, several studies have verified that individuals who expect to do better on an achievement task actually do perform at a higher level (Battle, 1965; Feather, 1966).

As mentioned above, an individual's status is somewhat deterministic of the expectations and ideologies of the many agents of socialisation and of the social factors and interactive human behaviour that influence the structure of society.

Numerous studies suggest that women, as with other minority groups including disabled people, are particularly influenced by the perceived acceptance or rejection of others of their achievements (Freeman, 1971; Horner, 1972). As Hendey (1999) suggests, norms prescribe roles for individuals in different situations, and informal as well as legal sanctions may be used to maintain expected behaviour. For example, according to traditional societal norms, women are expected to achieve less than their male counterparts and, similarly, disabled people are expected to adopt a passive, dependent role in society (Hendey, 1999).

When individuals start to deviate from the expected norm, they are likely to become victims of social rejection and discomfort. For example, women or disabled people with the reputation of low-achievers who have achieved a high, prestigious professional status may strike onlookers with a sense of 'status incongruency', a conflicting status level noted by Donelson and Gullahorn (1977). Status incongruency tends to make outsiders feel uncomfortable in dealing with people who have achieved or become something that was presumed beyond their ability. This state is likely to induce the employment of some sort of social sanction. Furthermore, Colwill (1984) maintains that the high-achievers themselves may tend to avoid this discomfort-producing situation by not aspiring to careers beyond their expected status level. Horner (1972) contends that even if expected low-achievers (i.e. members of some minority groups) do have an opportunity to become successful, many may avoid it in order to behave in a socially approved manner.

The unexpected success of members of minority groups, such as women or individuals with physical impairments, may cause success to be attributed to unstable factors such as luck (Deaux and Emswiller, 1974) or undue effort (Feldman-Saunders and Kiesler, 1974), which will rarely result in tangible organisational rewards, unlike success that is attributed to more stable factors such as ability. The relationship between expectancy and the stability dimension of the causal attributions was attempted to be verified by Valle and Frieze (1976) who proposed that the causal attribution made is strongly influenced by the extent to which an individual's performance violates the observer's initial expectations. An example of this is the increasing professional success of women in economic society, which contradicts general expectations of women being unemployed or concentrated in the secondary labour market (Frieze, 1975; White et al., 1992). The same is true for the disabled minority who, in accordance with societal norms, are expected to be passive and dependent, and unable to make any significant contribution to the economic development of society (Oliver, 1990). Therefore, it can be argued that disabled people occupying high-status professions have deviated from the stereotypical societal norm (of disabled people), so onlookers are more likely to attribute their success to chance factors rather than internal causes. However, as Colwill (1984) warns, for members of these minorities (e.g. women or disabled people) to attribute their own success to luck could have serious consequences. She argues that individuals who attribute their success to luck will not raise their expectancy of future success, which in expectancy/valence terms would leave motivation unchanged. In addition, they would learn nothing about how they achieved success, leaving self-esteem and self-efficacy beliefs unaltered. The failure to raise self-esteem is likely to inhibit career growth.

Predictions of future success and failure based on prior expectations

So, to sum up, if the individual is expected to perform well and actually does so, the performance will be attributed to internal, stable factors such as ability, and a high level of future performance will be predicted. If expectations are high but performance is low, the failure is attributed to bad luck, lack of effort or other unstable characteristics, and the expectations of future performance continue to be high. Conversely, if an individual performs well when expectations are low, the observer will tend to judge the outcome as a result of good luck, special effort or other unstable factors, which Frieze (1975) conceives as highly changeable. Finally, if expectations are low and performance levels are also low, the observer will be likely to predict future failure and to attribute this to a lack of ability (see Colwill, 1982).

Familial origins of locus of control

According to functionalist theorists (e.g. Parsons, 1956; Wallace and Jones, 1992), the family is responsible for teaching children to conform to social norms and learn culturally prescribed social and familial roles. However, they point out that for this to be successful, parents must allow children to be temporarily dependent on them but then, in time, facilitate in liberating the children from that dependency.

Katkovsky et al. (1967) believe that it seems likely that an individual's internal or external locus of control could be influenced by particular child-rearing patterns. For instance, the more a parent initiates and encourages their child's achievement behaviour and the development of skills, the more the child will learn that it is his/her own behaviour, and not external factors, that will determine the reinforcements he/she receives. Moreover, the extent to which parents are positively or negatively reinforcing also may have a significant bearing on the child's belief in internal versus external control. Katkovsky et al. (1967)

argue that the more positive parents' reactions are to their child's achievement behaviours, the more the child is likely to develop a belief in internal control of reinforcements; and the more negative the parents' reactions, the more a belief in external control will be fostered. Such a contention was supported by the results of Davis and Phares' (1967) interviews with university students which revealed that extreme internals recalled experiencing significant positive parent–child interaction, less rejection, hostile control, inconsistent discipline and less with-drawal than did extreme externals. This is consistent with Lefcourt's (1982) work which suggests that warmth, supportiveness and parental encouragement are essential for the development of an internal locus of control. Marcia (1966) suggests that this pattern of parent–child relationship permits and encourages decision making about future choices and orientation including occupations, and results in a conferred identity meaning that the individual's identity is a syn-thesis of childhood experiences.

Nurturance is conceptually and empirically different to protectiveness (McDonald, 1971) which, if on a random, over-abundant schedule, can lead to feelings of helplessness or a very external locus of control. Devereaux, Bronfenbrenner and Rogers (1969) suggest that nurturance is subsumed under supporting, but protectiveness is subsumed under a controlling dimension. Therefore, although a child requires a safe environment with a certain degree of security in order to explore and develop their sense of self as a causative agent, overprotective child-rearing practices may have the effect of suffocating the child's curiosity and intrinsic motivation. This can curb active exploration of the child's social and physical environment.

Although all children are said to be dependent, as maturity increases for the non-disabled child he/she will strive to become more independent (Sutherland, 1981). However, this is not always achievable for disabled children, who are very often prevented from developing social skills and self-confidence because their lives are controlled by other people (Alderson and Goodey, 1998; Morris, 1997; Norwich, 1997). A significant body of recently published research has pointed out that disabled children are often denied the same rights and choices as other children (Davis and Watson, 2001; Priestley, 1998), are under constant surveillance (Allan, 1996) and are cut off from the opportunities to interact in the same way as do non-disabled children. In accordance with Davis, Watson and Cunningham-Burley's (1999) work, parents, medical professionals and local authority officials are heavily implicated in this process.

It is not, however, correct to assume that all dependency equates to having an external locus of control. Existing literature fails to clarify that if individuals have difficulty in mobilising themselves and request facilitation from someone else, it does not necessarily mean that they are not in control of what happens to them. It simply means that the employment of a facilitator makes it easier for them to exercise control over their own lives. This book shows just this by illustrating how individuals with significant physical impairments, although often requiring the continuous assistance of others, believed that they were in control of their destiny and that their high-achieving status was due to their own hard work, ability and perseverance. It can be deduced already, from what has been discussed about patterns of motivation, that these people are likely to have an internal locus of control which can be perceived as a necessary condition for intrinsic motivation. However, the extent to which the disabled high-flyers perceive their successes and failures in life to be primarily as a result of their own behaviour or the behaviour of others will be demonstrated more clearly below.

THE LOCUS OF CONTROL OF DISABLED HIGH-FLYERS

The disabled high-flyers' stories indicate they are self-confident and able to take responsibility for their own action, both qualities of people with an internal locus of control. They also demonstrated competence, self-reliance, initiative and independence, which other authors (e.g. Andrisani and Nestel, 1976; Shapero, 1975) have implied are characteristic of true internals. Further, if the high-flyers were confronted with adversity, they felt they were always prepared, if necessary, to challenge and change the existing system and not be constrained by conventional assumptions or beliefs, thus enhancing feelings of competence and self-determination.

The fact that the individual disabled people had all reached relatively high and prestigious positions in their careers is indicative of their power to control their own destiny, which would reinforce a personal sense of internality. There was a strong belief, among the high-flyers, that it was primarily their behaviour, and not the behaviour of the external environment, that affected their life development. As Sunny pointed out, 'You can't sit back in this job because you can get forgotten. So you have to take opportunities when they present themselves and keep pushing.'

Similarly, Ali believes he has the ability and strength to achieve his own goals, so if he experiences setbacks or obstacles in the process, he feels it is his responsibility to overcome them:

> As soon as my work is assigned to me, I am able to make certain measurements to test how long I should spend on it, how long it should take to complete, how much effort I should put in it, what are the relevant and irrelevant references and who are the persons with whom I must consult to finish off the work.

This was echoed by Adrian, the senior architect:

> To be successful in your chosen career, I think you have to sit down and think it through, check out all the pros and cons; if it is viable then go for it. It's down to you as an individual and the people you work with.

Other high-flyers were also unlikely to be discouraged by barriers imposed on them by external factors. Rather they struggled to find strategies to overcome them. Rachel's story of her former teaching career illustrates this point:

> ...I've always won through in the end, but it's been touch and go on occasion. Not long after I took over as head of the department, it felt as if the department was failing around me because members of staff were leaving. A member of staff had a mental breakdown and another member of staff had serious disciplinary problems. It seemed as if it was just getting worse and worse so I had supply teachers in and the kids were behaving badly with them... I couldn't teach my class because I had to sort out the others, and as I did that my own class misbehaved. It seemed as though it was just a nightmare, but I kept working through that and I kept on putting things in place and it started to ease it and then someone else was promoted in the department and someone else came back into the department. Almost overnight the department was transformed, because I had been working for those two years. Almost at one stage I thought about giving up. I thought I don't need this, I don't need all this stress, but I didn't give up, I went on and it all came right in the end, and it turned out to be a really good department and it was worth all the struggle.

At the time of the interview Corin's biggest challenge was teaching applied computer science to a lecture theatre full of first-year undergraduates without being able to write notes and information on the blackboard (an action which is not physically possible for her). She explained the strategies she used to make the challenge of teaching a success:

> Teaching large groups means I have to work out the best way of getting the information to the students without being able to do things like scribbling on the blackboard... I use a lot of overheads. This is a lot of preparation as I have to anticipate any questions that might come up, which is very difficult with first-year computing students. I use a package called PowerPoint which enables me to create slides and project them to the class, but I don't actually like using that as it turns into a presentation rather than teaching. So I've got some tricks up my sleeve that I'm going to use this year, for instance I'm going to ask students to come up and write on the board when they have a problem. So they can

actually work through the problems themselves and help me to give feedback in a mentoring capacity.

When Ed, the TV critic, is confronted with a difficult situation or task he tends to analyse it first in order to determine why it may be difficult for him to handle, and based on what he has learned, seeks alternative ways of managing it:

> First of all you have to be able to analyse why the task is difficult. You need to analyse not just what is wrong, but why it's wrong, so you have an understanding of what you can do about it. And you have to see whether you can handle the problem yourself or whether you need help from someone else. If you do require assistance from someone else, you have to be able to communicate to them what you need and why you need it. I don't leave things and let them drift.

Several of the successful men and women trusted their own effectiveness, knowing when to continue fighting against obstacles and when to let go. It was inferred, from their stories, that their experience of living as a disabled person in a non-disabled society taught them when it is worth persisting and when it is not worth expending such energy on the impossible. As Lara reasons:

> I think, as a disabled person, I tend to be quite methodical because often if you have limited independence because of limited access, you tend to have to think things through throughout your day, from booking a cab, to booking the train three days ahead. I think, because of those life experiences, I'm quite patient and tolerant because you just say, 'Here we go again', you know that generally things are not worth getting yourself angry over. I think experience brings you the knowledge of when it's worth fighting and getting angry and frustrated and when it isn't.

Amanda, who acquired her impairment in her early adulthood and spent 16 years adapting to life as a disabled person before realising she could still have a valuable life and become a dancer again, believes '…you've got to weigh up the pros and cons and what's the profit at the end'.

A large number of the successful disabled people in this book perceived their success to be due to their perseverance, tenacity and innovation, traits identified by other studies (e.g. White et al., 1992) as being prevalent in people with an internal locus of control. Many felt that these traits were crucial for them to achieve their success goals despite meeting with several encounters of disability discrimination along the way. As Mary, a retired solicitor, recalls:

> I used to sit in my office and a client would come in for the first time and you could see them looking around for the solicitor. They couldn't really believe it was me. And I think I must be the only solicitor who's

> been tickled under the chin, in the middle of the High Street, by a client. I think you get over those by being damn good and actually proving that you are a jolly good solicitor!

Roger demonstrated his internal locus of control by his pursuit and completion of a PhD which required him to be intrinsically motivated, seeking to maximise satisfaction through responsibility, challenge and learning derived from the task. It can also be argued that Roger's doctorate and current profession, achieved in spite of his disabling life experiences, indicates his tenacity and perseverance.

Although the disabled high-flyers showed evidence of an internal locus of control, when they were asked if luck had any influence on their success, the initial response of many was that it did play a significant part in their overall success. Rotter (1966) would argue that individuals with an external locus of control believe that their rewards are controlled by external factors, such as luck, chance, fate or powerful others. Further, in Colwill's (1984) terms, attributing success to luck is detrimental to individuals' careers as they learn nothing about how they achieved their success, failing to raise self-esteem and self-efficacy beliefs and thus inhibiting career growth.

Although many of the disabled high-flyers felt that luck had played an important role in their career success, they thought it was also important to have the ability to capitalise on the opportunities luck presents. As Katey says:

> There are a lot of opportunities that I caught as they went past, so it was lucky they were there, but it was under my control that I recognised them!

Similarly, Corin feels luck played its part in her success. She believes everything happens for a reason: 'opportunities arise for everyone but it's up to them whether they take them.'

Jonathan perceived the opportunities that he was given to firstly help him to start a career in the entertainment industry, and secondly ensure it continued successfully, were dependent, to a large extent, on luck:

> I think the entertainment industry is very much luck-based. For example, some people could have been working on small shows for years but never make it to stardom. And someone could have just started and got a chance to do a popular show and the opportunity to be rich and famous! So a lot of it is to do with luck.

Timing, although not examined in detail, did emerge from the data and was considered, by a number of the high-flyers, to be an important element of their success. Timing seems to be based on the ability to overview a situation, to see the opportunities and pitfalls, to match available resources to the demands of a situation and finally formulate a clear plan that could be acted upon. This was expressed by Marty, who worked as an indoor postman for nine years before his professional life took a major turn, as a consequence of attending an integrated dance workshop. This was the beginning of his new career. Thus Marty saw timing as being significant to how his career panned out:

> The way things worked out, everything seemed to happen at the right time. I don't think they could have worked out any better. I met the right people at the right time. There's no way I can say I wish I had started dancing five years earlier, because the opportunity wasn't there! I needed to spend nine years in the Post Office to pass that time to meet that moment to start my dance career.

Likewise, Amanda, the director of the same dance company, also felt timing had an important part to play in her current professional situation. Sixteen years after her paralysing accident and thinking she would never be able to dance again, Amanda was asked to dance in a film for BBC2:

> During rehearsals and stuff, I found ways to move which didn't parody able-bodied dancers, it was movement very particular to me, I was expressing a very different kind of language really, but it was based on the knowledge I had before.

Having her talents exposed on national television was a significant turning point for Amanda and the start of a successful career. She teamed up with an arts graduate and started teaching integrated dance classes. The classes became more and more popular, and soon they were invited to perform and conduct workshops for various groups. From there, a team of seven dancers (four non-disabled and three wheelchair-users) were selected to form the first professional integrated dance company in the world: 'I wished I had started earlier, but maybe I wasn't ready to be as open as I was at the time I did start…'

Sunny, an established actor, believed his theatre company for disabled people was a success because it was launched at the right time, which was in 1981, the International Year of Disabled People.

CONCLUSION

It has been argued here that the constructs of personality: locus of control, need for achievement and work centrality, have an influence on success through their impact on motivational processes. The body of discourse reveals that high-flyers are more likely to have an internal locus of control, attributing success or failure predominantly to internal behaviours such as ability and effort rather than factors external to the individual. Such internality is established in childhood and influenced by child-rearing practices where parents have relatively strict expectations about right and wrong behaviour, and teach their children to take personal responsibility for their actions, thus engendering a high need for achievement which entails a single-minded preoccupation with task accomplishment. Altogether the disabled high-flyers had a sound record of past achievements, the success of which made them ambitious to achieve future goals.

The male and female high-flyers alike were intrinsically motivated, seeking to maximise their satisfaction through responsibility, challenge and learning derived from the task itself. They were ambitious and determined people with a high need for achievement, and the desire to perform an interesting, enjoyable and worthwhile activity. Many of the disabled high-flyers were driven to do a good job for other people but also saw work as a means to prove their self-worth by fulfilling a purposeful role in society. As Morse and Weiss (1955) assert, many workers are motivated to engage in the act of working as it grants them a sense of purpose in life, a psychological notion that is critical to increased self-esteem.

Although achievement, ambition, determination and purposefulness were identified as primary patterns of motivation for a large proportion of the sample, many respondents felt that they were inclined to expend more energy and enthusiasm in doing a better job if it was enjoyable and kept them stimulated. This is consistent with the managing directors in Cox and Cooper's (1988) study who were motivated to spend much time and effort on work-related activities because they enjoyed the job, sometimes believing it was the leading interest in their lives.

The successful people demonstrated high levels of career centrality, either in terms of behavioural elements such as hours worked, or by the fact that they perceived their work as being central to their self-identity. They had stories to tell about challenging tasks and how they resolved a problem in a logical and scientific way. Moreover, their stories demonstrate that they had a drive to persevere in the face of adversity, although they also knew when to stop. This infers that these disabled individuals had high mastery motivation which, for some, developed through their experiences of living and working in a disabling society. Like the successful people in White et al.'s (1992) study, the disabled high-flyers believed that their career success and indeed life success were due to their tenacity and perseverance combined with hard work. They were also less likely to attribute their success purely to luck, although perceived it as important in so much as it presented them with opportunities, which they could turn into successes. Several high-flyers, particularly artists, also considered timing to be important to their career success. They believed that certain turning points, significant to their life development, were triggered off as a consequence of being in the right place at the right time. This corresponds to Cooper and Hingley's (1985) theory which describes timing, in this context, as:

> ...based on an ability to overview a complex situation, to see the opportunities and pitfalls, to match available resources to the demands of the situation and finally, to formulate a clear plan which is then acted upon. (p.20)

CHAPTER 7

Career Choice and Experiences

> The strongest principle of growth lies in human choice.
>
> *George Elliott*

INTRODUCTION

Career choice not only refers to the choice of an occupation but also to the manner in which people arrive at an occupational choice. Hall (1976), along with other developmental theorists, recognises that an individual's career changes, and that different stages are marked by different needs, concerns, commitments, aspirations and interests. Hall (1976) maintains that careers are organic entities, with developing life-cycles, which interact and reflect the individual's life, past, present and future.

Traditional career models rest on the premise that individuals learn job-related skills and map career possibilities, then choose careers and move within them (Hall, 1976; Schein, 1979). Thus, career progression has been taken, by several researchers (e.g. Larwood and Gutek, 1987), to imply climbing a hierarchy; increased salary, increased recognition and respect; and greater freedom to enjoy interests. However, this conception of career progression is principally objective and neglects the more personal subjective side.

CAREER CHOICE AND DEVELOPMENT

Holland's theory, first presented in 1958, emphasised the 'searching' aspects of person-environment fit. He described the choice of an occupation as an expressive act reflecting a person's motivation, knowledge, personality and ability. Further, as understood by Hodkinson and Sparkes (1997), career decisions are context-related and cannot be separated from the individual's family background, culture and life history. Many researchers (e.g. Hall, 1969; Vondracek, Lerner and Schulenberg, 1986) agree that careers represent a way of life, an environment rather than a set of isolated work functions or skills.

Moreover, individuals see their careers as part of them, as something that can grow, change and develop with them throughout their lives. For example, as stated by Holland (1958):

> ...To work as a carpenter means not only to have a certain status, community role, and a special pattern of living. The choice of occupational title represents several kinds of information: the S's motivation, his knowledge of the occupation in question, his insight and understanding of himself, and his abilities. (cited in Brown, Brooks and Associates, 1996, pp.35–36)

The notion of developing one's career over an entire lifetime is an addition to the work on career theory. This approach, introduced by Super in the 1950s, as the 'life-span, life-space' approach to career development, brings together life-stage psychology and social role theory to convey a comprehensive picture of multiple-role careers, together with their determinants and interactions. As Super, Savickas and Super (1996) maintain, in order to understand an individual's career, it is important to know and appreciate the web of life roles that embeds the individual and his or her life concerns. Thus, the life-cycle approach addresses the individual's life situation, while focusing on how people change and make transitions as they prepare for, engage in, and reflect on their life roles, especially the work role. Furthermore, it acknowledges that a large and complex set of factors interact dynamically in determining the course of careers. Such factors include life events, conceived as ecological determinants of marked intra-individual changes. They also represent dynamic moments in person-environment interaction (Faltermaier, 1992).

Life events differ in their meaning for the subject; some are peripheral, others central. Sometimes they mark a turning point in one's life which, Strauss (1962) maintains, occurs when an individual has to take stock, to re-evaluate, revise, re-see and re-judge.

Strauss (1962) claims that turning points are or can occur in all parts of our lives. This includes occupational careers, where, according to Hodkinson (2003), a turning point is a short period when a person's career changes track. Turning points may be understood as a trigger to personal development: the beginning of an education, a job or a partnership. Hodkinson and Sparkes (1997), in their study, discern three different categories of turning points. The first category is structural and determined by the external structures of the institution involved. For instance, students go through one such structural turning point at the end of their compulsory schooling when they have to decide whether to stay on to further their education full-time or leave and pursue a different direction. Another is at compulsory retirement age. The next category of turning points are referred to as self-initiated, in that the individual concerned is instrumental in precipitating a transformation in response to a range of external factors in their personal life in the field. Finally, turning points can be forced onto some people by external events and/or the actions of others. One such turning point, experienced by several of the high-flyers in this research, is having a debilitating accident resulting in becoming disabled. Such an event would have a causal effect on the direction of one's future.

Empirically there is no doubt that life events influence individual development. Some researchers (e.g. Callahan and McCluskey, 1983) maintain that the individual is a passive recipient of external influences and is expected to adapt optimally to environmental changes. However, other researchers suggest that such an approach tends to obscure the developmental process in some respects, and stress that the individual should be seen as active and as the producer of his/her own development (Lerner and Busch-Rossnagel, 1981). Individuals interpret changes in their environment and are able to change the environment themselves by initiating life events, planning their future and even consciously promoting their personal development.

Vondracek, Lerner and Schulenberg (1983a, 1983b) point out that vocational and career development can be fully understood only from a relational perspective that focuses on the dynamic interaction between a changing individual in a changing context. Driver (1988) concurs with this, believing that there is a growing consensus that career includes both work and non-work activities. Super *et al.* (1996) argue that too many career theories ignore the fact that while making a living, people still have a life. The work role, albeit a critical role in contemporary society, is only one among many roles which an individual occupies. A person's multiple roles interact to shape each other. Thus, individuals make decisions about their professional life (i.e. career choices), within the circumstances imposed by the constellation of social roles that give meaning and focus to their lives. As Arthur, Inkson and Pringle (1999) suggest, careers are organic entities, developing through different stages which are shaped by complex interactions between personal make-up and choice, and the external forces of family, class and residential, economic and organisational circumstances. They illustrate this, in Chapter 5 of their book *The New Careers*, with the case of a trained and qualified nurse whose career has been interrupted, and contained periods of part-time employment while she gave priority to her family. Despite many transitions, and the risk of fracturing her career to accommodate family needs, the nurse advanced in her profession by using the expertise and confidence she had built up by her experiences over the years. Arthur *et al.* (1999) maintain that the data informing individuals' career directions come not only from their paid work role but also from their wider social roles as family members, partners, volunteers, members of ethnic or class groups and positions as privileged or underprivileged members of society.

The family, a principal agent of primary socialisation, has been noted by a significant body of evidence including that presented in Chapter 4, to be important to one's career choice. Osipow (1983) believes that parents influence their children in general, particularly in their vocational choices. The family has been perceived as a social institution in which an entire array of human experience exists, and in which early conceptualisations of work and the meaning attached to it are formed. Accordingly, a case can be made for the family's ability to influence members to choose careers traditionally considered gender-appropriate. Social norms and ideological patterns of behaviour have been noted for having a substantial influence on one's career aspirations and choices (Goodale and Hall, 1976; Kidd, 1984). For example, Astin (1984) recalls that her childhood socialisation had a profound impact on her career development. Although her first career choice was architecture, her dreams of becoming an architect never materialised because the social norms of the day dictated otherwise. She claims that her father saw architecture as a sub-field of his own field, engineering, which he considered to be an exclusively male field, and strongly discouraged her from pursuing it, believing it held no opportunities for women.

Goodale and Hall (1976) claim that sons are likely to inherit their father's occupational level. They postulate that a father's occupational status exerts a considerable influence over his son's career achievement by affecting his education and his first job. For example, Allen (1988), in her study of doctors and their careers, found that men's choice to study medicine was often related to the fact that their father or another member of the family was a doctor. She found that the women were more likely to have felt a strong desire to 'help' people from a young age. Fitzgerald and Betz (1983) suggest that the different expectations of the sexes in society can have a significant impact on the direction of an individual's vocational development. This is supported by Astin (1984) who argues that, although the basic work motivation is the same for men and women, their choices are different, as are the motives for their pursuits. This may be the result of their different early socialisation experiences, and the structure of opportunity that ultimately influences the values that are transmitted through the socialisation process (e.g. sex-typing of jobs, discrimination). Astin maintains that work expectations begin to develop early in childhood through the process of socialisation, whereby the values of a particular society are gradually inculcated through the spoken word and the examples of parents, teachers and other adults. As a result of childhood experiences including play, helping with household tasks and engaging in early paid work activities, individuals develop certain expectations as to what kind of adult work activities are available to them. Furthermore, they have an understanding of what activities they are best capable of performing, and the extent to which these activities will best satisfy their survival, pleasure and contribution needs. Therefore, in the process of satisfying these needs through childhood activities, the individual gets certain experiences that directly influence their career choice and work behaviour.

Interests

Vocational interests (i.e. people's patterns of likes, dislikes and indifferences regarding various occupations and career-relevant activities) have been assumed to be a potent ingredient for making career choices (Lent, Brown and Hackett, 1996). It has been asserted that people form enduring interest in an activity when they anticipate that performing it will produce valued outcomes (Bandura, 1982; Lent, Larkin and Brown, 1989). Conversely, people may form aversions to activities in which their self-efficacy is weak or where they anticipate receiving neutral or negative outcomes. According to a model developed by Lent et al. (1996), emergent interests promote particular goals for activity involvement. This means that as individuals develop an affinity for an activity at which they feel efficacious and expect positive outcomes, they form goals for sustaining or increasing their involvement in that activity. These goals, in turn, increase the likelihood of actual activity practice. The attainments accrued from activity practice, such as trophies, grades and self-satisfaction, form an important feedback loop which facilitates the culmination or reshaping of self-efficacy and outcome expectations. This promotes particular career interests that, in turn, are important to future intentions and plans to pursue a particular career path. This process is constantly in motion throughout a person's lifespan and it is through this process that people come to develop characteristic patterns of career interests.

Although career interests tend to stabilise by early adulthood (Hansen, 1984), change and growth in interests is theoretically possible at any point in life. From childhood, young people accumulate conceptual structures (schemata) which serve as tools for understanding their experiences. A schema structures what a person knows about the world, by filtering out the 'irrelevancies' and allowing sense to be made of partial information. As new experiences are gained, schemata are modified and as they change, so does what is recognised in the surrounding world. In this dialectical way, as Hodkinson and Sparkes (1997) argue, the life history of the individual shapes and is shaped by his/her practice. Therefore, when people are presented with environmental conditions or life challenges such as job restructuring, childbirth, acquisition of a disability or exposure to new activities, their schemata changes which, in turn, influences their actions. As well as environmental conditions, a number of personal and contextual variables – such as gender, race/ethnicity, physical health/disability, genetic endowment and socio-economic status – have been proposed to have a substantial impact on career choice and direction. For instance, gender and disablement, viewed as socially constructed aspects of people's experiences, shape the learning opportunities to which particular individuals are exposed, the interpersonal reactions (such as support and indifference) they receive for performing certain activities, and the future outcomes they come to anticipate. This is shown by Eccles (1987) and Kimball (1989), who argue that parents and teachers tend to treat boys and girls differently in terms of the activities they are encouraged to perform, how well they are expected to do and the sorts of social reactions that are provided. Such treatment is based on culturally shared experiences about gender-appropriate behaviour. Likewise, Hackett and Betz (1981) contend that girls are more likely to develop self-efficacy for female-type activities (e.g. artwork or domestic tasks) and to feel less efficacious at activities that are culturally defined as not feminine. This is as a result of the gender-biased access to opportunities for practising and observing particular behaviours. They propose that, as a result of socialisation, women's expectations of personal efficacy in relation to many career-related behaviours are different from men's and thus they are restricted to a limited range of occupations. This could also be true of men, who are just as likely to avoid traditionally female activities and behaviours due to being nurtured to behave according to norms acceptable to their gender. Such externally imposed barriers do, however, become internalised and could cause impediments to an individual's career options which, over the years, have been directed by societal ideologies and the expectations of men and women towards particular occupations. A similar psychosocial process may affect the career-related self-efficacy and outcome expectations in children and young adults with disabilities.

Patterns of career development for disabled people

The opportunities available to people to develop as individuals, citizens and workers are significantly influenced by ecological issues and social contexts composed of a combination of political, social and economic environments (Herr, 1996). These have an important impact on their possibilities for choice, the knowledge available about opportunities open to them and the reinforcement of their behaviours. Herr emphasises the invaluable effect that environmental stimuli, social metaphors, traditions and value structures have on human behaviour. These ecological constructs serve to define physical and psychological boundaries within which various individuals perform their daily transactions.

Many everyday activities such as the distance people walk, the steps they climb, the materials they read and the messages they receive, impose stringent requirements on persons with different levels of functional skills (Hahn, 1988). However, this is not necessarily a deterrent from pursuing a career. According to a study by the Chicago School of Sociology (Bulmer, 1984), a 'career' is a device for exploring the individual identity as it embraces non-work as well as work experiences, and subjective as well as objective components. Such a perspective broadens its focus from professionals and managers in traditional bureaucratic structures to all adults in more dynamic and flexible situations. Therefore, it succeeds in incorporating disabled employees who may, due to the threat of social or physical obstacles seen to prevent traditional hierarchical advancement, need to be flexible and innovative in order to advance by achievement. For example, Hendey (1999) maintains that disabled people in receipt of personal assistance, especially from communal care agencies or residential homes, are often denied the right to be flexible in their daily lives. Limiting flexibility and spontaneity, by predetermined support provision, makes it impossible for disabled people to integrate into the community or move to another city to develop professionally and respond to their changing needs.

A further way disabled people can advance is to follow individualised career paths and become sculptors of their own careers. This may help them to avoid barriers, have a constant awareness of opportunities to advance, and have the ability and application to capitalise on them. Being sculptors of their own careers gives individuals the flexibility to follow career routes which, they anticipate, may present them with opportunities to achieve and enhance productivity levels without being physically limited by demands of traditional mainstream competitive work settings. As Lysaght et al. (1994) argue, the success of people with severe disabilities is hampered by the full-time competitive work schedule that fails to account for the reduced activity tolerance levels of these persons. Thus there is a need to develop a means whereby workers with disabilities have opportunities to maximise their productivity and strive towards long-term success.

However, research has revealed that it is not uncommon for disabled employees to retain traditional views about employment and careers, expecting to stay with their current employer and to be promoted. According to the Labour Force Survey (1998), disabled people tend to be more loyal than many other employees and have a tendency to remain with employers for longer periods. A possible reason for this could be that many employees with disabilities require accommodations in their homes, and services in their communities that make them far less likely to make regular job and employer transitions during their working lives. This is contrary to the recent career path orientation of many non-disabled employees who, as indicated in King's (1999) study, are concerned with making sure they have the right range of skills and experience for future employability, and are not deterred from regularly changing job and employer to achieve this. As has been shown by OPCS surveys, it is common for people already in work to move to other parts of the country to acquire more skills and greater experience. In present circumstances, however, geographical mobility is difficult, if not impossible, for many disabled people. Many of them use personal and domestic services provided by local authorities or voluntary agencies (Barnes, 1991; Hendey, 1999). Begum (1990) argues that service delivery tends to be structured around predetermined tasks instead of user preferences and is often unpredictably timed.

A further barrier to geographical mobility is the short supply of housing accessible to disabled people. Despite the new Government Disability Bill (2004), disabled people in Britain are being forced to live in institutions or with people they do not wish to live with because there is not enough accessible housing. The 1995 Disability Discrimination Act claims to protect disabled people against discrimination in employment and education. However, if disabled people cannot get in and out of their own homes or get the personal assistance they need to get up out of bed in the morning, they are unable to work, attend school, college or university (Disability Rights Commission, 2004).

The majority of mainstream dwellings in both private and public sectors are designed explicitly for non-disabled people, in particular those who are 'male, fit and aged between 18 and 40' (Rowe, 1990). The housing needs of disabled people are rarely considered within the general area of housing provision and when they are it is usually within a ghetto of so-called 'special needs housing' (Morris, 1990), meaning small clusters of accessible homes set within mainstream housing estates. However, because the availability of this type of provision is limited throughout the country, disabled people may have to forego any career advancement opportunities that may involve moving to another area (Barnes, 1991). This could have a detrimental effect on the career development of many disabled people. Further, it serves to explain, in part, why disabled people tend to stay with one employer for a long time compared to their non-disabled colleagues. Thus, one may argue that although such a pattern of career development is not always, especially in the last decade, regarded as conventional for the non-disabled majority, it could be seen as relatively typical for disabled employees.

However, such a pattern of career development (i.e. working for one employer for a long time) was not unpopular for the female executives in Hennig and Jardim's (1978) study. The women were unlikely to take advantage of advancement opportunities that involved regular company moves. In fact, having found a suitable organisation, none of the women worked for any other firm because they felt that once they had established good working relationships it would be unproductive to move to another company where they would have to go through the process all over again.

CAREER CHOICE AND PROGRESSION AMONG DISABLED HIGH-FLYERS

The stories of the high-flyers' career development uncovered the external barriers they encountered during their journey to meet their occupational goals and the turning points which they considered to be significant to their current occupational position. Sometimes turning points were, as Hodkinson and Sparkes (1997) pointed out, forced onto some people by external events. These were connected to the high-flyers' impairments that caused certain diversions or reorientations. However, for others, turning points involved simply getting a job, watching a play or meeting a significant other, and were not influenced by their impairment.

The findings revealed that disability certainly impacted, although to varying degrees, on the career development of several of the disabled high-flyers. It was sometimes perceived to be a critical determinant in terms of informing the career choice, aspirations and development of these successful people. However, their interviews showed that there was a significant difference in the extent to which disability affected the life-cycle of individuals with acquired impairments and those with birth/post-birth impairments. As Priestley (1998) contends, children/adults with congenital disabilities may be excluded from important social processes through different mechanisms of medicalisation and administrative segregation. Furthermore, if a disabled child is raised in an overprotective environment where independence is not encouraged and they are not challenged, the child will probably evolve into the stereotypical disabled person, i.e. passive and dependent.

Sutherland (1981) argues that this is the difference between children with congenital disabilities and those who have acquired disabilities in adult life. The latter often have much more power in terms of money, legal status, position in the social structure and experiences in dealing with encounters with other people, all of which makes it easier for them to reject attempts made to coerce them into conforming to a stereotypical role. On the other hand, it may be suggested, both from the disabled high-flyers' stories as well as my own experience of disability and professional progression, that people with a congenital disability have 'grown up with it', know their abilities and limitations well and try to overcome them. Furthermore, when the child is nurtured within a family who challenges them and treats them as normally as possible, the child is more likely to stretch to meet their expectations (Thomas, 1998). People with acquired disabilities (especially when the change has been sudden, e.g. road traffic accident) usually have two serious opponents to overcome: anxiety and psychological problems first, and lack of relevant knowledge about their 'new' situation second.

The interviews with the high-flyers uncovered some very interesting information about their work histories and the different routes they took to meet their career goals. Analysis of their descriptions of their work histories revealed three different patterns of career progression experienced by the disabled people. The three patterns of career progression are defined as:

Education-related career progression – a pattern where there is a direct connection between education and work (i.e. people enter an occupation after taking specialist training and qualifications), and a tendency to be promoted in a specialised field with minimal, if any, geographical mobility.

Individualised career progression – a flexible and dynamic career path composed of a series of challenging jobs with no obvious connection to previous educational training. Such a pattern of career progression is facilitated by the ability to manage one's own time, and seek out and capitalise on new opportunities to progress. Individuals who were not able to pursue their initial career choice but instead took a different career route, unrelated to their original training and choice, may follow this pattern.

Redirected career progression – the pursuit of a completely different career route as a result of external life events, the actions of others or personal decisions. For instance, an army officer may be prevented from moving up the career ladder after a disabling accident, and thus may choose to pursue a different career which offers him/her opportunities for promotion.

The number of disabled high-flyers who followed each career path can be seen in Table 7.1. As indicated by the table, the career paths followed by some of them may fall into more than one of the categories. For example, one of the men was forced to redirect his former education-related career path in law, after a disabling accident. However, his redirected career in architecture also followed an education-related pattern of progression as it was directly related to specialised training and qualifications obtained prior to starting work.

Education-related career progression

Nineteen of the high-flyers followed relatively education-related career paths, entering their occupations after taking qualifications in a related subject and experiencing the opportunity to move further by specialising or applying for promotion. Several of them advanced in their career without necessarily moving employer. As Table 7.1 indicates, these were men or women with a congenital or acquired disability. The impact that gender and disability had, or did not have, on the respondents' career progression will be discussed later in the chapter.

Four men with congenital disabilities entered their career after undertaking educational training in the same field. One of these men was Harry (senior

Table 7.1 Career patterns and decisions
followed by disabled high-flyers

Respondent group	Education-related progression	Individualised progression	Redirected progression
M/A[1]	8	0	2
M/C[2]	4	6	4
F/A[3]	2	1	0
F/C[4]	5	4	1
Total	19	11	7

[1]Males with acquired disabilities = 8   [3]Females with acquired disabilities = 3

[2]Males with congenital disabilities = 11   [4]Females with congenital disabilities = 9

computer analyst), who remained with the same employer for eight or nine years, entering his occupation immediately after graduating with a computer science degree:

> I have done this job for a number of years, about eight or nine years, more or less doing the same job, but the responsibilities have got stronger and harder. Before that I was at university from where I graduated with a 2.1 (Hons) degree in computer science. So this was my first job and basically I have stayed.

He identifies a significant milestone as qualifying for the role of certified Microsoft systems engineer, an industry-recognised qualification which, he believes, will give him the opportunity to move within the company and within the industry. As he says, 'it just gives you freedom to go on the market.'

Bob, a financial planner, followed a similar career pattern. After graduating from university with a degree in economics and accounting, he did four years professional training with an accounting firm, then decided to specialise, after which he started working as a financial advisor for another accounting firm. He started this job in 1987 and was still in their employ at the time of the research interview. As he states, 'in my working career I have only ever had two employers, two jobs.' Although Bob realised that this did not give him the wide experience he required, and would prevent him from climbing up the occupational hierarchy at the same pace as his non-disabled colleagues, he considered it more practical for him, as a disabled person, to remain with the same employer:

> I think it's quite important that everybody in the organisation can get to every other part of the office, can get to see everybody, can get to do

things and don't have to rely on other people always to come to you because steps get in the way. This is important, particularly with the sort of job I have got at the moment. Most of the companies are very small, less than ten people. Most of them operate from first and second floors in old office buildings with no lifts, steps up to the doors and so on, so it would be very difficult for me to move within the industry to another company. Therefore, unlike a lot of people, I can't keep changing jobs to get wider experience. So the physical limitations, projected as a result of disability, mean that you are very limited as to how often you can change jobs.

All of the men with acquired disabilities followed 'education-related' career paths. Clint has been employed by the same company for 25 years, ever since leaving university from where he graduated with a BSc (Hons) degree in international economics:

At the age of 21 I applied to work for my present employers, which is 25 years ago now, with a view to gaining a few years' international experience. But in the early years every time I thought about moving they made me an offer of promotion I couldn't refuse. Since then I've been promoted four times.

Similarly, Amil, a computer science graduate, joined his company to work as a computer programmer and analyst, which he claimed to be a major turning point:

At the time I was looking, there was a recession so it was hard enough to find a job and harder still if you are disabled... I only have ever had one job, working for [X company]. I joined them a year after leaving university, and have been there six years now. After a couple of years of being employed with [X company] I started to get a lot more responsibility in terms of doing more project management-type work, becoming team leader. The next turning point was last year when I got a promotion.

Roger, a university professor, spent many years of hard work and determination working to achieve the next goal in his academic career. However, his career path was not altogether smooth. Roger mentioned a few major turning points he experienced during his career development. For instance, he identifies a major one to be his viva examination for his undergraduate degree, which determined whether he would graduate with a first class or second class degree which, in turn, would influence the subject of PhD research and where it was to be conducted. But when Roger learned he had a muscle deteriorating condition he became apathetic and contemplated not finishing his PhD, not expecting to live long enough anyway. However, this was before the second major turning point, as he explains:

> I got engaged to a girl, whom I had met about the time I was diagnosed with my impairment. This gave me something to live for. If we were to get married, I had to get a job, and to get a job I had to finish my PhD.

Maria was one of the five women with a congenital disability who followed an 'education-related' career path, as she entered her professional role of speech and language therapist after qualifying with a degree in speech and language therapy. Although she worked in this field for many years, her role became more specialised since she got a post as clinician. She considered this to be a major turning point in her career.

Corin, the university lecturer, also followed this career pattern. After graduating with a university degree in computer science, and failing to get a job in a related field, she went on to do an MSc and then a PhD that opened doors to the field of research and academia. Before getting a full-time lectureship at a Scottish university in 1997, she worked in research for some years, first as a research assistant to carry on with her PhD research and then on several short-term contracts. Although it could be argued that this is a conventional pattern of career development for anyone working in the academic field, Corin felt that her disability provoked some prejudice for her when trying to get a permanent contract as a lecturer. Even though she did not encounter any negative prejudice in her university department, having proven her abilities which, in time, served to override her disabilities, it was always a challenge when she was looking for work elsewhere:

> There have been a lot of negative hurdles which I have had to jump over along the way. People have denied me access to things because of my disability. As soon as I go out of the department it's always been a matter of proving myself every time.

Judith, an education and training development officer, who acquired a hearing impairment before going to university, believed her education has proved to be positively influential to her current occupation in the arts. Thus her career progression can be described as 'education-related':

> Definitely my education at a higher level has all been connected to the visual arts and I use that such a lot now. But I think people who work in the arts have these all-over-the-place sort of careers. You do one thing then you do something else, thought of as portfolio careers. I think people who work in the arts tend to work over a broader spectrum than, perhaps, people in different industries who specialise more. I've proba-

bly specialised at a later stage in my life. I've kept my hand in with the visual arts: I'm a visual arts assessor for the [southern] Arts Board.

After university Judith worked on several arts projects, but claims the major turning point was her work as an arts association trainee: 'Without that I wouldn't be doing what I'm doing now.'

Indivdualised career progression

Eleven of the high-flyers achieved their success by following this type of career progression, not directly related to their previous education and training but rather formulated by a series of challenging jobs. Furthermore, they considered their progression to be determined by being in the right place at the right time to seek out and take advantage of opportunities as and when they presented themselves, and by certain events and life-changing experiences that served to be significant to their career progression.

Ten of the eleven people who followed an indivdualised pattern of career progression had a congenital disability. One of these was Sunny, who graduated with a university degree in social sciences but, since a child, had always wanted to be an actor. However, he believed disability discrimination had prevented him from going to drama school to acquire specialist training and qualifications: 'I did a degree in psychology, philosophy and sociology which has nothing to do with acting.' The denied opportunity to undertake specialist training and qualifications in acting meant he had to follow an individualised career path, and one that he had created himself, which was facilitated by a combination of hard work to seek out opportunities, perseverance, luck and timing. According to Sunny:

> ...drama schools didn't accept disabled people. When I was a kid, they didn't... So it basically took me about 12 years to achieve my child-hood ambition. I had to do it unconventionally. The only way it could be done, at that time, was to create a theatre company of disabled peo-ple, write your own shows, perform them and hope other people will be interested in what we were doing and see what we were capable of.

Sunny believed 1981 was significant to his career progression because, being the International Year of Disabled People, it proved to be a good time to launch and publicise his theatre company for disabled actors. His work at this theatre company was not only considered to be a self-initiated turning point, but also the start of Sunny's successful acting career: 'Since then, I worked in stage plays ... then there's been television ... and a few other small dramas, a Channel 4 production in which I had the leading role.'

Similarly, Sam, who graduated with an upper second class degree in communication studies, followed an individualised career pattern. He decided to combine his personal interests with his professional interests, as he states:

> My work is also part of my private life. I spend about 75 per cent of my time in work or in work-related activities. I'm in the type of work where my paid employment can and does overlap with the work I do voluntarily.

He achieved his professional position as sports development officer for a national charity by working in a number of unrelated jobs and being influenced by a number of life events which triggered certain changes:

> After university, I went into a two-year training program called Fast Track which was pretty good but I soon found out it wasn't for me. It gave me certain skills and work experience, but I just didn't seem to get on so I quit after six months. I then was out of work for six months and then was offered a post with the local authority as a disability sports development officer. But it got a little frustrating as the post didn't demand enough responsibility. Also there were various issues concerning physical access around the work place which caused some distress because the offices that we used were located in such a place that it meant that I only had access to my own office and no other part of the building. This restricted me for playing a full part in my department. And then I applied for my current job.

One of the other six men, Jonathan, a TV presenter, began his career as a consequence of luck and being in the right place at the right time:

> I got spotted by a talent scout from Thames TV who asked if I would like to do a screen test for a show. I ended up presenting a children's show on Channel 4 twice a week.

According to this book, Jonathan's career followed an individualised pattern of progression, but he perceives that the way his career was progressing was conventional for the television industry: that is to start off doing bits and bobs, 'do a children's series on Channel 4 and then a children's series on BBC1'. However, this was stopped as a result of bad press, proving to be a significant turning point in his career:

> I got a children's show on BBC1. At the same time I started my band, a sexy pop act. But a national newspaper got hold of the fact I was in a fetish band, going to fetish clubs and also presenting children's television, so they printed something that implied the BBC had employed a

pervert to work with children. That incident stopped my career from going further.

After that Jonathan grabbed what opportunities came his way, using his disability to get him more work so he could be seen and get his mainstream career back on track. He took advantage of the fact that the TV industry has cycles of disability programmes that offered him potential work opportunities:

> I got picked up on the first cycle of disability TV. Then they went off disability for a year. Then they included it again… So the television industry goes in cycles and I think, by the end of next year, disabled actors are going to be employed more and more by the BBC. So suddenly people with disabilities get a chance to move up a step. Once you are on the inside and know when these opportunities are going to occur, you can grab them.

As Table 7.1 (p.149) indicates, four of the women with a congenital disability took an individualised career route to reach their professional goals. One example is the case of a freelance journalist, Katey, who attempted to follow an education-related pattern of career progression, starting with a postgraduate diploma in journalism. However, she was driven to revise her career route, by negative reactions towards her disability:

> I did English at university and went on to do a postgraduate diploma in journalism studies at [X] University. But I left that early due to encountering overt prejudice. On a number of occasions I was told I wasn't suited as a journalist because I was disabled but I could be a subeditor which involved sitting in the office editing other people's work. The tutors basically did things to prove their theory that I couldn't keep up. So they worked me as hard and for as many hours as possible until I cracked.

So she pursued her career aspirations via a more individualised route, gaining entrance to her career by perseverance, hard work, seeking out and capitalising on opportunities when they presented themselves. Katey confirms that her career started making great progress after getting a job with a local newspaper in the town where she grew up. She worked there for six years, first as a reporter and then as editor. She claims this to be a major turning point in her career, which '…has progressed by me being opportunistic – grabbing opportunities when I see them, and just going for what I want and don't let anyone stand in my way'.

Two other women chose not to enter or pursue a career in the field in which they had been trained and qualified. Instead they decided to enter a completely different field and progress via individualised career routes. As Lara comments:

I had no plans to go into a career in the arts. I was trained as a sociologist, contemplating social work, welfare rights, that kind of thing. When I left college I applied for a part-time job, simply because the advert said 'disabled people welcome to apply', because I hadn't worked up to then at all, so I thought a part-time job would be good to see how I'd manage, and because the advert said 'disabled people welcome to apply', I thought at least I would get an interview. It was for a job-share post, to co-run an arts project involving disabled people. That was a major turning point.

Similarly, Kay's initial degree qualifications did not provide her with any realistic career openings. She did a degree in linguistics which she perceives did not prepare her for 'anything in working terms'. So she followed an individualised career path, working in a series of challenging jobs, unrelated to her previous education, but climbing up the status ladder with each job. Progression was facilitated by a series of turning points. One big one was redundancy:

Although being made redundant was a disaster for us (me and my husband), having a large mortgage hanging around our necks, it was quite a positive thing because it meant I got the disability strategy manager job.

Amanda, the artistic director and dancer of an international integrated dance company, achieved her professional position via a partially individualised career path. Although her career as a dancer started via educational training in the same field, it stopped rather abruptly as a consequence of a paralysing accident, noted as a significant turning point in the respondent's professional life. As she recalls:

I went to dance college. I went to the [X] Dance School as soon as I left school, from when I was 16 till 19 then I joined a dance company. At the age of 22 I had an accident, so it was a very short career. This integrated dance company started in 1991. From the end of 1973 to 1990 I didn't do anything.

For Amanda it was not an option to continue along the same career route after the acquisition of her impairment. As a newly disabled person, she was presented with two possible alternatives: to change her career altogether or to find another way of achieving success in her original career. She explains:

For many years after my accident I did not partake in dance at all. Sixteen years later I was asked to dance in a film, on BBC2, for the *Ten by Ten* series, by a well-known choreographer and director. That was the beginning of it all.

This was a significant turning point in her life, giving her the confidence to try dancing again and take a more individualised career path, developing by seeking out and building on new opportunities such as:

> ...meeting a guy who has been my co-artistic director until just recently. We started teaching at an integrated sports centre giving disabled people the opportunity to do something other than sport which was the only thing on offer... From there, the company grew and my career certainly progressed. I never thought I would be the artistic director for the only professional integrated dance company around at the moment.

So Amanda's career path was formulated by a series of turning points, the luck of meeting the right people and being in the right place at the right time. As she reflects:

> I think my former co-artistic director was a great influence because, after I had worked on the film, he was the one who really convinced me that this is what I should be doing and he couldn't do it on his own. And together we were a good team: he was able-bodied, I was disabled, and we came from different backgrounds, we had different skills, and I think he was very inspiring. So it was lucky meeting him and lucky meeting the people we met on various workshops who are now in the company.

Redirected career progression

Seven of the respondents had followed redirected career progression. There were many reasons why they reorientated their original career, both internal and external to the individual. These included the result of a single event, a religious calling or issues surrounding disability. For example, Greg, previously a drummer in a rock and roll band, redirected his career as a result of 'coming out' as a disabled person. He explains:

> I decided to be a drummer behind a drum-kit rather than be at the front of the stage singing because I had plenty of ego to push me to the front of the stage, but it was the realisation that people would look at me as a freak that pushed me to the back of the stage. But the disability stuff hit in 1992. The new reclaimed 'I'm disabled and proud' attitude culminated with my interest in acting.

He recalls watching a play by a professional theatre company for disabled actors, founded by Sunny, as being a major turning point in his professional life:

> I saw a production that totally blew my head off, because I had never seen disabled people perform before. I suddenly realised that I could do what I really wanted to do all along, which was act! So I slowly moved out of mainstream music, and I auditioned for [X theatre company] and trained up as an actor for three years!

So, for Greg, watching the performance by disabled actors was the principal turning point in his life not only in terms of cultivating his professional potential as an actor, but also helping him to accept a component part of his self-concept, his disability.

Two other men were forced to rethink their professional future after acquiring a physical impairment. They both were confronted with disability in their adult years, after being educated and/or trained for a specific occupation as a non-disabled person. Adrian, a trained lawyer in his former life, had to retrain after becoming disabled: 'I wanted to be a barrister. But following my accident, I couldn't return to law because the courts were then too inaccessible. So I went into architecture.'

Likewise Nick, now retired from his full-time occupation of careers officer, specialising in advising disabled young school leavers of their post-school options, recollects:

> Before my illness, I wanted to go into the Navy. I wanted to be physically active, I wanted to go into the officers' training school in [X city]. I had a job with, or training with, the public school's and university's branch of the Royal Navy volunteer reserves. It all just disappeared – went down the plughole, as it were! So I reorientated my dreams; I had to.

Other high-flyers also followed a pattern of reoriented career progression, although it was not necessarily influenced by disability. For example, Marty's internal feeling of boredom together with his decision to do something about it changed his professional status from postman to that of dancer:

> I was an indoor postman for nine years, but by the end of nine years, I really needed to do something very, very different. This feeling of boredom inspired me to go to an integrated dance workshop, not with any view to take it up as a career, but as something that was going to break up my week. One thing led to another and after a couple of months I was invited to join the dance company. So I left the Post Office, joined the dance company and it went from there really.

Jude's first career started after she achieved a Masters degree in information technology but underwent a severe career change, not as a result of her disability but by being called to serve God. However, she did undergo a period of educational training before becoming a vicar, therefore once again following an education-related pattern of career progression.

Tom and Timmy told similar stories as they also reoriented their careers as a result of a religious calling to work for the Church. This calling was considered to be a major turning point for both of them, causing them to redirect their career route completely. As Tom comments:

> I thoroughly enjoyed my consultancy work. I was a disability trainer. I loved it, had a good reputation and good pay. But I went into the Church because I felt it was where God wanted me to go.

Likewise, Timmy, a baptist minister, graduated from university as an economist but having worked in that occupation for two years, recognised his calling and, as a result, changed his career path and what he conceptualised as a career:

> My idea of a career path has changed and it's got something to do with the work I am doing. I used to think of a career in terms of business. But that evaporated at the same time that I recognised this was what I was called to do.

Like Jude, both Timmy's and Tom's new career path could be described as being *education-related*, as defined in this book, because after recognising their calling they underwent specialist educational training which provided a key to work with the Church.

Impact of disability and gender on career progression

The stories reveal that disability did not always influence the high-flyers' decisions to follow certain patterns of career progression. At times the ways in which the disabled high-flyers perceived their careers to have developed were no different to what is known about how the careers of non-disabled high-flyers, in the same field, develop. For example, the three vicars in the sample had to redirect their original career as the result of a religious calling.

However, issues surrounding disability did, in fact, influence a number of the respondents following education-related patterns of career progression (as defined above) to stay with one employer for several years. Although this is not regarded as conventional for non-disabled high-flyers, who are more likely to move job and employer to progress in their career, it is different for disabled workers who are more inclined to stay with one employer longer for purposes of convenience and ease. As discussed earlier, the services and resources required by many disabled people often impede successful employer transitions or job moves.

The evidence above also suggests that disability did have an impact on the different patterns of career progression followed by high-flyers. It shows how the respondents with acquired impairments were more likely to pursue traditional patterns of career progression (i.e. enter a career directly related to prior educational training) than those with congenital impairments. It is possible that this may be influenced by two factors. First, the former group had a non-disabled childhood where parental expectations of them were high and they were encouraged to achieve to a high standard and, at times, were directed towards particular goals. This was unlike the successful individuals with congenital disabilities who, as disabled children, were not exposed to the same standard of expectations. This was due to parents being unsure of how their child's disability would evolve and thus what they would be permitted to achieve (as discussed in Chapter 4). The second factor is that the respondents with acquired impairments attended mainstream educational institutions with a wider range of subjects, whereas several individuals with congenital impairments went to segregated schools and/or colleges where the curriculum and teaching expertise were limited (see Chapter 5). As a consequence, some of them studied the subjects that were available as opposed to subjects related to their preferable career choice.

On several occasions, the high-flyers perceived their disability as beneficial to their career development. Twelve of the 20 individuals with congenital disabilities currently work or have worked in areas focusing on disability. However, only a few were actually employed by disability organisations or institutions, such as Scope and the Muscular Dystrophy Group. Most of these 12 high-flyers were employed in disability-related work roles in mainstream organisations. For example, Kay is employed by a large rail organisation as disability strategy manager, and has the responsibility of ensuring that the rail network is accessible to disabled people. Her role within the organisation is considered to be very important, because, as she explains:

> Although they have already been doing stuff around disability, it has been quite fragmented and they haven't really known what they were doing essentially. So they wanted somebody to come and pull it together and also have the outside contact with disabled people.

The whole concept of having a disability focus within mainstream organisations can also be demonstrated by Anna's work situation. As well as being a professional wheelchair athlete, Anna is employed by the British Athletic Federation to work with disabled people with an interest in athletics.

Although these disabled professionals had no real preference of whether to work in the mainstream or disability sector, a few of them perceived their disability as an asset to their current career success. As Christian, a parliamentary officer, states, 'I work for a disability charity, not because it's a soft option but I can use my experiences, frustrations and persecutions to help other disabled people.'

Another example of disability being more of a help than a hindrance in an employment situation is demonstrated through the experiences of Marty, who considered his disability to be an important determinant of his career development and advancement, as he reveals:

> I'm a dancer in an integrated dance company, which is made up of seven dancers at this present time: four able-bodied dancers and three who use wheelchairs. When I started dancing, my disability proved to be a major advantage. In the last six or seven years, we have developed a new style of dance and vocabulary which has proved rather successful. If I hadn't the disability that I have, I wouldn't be doing what I'm doing in the style that I'm doing it in. So my disability has worked in my favour.

A small number of high-flyers who had acquired a disability also saw it as a causal factor in their professional success. For Adrian, the architect, acquiring a disability not only forced him to change careers, but also increased his professional position in society:

> Had I not had my accident, I would have probably stayed in law and gone to the bar and would have been a very junior barrister doing things like probate. But since I couldn't physically return to law after my accident, I went into architecture. Now I'm joint senior partner in three private practices, one of which is a limited company.

Further, through his work as an architect with/for people with disabilities he earned one of his most prized achievements, an MBE. Adrian also recognised that being mobility-impaired had ignited latent personality traits such as determination which encouraged him to learn skills that have been beneficial to his career development. He feels that he would not have considered attempting to pursue these in his former life as a non-disabled person:

> Since my accident I think my personality has changed and that has had an obvious impact on my practice. I'm not what people would normally associate with an architect – a stuffy academic.

Cane also considered his disability to be a positive influence on his high-flying status. Prior to the acquisition of his disability, he was keen to pursue a career in acting. However, after his accident, he become more and more interested in directing, which he thinks may have been influenced by '...practicality a bit; it's probably easier to do as my physical impairment is not in the way of me directing'.

Further, Cane's disability served to promote his suitability for a job with a theatre company for and run by disabled people. He identifies his work with the company as a significant turning point in his career, giving him a possible career opportunity and influencing his '... politics, personal politics and confidence'.

It may be argued that, in order to break free from the web of dependency, people with disabilities feel they must work harder than their non-disabled counterparts to gain the key to mainstream society, become autonomous and thus become accepted. One can suggest that together with disability come latent personality traits which are regarded as essential in order to survive in a mainstream society. Several high-flyers identified disability as making a positive contribution to their career success in terms of their determination and drive to achieve. Judith speculates:

> I wonder if I would have fought so hard for what I've got if I hadn't been deaf... I'm very stubborn, so if people tell me I can't do something I just say 'watch me' and go and do it.

No significant gender differences were identified from the high-flyers' stories of their career progression. Although they all spoke of important life events and people that had a major influence on their career choices and patterns of development, gender was not highlighted as being a factor in these.

CONCLUSION

As indicated in earlier chapters, the 31 high-flyers entered their careers from a wide variety of backgrounds and educational levels. They all followed one of three patterns of career progression, defined in this book as 'education-related', 'individualised' or 'redirected'. Several high-flyers decided to enter and pursue a career totally unrelated to their original education. Others experienced dramatic career changes, initiated by external events such as the acquisition of an impairment, personal life developments or the actions of others, which marked a turning point in their lives and the beginning of their 'redirected' career progression.

Disability had a significant influence on the routes of career progression the high-flyers followed. For instance, some of the high-flyers, particularly those with childhood disabilities, were less likely to follow education-related career progression due to the lack of education and training choices available to them as young disabled people. To achieve success in a career of their choice, they had to take a more individualised route.

So in order to understand an individual's career, it is important to know and appreciate the web of life roles that embed the individual and his/her life concerns. No decisions concerning individuals' work role behaviour, such as occupational choice and organisational commitment, are made without the influence of other social roles, relationships and life events. Life events are noted as causal triggers or turning points in an individual's career development. These could be central or peripheral, planned or unforeseen, but nevertheless have the potential of fuelling, changing or suppressing individuals' life development.

CHAPTER 8

A Portrait of the Disabled High-Flyer

> Success is getting what you want. Happiness is wanting
> what you get.
>
> *Dale Carnegie*

This chapter attempts to summarise and collate all the information gathered during this study, concerning the perceptions, experiences and background of 31 disabled people who have reached successful positions in their career, and exceeded the employment expectations society generally has of the disabled population. The research has provided insights into what disabled high-flyers consider are the factors that determined their success. There are two major reasons for doing this. One is to facilitate the processes of personal development and selection of jobs for disabled professionals, by providing knowledge of the disabled high-flyers' progressive journey to career success, including significant turning points, obstacles encountered and specific strategies adopted to combat them. Furthermore, it serves to link various areas of previous research about disabled people, which have tended to focus only on single aspects of career development, such as childhood, education, personality, employment, disability or discrimination. The second aim is to provide role models and guidelines for young disabled people in their own development, as well as potential teaching material for case study and workshop exercises in education and training about citizenship and diversity. This will contribute significantly to the educational process of disability and equality in schools, employment and society in general.

In order to illustrate what makes the disabled high-flyer successful, and how they define career success, a description of the major findings will be reported under the same broad headings that have been used throughout: namely, conceptions of success; childhood; education; individual personality and motivation; and career choice and progression. These findings also reveal the differences between males and females, and individuals with acquired and congenital disabilities in terms of the extent to which they consider these five attributes contribute to their career development and career success.

SUCCESS

While success has traditionally been seen purely in the external, organisational terms of hierarchical seniority and salary level (Melamed, 1995; O'Reilly and Chatman, 1994), widespread evidence suggests that is not always how individual professionals themselves see it (e.g. Sturges, 1999). It is now imperative to give serious consideration to individuals' subjective conceptions of career success in order to gain an improved understanding of what they actually want from their careers, and the impact this has on their career development (Parker and Arthur, 2000; Sturges, 1996). Further, such knowledge about subjective career success will provide organisations with some indication of potential alternative focuses for future career development and human resource management initiatives.

It has been argued that the multinational success of organisations has stemmed from the diversity of their employees including disabled people (Cox and Blake, 1991; Kandola, 1995), and if it is to continue they need to have an understanding of how disabled professionals define success for themselves. This book shows that the disabled professionals' conceptions of career success are removed from traditional notions of organisational success, such as hierarchical position and level of pay. This may be due to attitudinal, physical and social discrimination blocking opportunities for disabled employees to progress in their career, and thus achieve objective success alongside their non-disabled colleagues. However, disabled people, given their differential psychosocial development, may still perceive hierarchical position and level of financial reward as important to their own definitions of career success, but have expanded definitions of career success which incorporate both internal subjective criteria, and external objective criteria.

This research suggests that success for disabled high-flyers is a concept that involves two large dimensions: *internal* and *external*, each of which are composed of smaller themes. In total, seven criteria (five internal and two external) were identified as important to the 31 disabled people's perceptions of career success. The five internal criteria are *personal satisfaction/happiness, achievement, service, personal development* and *equality*; while the two external criteria identified are *material wealth* and *career progression*. Describing career success exclusively in the external terms of material wealth and hierarchical position does not represent what individuals feel about their own success. Although the 31 high-flyers in the study measured success in terms of internal criteria, only a minority were primarily concerned with career progression and material wealth. A plausible argument for this is that the causal effects of pay inequity and restricted advancement limit the progression of disabled people in the work place. Furthermore, career progression may be restricted if disabled people require accessible accommodations, specialist equipment in their homes and services in their communities. As Watson (1997) found, the lack of specialised and supported housing in many areas has led to disabled people being denied a choice and forced to live in the most run-down neighbourhoods where the concentration of available 'accessible' accommodation seems to be. This makes it difficult for them to make regular job and employer transitions during their working lives.

It was mostly the males in the study who thought of career success in external terms. This endorses a significant body of work about career success suggesting that men are more concerned with the conventional idea of career success than females (e.g. Cox and Cooper, 1988; Sturges, 1996). However, the majority of the disabled high-flyers in this study expressed their success in terms of internal criteria of achieving personal goals, equality, and being happy and satisfied with what they do. This is contrary to non-disabled male high-flyers' conceptions of success which, Sturges (1996) suggests, are defined in terms of salary and hierarchical position. However, there is no significant difference between how the disabled female high-flyers (especially with a congenital disability) in this study and non-disabled successful women in other studies (e.g. White *et al.*, 1992) see career success. Both tend to see it more in terms of personal growth and serving others.

Onset of disability did not always make a major difference to the high-flyers' perceptions of success. However, those with congenital disabilities expressed a stronger concern with personal development and equality than high-flyers who acquired their impairment later in life. A likely explanation for this is that the successful individuals with acquired disabilities had already defined success as a non-disabled person prior to their life as a disabled person. For example, according to previous studies based on non-disabled high-flyers, women are more likely to define success in terms of being happy. This was also true for all three women in this study who acquired their disability in early adulthood.

Doing a good job and being of service to others were equally important to the men and women in this research. This is contrary to a significant body of literature (e.g. Sturges, 1996; White *et al.*, 1992) relating to non-disabled high-flyers, which saw serving others and doing a good job to be predominately female aspirations. This research indicates that these aspirations were more prevalent for the high-flyers with congenital disabilities who felt that by serving others they could prove their self-worth to society. They believed success to be about being on an occupational and social equilibrium with their non-disabled contemporaries. However, this was not an issue for high-flyers with acquired disabilities who, it may be argued, had already experienced non-disabled status and, for most, it remained. As Sutherland (1981) maintains, individuals who acquired disabilities in adult life have much more power than those with congenital disabilities, in terms of factors such as money, legal status, position in the social structure and experiences in dealing with other people.

This book illustrates the kinds of criteria disabled high-flyers use to define their own success. It shows that success means much more than pay and hierarchical advancement and so if employers became aware of this, the feelings of insecurity and instability which many disabled employees may endure, could be reduced. This could enable disabled people to feel more confident about pursuing success on their own terms, which, as this research suggests, may often not relate to pay and advancement at all.

CHILDHOOD

The research has shown that disabled high-flyers in this study were similar, in terms of their childhoods, to non-disabled high-flyers in previous studies (e.g. White, Cox and Cooper 1992; Cox and Cooper 1998). They are both within a middle-class culture which emphasises the value of hard work and accomplishment. They all felt that they were supported by significant adults during their formative years, and encouraged to achieve at a high level and do their best.

Parental influence and social class

The majority of the sample identified their parents as significant to the cultivation of their potential, both in terms of social and professional progress. However, as the individuals with congenital disabilities became disabled during or immediately after birth, disability inevitably became a major factor in their childhood socialisation, especially influencing what was expected of them. It was noted that, in many cases, although the parents of children with congenital disabilities supported them to do whatever made them happy and encouraged them in their chosen pursuits, they had no prescribed expectations for their children to undertake any particular occupational direction. This lack of perception for the disabled child's development was likely to be influenced by the fact that they were born between the 1940s and early 1970s, in an era when disability politics had not been established and the whole concept of what it meant to bring up a disabled child was not really understood by the average parent. At that time disabled children were characterised by narratives of dependence, vulnerability and exclusion (Priestley, 1998). Society perceived them as socially and physically deviant, and incapable of contributing to the development of the economy (Oliver, 1990). This notion was reinforced by the medical model of disability which dictated that disabled people retained dependency even as maturity increased, thus were perceived as 'eternal children'. Unfortunately, during the time the high-flyers were growing up, there was a severe lack of positive disabled role models, thus parents were unlikely to challenge the respected opinions expressed by the medical profession.

Therefore the stereotypes of disabled people being passive and dependent conjured up by the medical profession and society as a whole, influenced parental expectations concerning the future development of their disabled child.

Social class also had an impact on what parents expected of their disabled child. Certain observable cues and abstract social class symbols (e.g. education, parents' jobs) within the family unit were recognised by the high-flyers during their childhood and inevitably influenced their occupational preferences and their lifestyle. For example, middle-class culture placed a high value on achievement and encouraged the attainment of high-flying goals, particularly in academic pursuits. Parents from the middle classes may have had slightly less rigid expectations of their congenitally disabled child than they may have had from a non-disabled child. However, they were still keen for the disabled child/children to conform to the norms and values of the middle-class culture, including achievement, as much as possible.

Several of the individuals with congenital impairments felt that although their parents had no prescribed expectations for them to succeed in a particular occupational field, they were encouraged to work hard and achieve as well as they could, and were given the financial and emotional support to do so. These individuals originated from middle-class backgrounds and had parents who occupied professional-status occupations. This lends support to the contention that high-achievers are more often encountered in affluent families where parental occupations are of a high status and the practised culture values achievement and the attainment of high-flying goals (Eysenck and Cookson, 1970). Further, the finding endorses arguments presented in disability research expressing the view that the social class structure which determines access to things such as education, jobs and higher income still prevails in the disability community (e.g. Pfeiffer, 1991). Socio-economic background was perceived to be important to the success of high-flyers from middle-class origins. This was because not only were they exposed to values and practices of working hard and doing well, but also they had greater access to services and facilities which were required to facilitate and support occupational participation, enhancing opportunities for success.

Not all of the high-flyers, however, were from middle-class backgrounds, yet they still managed to achieve career success. This confronts much work on career success and on disability suggesting that individuals originating from lower classes tend to have weak need for achievement (uncharacteristic of high-flyers) and low chances of occupational success. However, this study shows that a great number of the disabled people, regardless of their socio-economic background, had parents who provided them with love and support in whatever they chose to do. This supports Wood's (1973) argument that the provision of a home environment where parents are warm, loving and respectful to their child as a valued individual permits the cultivation of individual potential.

The impact of disability on childhood socialisation was not an issue for the high-flyers with acquired disabilities, as they acquired a disability status when they were in their late teens or early adulthood, and therefore grew up and were socialised as non-disabled children. However, gender did influence how these individuals were brought up. Several males had parents who were ambitious for them to become high-achievers. Interestingly, these men came from a middle-class culture emphasising the value of hard work and achievement striving. However, the women who had a non-disabled childhood recalled their upbringing as being primarily working class and their parents as supportive and loving, and permitting them to do anything that would generate happiness, rather than pushing them to become great achievers as the men were expected to be.

The women with acquired disabilities tended to pursue traditional female careers, influenced by their gender-related experiences in childhood. Although these women pursued relatively low-status careers before becoming disabled, the findings showed that the acquisition of their disability activated latent personality traits of determination and ambition which energised the women's need for achievement and drove them to pursue high-flying goals.

The career orientations of the females with childhood disabilities were unlikely to be influenced by their gender. It seems that disability was the master status, overriding all other attributes. These women were not expected, and thus not socialised, to pursue traditional female roles of housewife or mother. This may be, as Russo (1988) suggests, in part, due to the societal myth that disabled women are asexual, and incapable of leading socially and sexually fulfilling lives. However, this was not altogether negative as it permitted the women to compete against men in the professional sector and succeed in gender-atypical careers. Baumann (1997) believes that the relative lack of options available to disabled women could make them more dedicated towards a career. She suggests that because disabled women grow up with the expectation that they will not have families, they tend to focus on their career, intending to leave a legacy through their work. However, this research showed that even when the women did have roles of wife or/and mother (as did a third of the women with congenital disabilities), they still felt the need to pursue a successful career. This contradicts the stereotypical conception of disabled women being passive, dependent and helpless (Lang, 1982), and in a situation resulting in rolelessness. Moreover, it shows that disabled women are not only capable of achieving a status equal to non-disabled women in the home, but also have the potential to compete with non-disabled men and women in the work place.

Given that the disabled women are not expected or socialised to pursue traditional female roles, it is not really surprising that several of the successful women with congenital disabilities believed their fathers had been most influential in their occupational development, encouraging their achievement and directing their career orientation. It can be argued that the lack of emphasis on appropriate sex-role behaviour in childhood could have caused these women to develop what are often regarded as innate masculine traits. Such evidence endorses White *et al.*'s (1992) work which found that many successful women identify strongly with their fathers and engage in risk-taking gender-atypical activities with them.

Only a minority of the high-achievers were first-born or only children, thus contradicting earlier theory noting the predominance of first-born and only children among high-achievers (Helmreich *et al.* 1980; White *et al.* 1992). However, in their early years, the disabled high-flyers, like the first-born/only children, recalled receiving significant amounts of parental affection and attention, had their needs gratified quickly and received help promptly when in distress. This was perhaps due to their extensive physical care demands rather than birth order as has been suggested in theory of non-disabled high-flyers.

Childhood traumas

Many of the disabled high-flyers were able to highlight periods of trauma, deprivation and loss during their childhood. Deprivation was seen not necessarily in terms of grinding poverty, but rather in a psychological sense – a loss of, or separation from, parents at a crucial stage of emotional development. In their formative years, several men with acquired or congenital disabilities suffered the death or loss of a parent (the father in most cases) at a young age. This generated an early sense of responsibility and the child moved into an adult role before the end of childhood. This was particularly apparent for men with only-son status who felt that, in their father's absence, they had a responsibility to take care of their mother and sisters.

Several of the disabled high-achievers were separated from their parents at a young age by being sent away to boarding school and experiencing the traumas of an 'orphanic existence'. The negative effects of uprooting a child have been documented by other researchers including Shakespeare and Watson (1998), who argue that segregated education may result in isolation as it may mean losing regular contact with non-disabled peers and family because it involves attending a school well outside the local community. However, the male high-flyers in Cox and Cooper's (1988) study believed traumas of orphanic existence, through death of parent(s) or being sent to boarding school at an early age, to be significant to their future orientations. These experiences could be seen as propagating a general sense of independence and self-sufficiency.

Other early traumas included substantial periods of hospitalisation, medical intervention and negative prognosis. These were most recalled by many of the disabled people with childhood disabilities. However, their supportive upbringing, which encouraged personal internal locus of control and a strong need to achieve, helped the high-achievers survive such early adverse experiences. This, in turn, led to a basic feeling of strength, independence and self-sufficiency, responsibility and an early sense of mastery. Development of these traits was seen as critical to the sample group's present occupational situation and drive for achievement. This is supported by previous work (e.g. Cooper and Hingley, 1985; Cox and Cooper, 1988), which reports the positive causal effects of early adverse experiences on the future actions of high-flyers. However, as mentioned in Chapter 2, care must be taken not to assume that all disabled people who experience some kind of childhood trauma grow up to be successful in their careers. As this book indicates, it is, in fact, a combination of factors that facilitates such success. For example, if a person has experienced childhood trauma but has an internal locus of control, they may have the self-confidence to learn from the trauma and enable it to make them stronger and able to handle future events successfully. This contrasts with other people, who lack self-confidence and believe their destiny is controlled by others and are likely to be crushed by trauma. Such was the case with William Hay, born in 1754, who believed that the socio-psychological difficulties he experienced because of his impairment had caused him to be bashful, uneasy and unsure of himself. However, such experiences can also induce perseverance, stubbornness and problem-solving skills that will be valuable in future orientations.

EDUCATION

Level and subject of education

As a group, a large number of the disabled high-flyers have achieved a relatively high level of education. Of the 31 high-flyers, 27 had undergraduate degrees, and ten of those also hold postgraduate qualifications. However, four of the males with congenital disabilities did not attend university after achieving their A levels, and either undertook professional training directly related to their intended career or went straight into employment, learning on the job. Three of these men became established as professional artists.

Education, for over half of the high-flyers, was perceived as important to their current occupational and life situation. They considered their education to be a prerequisite to their occupational success, choosing their academic subjects with a specific career in mind; the majority of these were males who had acquired their disabilities during adulthood. A possible explanation for this could be that these individuals were educated before the acquisition of their disability and thus, unlike those with congenital disabilities, went to mainstream schools and were not restricted or limited in terms of what subjects they could pursue. Many of the high-achievers with childhood disabilities were subjected to attitudinal prejudice or physical access restrictions in mainstream schools. However, segregated school was often criticised for its limited curriculum and deficient teaching expertise. These points would serve to explain why only a small number pursued a field of study that was directly related to their career.

Two-thirds of the women with congenital disabilities obtained educational qualifications that were seen as imperative to gain entrance into their current occupations. Interestingly the majority of these women and the small group of men whose choice of education permitted their career choice were educated in mainstream institutions, either throughout or for a substantial part of their educational career. These disabled people had a wider range of subjects to choose from in mainstream schools; subjects that matched their original aspirations and would guarantee entrance into a respectable and prestigious career. Further, it could be argued that the mainstream education system taught the young disabled people that in order to conform to the norms and values of society they needed to learn the formal and informal skills necessary to pursue a valuable position in the labour force. As Warnock (1978) reports, education prepares individuals to become economically participative members of society. So, experience of the rules, regulations and expectations of the mainstream education system would invariably influence one's future educational and career decisions.

Education was also identified as a primary ingredient in the disabled high-flyer's social, psychological and cultural development. Further, it was noted as the source by which the group, as children and young people, could learn the basic norms and values of the society in which they live in order to function safely and harmoniously. This finding is consistent with much sociological theory, including Giddens (1997) who suggests that by socialising generations of young people to accept dominant norms and values, education plays an important role in the maintenance of social conformity, both in formal and also less obvious ways.

Segregated schools

Segregated schools were perceived by the high-flyers to offer a limited curriculum and poor teaching expertise, thus the disabled people who were products of the segregated education system had very limited control over the subjects they studied. It was never an option to decide on a career first and choose the corresponding subjects second. So, in this respect, segregated education had a major part to play in the discriminatory process by denying disabled individuals the freedom to choose how they intended to contribute to society's developing economy. However, although segregated education does indeed restrict the educational and, therefore, occupational choices of young disabled people, this book shows that it is nonetheless essential to the social, physical and psychological development of some disabled children. Furthermore, in support of Pitta and Curtin's (2004) work, the disabled people considered segregated education to have encouraged their feeling of security and enhanced their self-esteem by avoiding continual comparison of their achievements with other, more physically competent students. Just under half of the high-flyers with congenital disabilities attended segregated educational institutions exclusively throughout their compulsory education and further education. Several of them considered their segregated education to be paramount to their current career success. They believed it to be critical to their character formation and the cultivation of their developing personality, as it provided an environment free from the intervention of mainstream barriers, permitting them, as children, to explore and develop a sense of self. This is consistent with Jenkinson's (1997) argument that segregated schools are perceived as more supportive, both physically and socially, and less threatening to students with disabilities than the regular schools.

The research in this book accepts that segregated education can impede the economic future of disabled people, by restricting the range of educational and occupational choices available to them. However, it rejects the claims made that segregated education inhibits exploration of the self by its unreal protected environment which shields disabled individuals from the realities of society (e.g. Alderson and Goodey, 1998; Barnes, 1991). The research indicates that disabled children need a protective accessible environment, free of mainstream barriers, to develop their personality and character fully with the support of assistive devices and high-quality support. Furthermore, because the classes are usually small with high teacher–student ratios, disabled children can receive one-to-one attention and instruction which can be pitched at a level appropriate to their individual needs. Such heterogeneity would not be accommodated in mainstream schools as, Tomlinson (1995) argues, they still operate on the prin-ciple of standardisation, force students into standard curriculum programmes and have standard expectations for 'normal' behaviour. Alternatively, they force the students out of the system altogether and make them go into a separate room with a teaching support assistant as many teachers are not comfortable respond-ing to individual differences within a whole-class setting (Pitta and Curtin, 2004).

This is disappointing given the ongoing policy drive towards inclusion. The Disability Discrimination Act (1995), the Special Educational Needs and Disability Act (2001) and the recent White Paper *Removing Barriers to Achievement* (Department for Education and Skills, 2004) emphasise a need to move towards educational inclusion and to accommodate the needs of young disabled people in mainstream schools. Supporting the *Salamanca Statement on Principles, Policies and Practice in Special Needs Education* (UNESCO, 1994), which calls for inclusion to be the norm in the education of all disabled people, legislation in Britain now makes it unlawful for schools and colleges to discriminate against disabled people. All educational establishments are now legally obliged to take reasonable steps to amend any policies, practices or procedures that may discriminate against disabled pupils so they can receive their education in the 'least restrictive' environment. However, 'least restrictive' can be interpreted in different ways and does not always lead to full inclusion. Zigler and Hall (1995) suggest that in a climate of economic stringency, 'least restrictive' might be interpreted to mean 'least expensive'. Furthermore, the least restrictive environment principle can be criticised for focusing on physical settings and impairments, and failing to give attention to the supports needed by students with disabilities to fully participate in mainstream environments. As reported in a recent briefing document (Audit Commission, 2003), schools remain dissatisfied with the level of support they receive for pupils with special educational needs. The non-availability of adequate support may have a detrimental impact on the school performance and social interaction of disabled pupils within the school setting as well as their post-16 outcomes.

Growing up in a barrier-free environment gives disabled children the opportunity to be 'children' first and to have dreams and aspirations without the constraints of a disabling environment. If these dreams and aspirations are strong enough, they could help to overcome the barriers encountered in mainstream society when these children try to achieve their goals as disabled adults. This is consistent with Pearse (1996) who considered segregated institutions to be an integral ingredient to the social and psychological independence of disabled children. As Watson *et al.* (1999) affirmed, a segregated setting offers much more autonomy than a mainstream setting as children have the freedom to associate with others in child-defined spaces, albeit within the usual parameters of the school environment. Several high-flyers perceived that the special education they received provided them with a supportive peer group who shared their experiences of disablement. In this environment they did not feel 'different' as they perceived they could have felt in a mainstream school. This is in accord with many accounts by disabled adults who testify to the importance of the friendships they made with other young people in special schools (French and Swain, 2000). So, while some disabled high-achievers believed that special education could impede their economic future, isolate them from the non-disabled world, and restrict the range of educational and occupational choices available to them, several believed that it was crucial to their success in adulthood, in terms of permitting the exploration and development of the self.

However, a number of the high-achievers who participated in mainstream education saw their social experiences of it as valuable to their current occupational and social situation. It can be suggested, then, that inclusive education can (for some people) facilitate the establishment of social relationships between disabled and non-disabled peers, as awareness and understanding of disability is said to engender an increasing acceptance of it. Furthermore, it presents disabled people with a training equal to their non-disabled counterparts and, therefore, they were qualified to compete with them in mainstream economic society.

Although many of the successful disabled men and women favoured educational segregation, others uncovered a number of deficiencies with total segregation. Many argued that special education prevented disabled children from interacting with non-disabled peers, thus inhibiting social integration between the disabled and non-disabled world. This is consistent with Barnes (1991) who asserts that disabled children who attend special schools normally stay there until their late teens, and are therefore denied some experiences considered essential for the transition from childhood to adulthood, and are shielded from the realities of society. Jenkinson (1997) contends that lack of feedback from non-disabled peers and removal from the common culture of childhood and adolescence contributes to later isolation in the community. However, this work shows that the high-flyers perceived that their experiences of early separation engendered basic feelings of strength, self-sufficiency and independence – 'survival skills' which served them well in successfully meeting career goals and establishing their current position in society.

Several high-achievers believed that special education provided role models to inspire disabled young people, not only in terms of what they achieved but how they overcame disabling barriers to do so, while maintaining a positive disability identity. So, although mainstream education can provide role models that inspire young people to achieve successful adulthoods, this book shows that this is based on a non-disabled culture in which it might be difficult to identify favourably with their disability, or know how to negotiate disabling barriers. Mrug and Wallander (2002) argue that social environment plays a crucial role in the formation of and changes in self-concept.

Education and economic participation for disabled people

This book recognises that education has a significant part to play in the career and life success of the disabled high-flyers. However, it also highlights the importance, and the constraints, of both segregated and mainstream education, and how disabled people perceive them to both facilitate and impede their successful career and life progression. Disabled people are not a homogeneous group and have different needs, wants, abilities and aspirations, which may not be wholly satisfied by total integration or total segregation. Therefore, an alternative system is needed which facilitates disabled students to develop psychologically, socially and cognitively at the rate of their non-disabled peers, which permits disabled students, who are able, to choose to pursue subjects not available in the special school's limited curriculum, and achieve the prerequisites regarded as essential for successful vocational participation and career development. Further, it should enable disabled and non-disabled students to share similar situations and build friendships and other relationships, while allowing disabled students to retain access to the support, facilities and resources provided in special school that may not be available in the mainstream school.

PERSONALITY, MOTIVATION AND WORK CENTRALITY

Many of the disabled high-flyers had intrinsic motivational tendencies. Like previous studies of non-disabled high-flyers, there were no noticeable differences in motivation between the men and women in this study. All were ambitious people, with a determination to achieve interesting and worthwhile goals which would also give them a purposeful role in society. Their good record of past achievements had motivated them to set and achieve increasingly higher goals. Several admitted that their need for achievement was energised by the attitudinal and social prejudice they encountered as disabled people and the low status which they were automatically ascribed by society. Further, their need for achievement was significantly influenced by the inequality between the disabled minority and the non-disabled majority in society. Adams' (1965) equity theory suggests that an individual's motivation is influenced by how they feel they are being treated in comparison to others of similar status. The majority of successful individuals with congenital disabilities in the study maintained that they were driven by the need to prove their self-worth and to compete on an equal level with their non-disabled colleagues.

The high-flyers felt they had demonstrated high levels of determination and stubbornness, considered essential for them to persist in the face of adversity and overcome obstacles. They had a tendency to prefer challenging tasks, which could be interpreted as high mastery motivation. Most mentioned that they were unlikely to be inhibited by negative attitudes and experiences, but tended to persevere to overcome challenges, treating each as an opportunity that could be learned from, rather than being discouraged by it. These traits and characteristics were thought to become stronger for several of those who acquired their disabilities later in life. This book demonstrates that although the disabled high-flyers were not easily defeated, they knew when to persevere and when it was not worth it. This is consistent with the previous studies of non-disabled high-flyers, implying that successful people have clear objectives and the ability to control the direction of their careers.

The characteristics of high-flyers are often associated with individual childhood experiences of separation and early responsibility. Furthermore, and especially for those successful individuals with congenital disabilities, it could have been built up from their experiences of growing up and living as a disabled person in a predominantly non-disabled society. As Freund (1973) points out, people with disabilities are good at solving problems as they encounter them nearly every day of their lives.

A number of the disabled people maintained that they were motivated to work by the actual purpose of the job and the moral satisfaction they received from serving others. They felt that their work was a means of demonstrating their worth and value to society. Further, it provided opportunities for them to experience a continually changing environment, to play an active part in inducing change in that environment and, in doing so, to use and develop further their skills and capacities. A few of the individuals, who felt that they had been victims of disability discrimination and prejudice, were motivated to work to ensure the same did not happen to other disabled people. So, the disabled high-flyer is not only contributing to the welfare of the economy, and the happiness and well-being of society, but also to the advancement of their own social status as a disabled person. Fulfilling a purposeful role in society and serving others, as opposed to being served by others, goes some way to disproving the traditional stereotype of disabled people being passive and dependent with an ascribed underclass status. It was the belief of many of the people in the study that occupying a purposeful, respectable and prestigious position in society's economic structure would serve to divert attention away from their disability, increasing acceptance and reducing discrimination. As Sutherland (1981) argues, acceptance becomes easier the more one conforms to the norm of the societal majority.

The sense of purpose that work gives disabled people also has psychological consequences, in that it serves to increase their self-esteem and self-confidence. Furthermore, it permits a healthier lifestyle not only by satisfying economic needs but also by providing fellowship, social life, respect and admiration for others. By showing disabled people in purposeful economic roles, building relationships with and earning respect from colleagues, this book serves to provide role models for disabled and non-disabled people and emphasises the economic value of employing them to help serve the demands of increasing globalisation and a multiculturalism.

Feedback and recognition were cited as significant driving forces for several of the high-flyers. The women claimed to be externally driven by the need to see concrete results of their efforts and obtain recognition from others for their successes. The small percentage of both men and women who felt feedback and recognition were important driving forces were mostly those with congenital disabilities and based in the arts sector. They needed to see concrete results for fulfilling a purposeful role, being a success and doing a good job. The artists were particularly driven by recognition and feedback, as their career progression and success were largely dependent on being seen, on who saw them and how were they rated by others. This need for concrete feedback is a characteristic that has often been associated with a high need for achievement (McClelland et al., 1953). However, although the artists could be described as having an internal locus of control as they displayed a strong belief in their ability to control the direction of their careers, the very nature of their work meant they were not exclusively in control of their professional successes or failures. They felt the luck factor had an important part to play in their current success, but they were more likely to refer to it as a willingness to take advantage of the opportunities that luck presented.

Although money was not considered to be a primary driving force to work, most of the high-flyers mentioned that money was indeed necessary for a decent level of subsistence, and a respectable independent lifestyle for themselves and their families. This is supported by Vroom (1964) who maintains that despite the old saying, 'money can't buy happiness', it can be exchanged for many commodities that are necessary for survival and comfort. For the disabled high-flyers, money goes far beyond the satisfaction of biological needs. The goods and services purchased with the money grant them a comfortable lifestyle. However, the research suggests the disabled individuals are intrinsically motivated in that they seek to maximise their satisfaction through responsibility, challenge and learning derived from the task itself. As has been shown in other studies (e.g. Cox and Cooper, 1988; White et al., 1992), this is also characteristic of non-disabled high-flyers.

This book provides an insight into the life and career development of the disabled high-flyers, as they perceive it, and a knowledge of how they overcame encounters of disability discrimination in the home, in education, in the work place and in society to achieve their personal goals and current success. It could be argued that the disabled people were destined to become high-flyers because their characteristics were prerequisites to their life successes and not dissimilar to those required to achieve career success.

Locus of control

Like the non-disabled high-flyers in Cox and Cooper's (1988) and White et al.'s (1992) studies, the disabled high-flyers in this book perceived that they had an internal locus of control in that they were self-controlled as opposed to controlled by others. They believed it was their own behaviour that determined the success or failure of their future life prospects, and not purely external factors such as luck, chance or significant others. The successful men and women experienced lucky breaks but felt it was necessary to have the ability to capitalise on them. Therefore, this would suggest that individuals can create their own luck by making certain choices, working hard, and being in the right place at the right time. So, if people are proactive and selective with the opportunities luck presents, it serves not to inhibit but to facilitate career growth.

Work centrality

Several of the high-flyers saw their work as instrumental to their self-image. This was more significant for those with congenital disabilities, who viewed work as something for which they could be valued and also as a means of proving their worth to society. Further, by developing a positional identity – defining themselves in terms of their career achievements – they considered diagnostic overshadowing to be reduced. So, disabled high-flyers are identified by their professional status, which becomes the master status, and not their disability, a low status attributed to them as a result of medical diagnosis of their impairment. Several high-flyers believed that by occupying a responsible, prestigious role in the developing economy they would have a greater chance of being respected and accepted into mainstream society. They considered this to be a successful coping and survival strategy.

Both the males and females in the study considered the act of working to be imperative to them. Even since taking on the roles of wife and/or mother, the women described their work as crucial to their psychological well-being, although they saw it as more of a peripheral rather than central part of self-iden-tification. Further, since marrying or being in a stable partnership, the women felt less of a need to prove their worth to society than they did previously through their work.

A few high-flyers with acquired disabilities felt their career was not always central to their identity. This could be correlated with the fact that most had families and concerns outside work. However, they conceived their work as invaluable to the enhancement of their position and respect within the commu-nity. The women saw their occupational position as satisfying an obligation in terms of personal responsibility or internalised norms of duty and as a means of contributing to societal economic growth.

The majority of high-flyers spent significant amounts of time, energy and commitment on work-related pursuits. They explained that they were likely to complete tasks successfully even when confronted with aversive experiences, therefore demonstrating high self-efficacy expectations. Many occupied their professional roles after many years of training which involved hard work, dedication and perpetual successes. These early challenges enabled the high-flyers to test out their abilities, and their experience of success served to further raise their self-efficacy beliefs. In addition, these individuals expressed futuristic visions, believing they had the ability to satisfy their long-term aspirations and ambitions. They demonstrated their dedication and commitment to work either by working beyond their statutory working hours (including evenings and weekends) and/or attaching personal value to their work and having long-term goals. Further, the individuals with congenital disabilities were driven by the need to 'make a difference' by working to bring social justice to society and make it more inclusive. Many considered their work as a means by which they could 'change the world' by helping minority groups, including other disabled people, to achieve their aspirations by influencing public policies and Government legislation. This was displayed by their thirst for new skills, advancement and achieving new goals. This is not dissimilar to the syndrome of 'creative discontent' mentioned in Cox and Cooper's (1988) study of male high-flyers. The respondents in their sample were driven, by a general restlessness and discontent with the world as it is, to do something positive to improve it.

Thus, the majority of the disabled high-flyers considered their work to be extremely important to their lives. The fact that most used work as a means of self-identification, had a future intentional focus and believed they could execute the required behaviour to achieve challenging goals demonstrates their high need for achievement, strong internal locus of control and high career centrality.

CAREER CHOICE AND EXPERIENCES

Career choice and progression

As Hodkinson and Sparkes (1997) state, all individuals experience career and life changes which are triggered by three different categories of turning points, namely structural, self-initiated and forced by external events or the action of others.

Educational training and qualifications seemed to be prerequisites to the career choice of many of the disabled high-flyers. Many individuals followed a pattern of 'education-related' career progression, which, according to this book, involves taking specialist training and qualifications, entering an occupation in that field, and undergoing several promotions to reach a respectable and aspired status, with minimal geographical mobility. A large number of these individuals were men who had acquired their disabilities in adulthood, thus having experience of non-disabled childhoods with high parental expectations and mainstream schooling. Several high-flyers who followed this 'education-related' pattern of progression saw the benefits of remaining with a single employer for several years, experiencing promotion and advancement over the years in the same organisation, as opposed to progressing up the occupational hierarchy via several organisation and employer moves. As indicated in King's (1999) study, career progression via several employer moves is regarded as a conventional career orientation for non-disabled high-flyers who are concerned with making sure they have the right range of skills and experience for future employability. However, this book illustrates that staying with the same employer for many years has been proposed, by the disabled high-flyers, as being a good strategy for success for disabled people. It can be argued that this differential conception of conventional career progression is significantly influenced by political, social and economic issues (Herr, 1996). For example, according to the Labour Force Survey (1998), disabled people may need assistive accommodations in the work place and home, and services in the community, and a lack of these may make geographical mobility difficult, thus encouraging them to stay in one place for as long as possible, if only for the sake of convenience. Furthermore, as Hendey (1999) maintains, disabled people in receipt of personal assistance are often denied the right to be flexible in their daily lives. The limitations placed on flexibility and spontaneity, by predetermined support provision and the built environment, make it impossible for disabled people to move to another city to develop professionally on par with their non-disabled counterparts.

In recent years, more and more careers are seen as 'boundary-free' entities, which move across boundaries between different employers and as such are independent of conventional organisational principles (Arthur, 1994; Mirvis and Hall, 1994). The responsibility for development rests not with the employer but with the individual, who will have to acquire the right mix of skills to survive in a 'freelance' environment. If this continues, many disabled people could be at a disadvantage due to their restricted opportunity to move jobs and attain a range of experience. This book suggests that old-style careers, operating in stable and supportive organisations, are more beneficial to disabled people. This is especially the case for those who entered their career as a direct result of their education, than some forms of new careers which are known as 'boundaryless' and which require more flexibility and moving from place to place. However, on the other hand, this book shows that some of the disabled high-flyers were in fact restricted by the glass ceiling advancement of old-style careers and opted to redirect their career path, pursuing a career with opportunities for promotion. It also illustrates why the individuals with congenital disabilities perceived themselves as often likely to follow more of a boundaryless approach to career progression in order to meet their initial career aspirations. This book suggests that people with childhood disabilities may be victims of prejudice by many important agents of socialisation such as family and education which can impose significant restrictions on them, limiting their career choices and opportunities.

Shepherd (1997) notes that there are very few examples of a co-ordinated range of opportunities that would offer disabled people a number of different options, geared to different abilities and aspirations. Therefore, this book points out that unless disabled people are driven enough to combat disabling barriers to meet their own desired goals, they may never attain personal career success.

In this study, the high-flyers with childhood disabilities did demonstrate a strong need to achieve their personal goals and, therefore, when denied the opportunity to meet them by more conventional means, they followed what was identified as 'individualised career progression'. In the context of this study, this type of career progression has been described as a pattern constructed of a series of challenging jobs that have no obvious connection with prior educational training. When facilitated by hard work, timing and significant life events, these jobs can act as steps to career progression and individual achievement. This was the career pattern followed by a number of high-flyers with congenital disabilities, several of whom worked as artists and recognised it as being the only way they could achieve career success in their desired occupation. Several of them had experienced disability discrimination in various aspects of life, including education and society as a whole, which served to impede education-related career progression and had influenced their decision to follow such individualised career paths. It was noted that this type of career progression was facilitated by a series of life events that marked significant turning points in their career route. These turning points led the high-flyers down a path that enabled them to meet the right people and be in the right place at the right time in order to take advantage of opportunities to achieve and advance in their chosen profession. However, although this was important, hard work, perseverance and strong self-efficacy beliefs were thought to be imperative to turn the opportunities into achievements and to perpetually progress along such career routes. This is consistent with White et al.'s (1992) study of non-disabled female high-flyers who also considered chances presented by luck and external events to be important to their success, although only when they had the ability and application to capitalise on them.

A third pattern of career progression that emerged from this research was conceptualised as 'redirected career progression'. A number of the high-flyers in this book were influenced by external life events to change their career completely. Many saw their career change as a consequence of them being victims of disabling barriers which hampered or prevented their progression in their original aspired career. A small number of individuals with acquired disabilities could not physically continue to work in their original careers after becoming disabled merely because the work environment was not accessible and supporting to disabled workers. Similarly, a number of those with congenital disabilities had to change their careers if they wanted to 'get to the top' (i.e. have a prestigious position and a respectable income) because they were being denied the opportunity to climb the career ladder due to issues surrounding their disability. This indicates the existence of the 'glass ceiling' in many sectors of the labour market, and, consistent with Jolly (2000), shows this to be a possible reason for the under-representation of disabled people in managerial and professional status occupations. Furthermore, it demonstrates how the social model of disability has an impact on what disabled people perceive as barriers to their career development.

Career change was also the result of self-initiated turning points (Hodkinson and Sparkes, 1997); that is, in response to personal feelings of boredom and lack of interest, and the need to do something different using individual abilities and disabilities to achieve desirable goals. Some disabled high-flyers had to redirect the original career choice due to a religious calling, or the actions of others preventing them from pursuing a career in the field in which they were previously trained and qualified. Therefore, it must be emphasised that, contrary to what may have been expected, being disabled was not always the cause of career change and redirection. Several of the disabled people perceived their career to have developed in much the same way as that of their non-disabled colleagues.

It was clear that several of the disabled people who had achieved their prestigious position in a high-status career had done so by reorientating their initial career path. Furthermore, it can be suggested that for this group, disability was not only a causal attribute of redirected career progression, but also at times a precursor of career choice and success. A majority of the disabled high-flyers experienced an early challenge in their occupational and personal lives, but coped successfully with this challenge. The acquisition of evidence of their competence, through performance accomplishment and experience of psychological success, should raise self-efficacy beliefs and hence the setting of more challenging goals in the future. Therefore it seems that, according to the narratives of the disabled professionals, success generates success. This was also indicated with White et al.'s (1992) successful women.

Although the disabled high-flyers' journeys through life were perceived to be significantly scattered with challenging and traumatic experiences, their stories illustrate that they all managed to learn from adversity, overcome challenges, solve any problems encountered and move on. Most felt that they had emerged from the experiences with added strengths and skills thought to be valuable to be a successful competitor in the mainstream global economy. Thus, this book suggests that employers should be aware that the skills a disabled person has to gain to survive and attain equality and acceptance in mainstream society are beneficial to employment. This is supported by Duckworth (1995), who argues that disabled people living in a predominantly inaccessible world have to develop highly refined problem-solving skills, which can be seen as paramount in today's employment. Furthermore, in a society where workforce diversity is critical to survive in the competitive global economy, disabled people should be encouraged more and more to join the labour market to meet the needs of an increasingly diverse customer base including disabled people.

So, overall, this book demonstrates that the factors disabled high-flyers perceived to be important to their career development and success are not dissimilar from those found, in previous studies, to be significant to the career success of non-disabled people. Furthermore, it shows that, when coupled with a supportive childhood background, persistence, drive and an internal belief in one's actions, several of the high-flyers perceived being disabled to be beneficial to their career success rather than being a hindrance. They felt they had developed certain characteristics and strategies, as a result of being disabled, that have certainly helped their career progression.

PRACTICAL IMPLICATIONS AND RECOMMENDATIONS

This book fills an identified gap in the field of disability, career development and career success. The study, based on subjective accounts of 31 disabled high-flyers, includes the life space of the individual by recognising both the individual/personal space and the work and non-work contexts within which the individual functions. It integrates findings and concepts from within multidisciplinary approaches which focus primarily on the disabled individual (child psychology, developmental psychology, education and disability theory), and those that focus primarily on the group (social psychology, sociology and anthropology). From such a multidisciplinary integration, this book can make a significant contribution to knowledge as it recognises that various situational and individual factors operate to influence the career behaviour and success of disabled people.

As has been noted in Chapter 1, the body of literature on career success and career development has hitherto been based on the non-disabled individual. Thus, this research serves to contribute to the realm of academia by illustrating how a group of disabled people perceived how they achieved success. The value of the research findings to disabled people chiefly relates to the fact that they have shown that subjective career success is as important as objective career success. Although, in the past, career success was based on hierarchical position and level of pay, this research has demonstrated that disabled people have different ideas about what it means to them. Therefore it indicates that no such narrow definition of career success exists from the point of view of the individual. Further, it appreciates that it is not a homogeneous concept founded on the criteria of pay and position alone, therefore may prove beneficial for disabled professionals' self-awareness and self-esteem if facets of organisational life were based on non-disabled values.

The primary aim of this book is to inspire other disabled people who aspire to become high-flyers by reporting the personal experiences, views and reflections of 31 disabled people on how they achieved career success and became 'high-flyers'. Furthermore, it serves as an important contribution to the learning process, as disabled people can learn from the experiences of their disabled counterparts featured in this study about ways to overcome discrimination, oppression and barriers to progression. The book shows that the present legislative climate ensures that work is being done to provide young disabled people with equal opportunities to their non-disabled counterparts, giving them a stake in policy-making processes and due weight to their views. This includes making decisions about their occupational futures, which is not only important to the individual concerned, but to the future of society as a whole. However, this can only lead to personal success if disabled people themselves are ambitious, determined and sufficiently able to put it into practice.

This research is micro-social, based on small-scale, personal, disaggregated and dynamic findings, and therefore it provides an in-depth insight into the journey to success travelled, as perceived by each of the disabled people, including the obstacles encountered and the strategies adopted to overcome these obstacles. Thus, it can contribute to the educational process of equality and awareness by providing positive literature about disabled people, which could be used as teaching material in case study and workshop exercises in education and training. It also could help to inform policy and practice in educational services by giving an understanding of significant educational experiences, needs and views of disabled people.

The research reported in this book suggests that disabled children who attend segregated schools may often receive a lower standard of education and more limited choice of employment options than those who attended mainstream schools. For this reason, disabled children need to be increasingly exposed to the culture and expectations of mainstream education, while maintaining the appropriate support and services available in segregated schools. This presents disabled children with the opportunity to have an education equal to their non-disabled peers and enables disabled adults to have career opportunities equal to their non-disabled colleagues.

This book can be used to help mainstream institutions and gatekeepers, including employers, to become aware of what disabled people can achieve, and how their worth is valuable to the development of a multicultural global economy. This should open up doors to disabled people along the road of career success that were previously closed to them, and in turn lead to the removal of the glass ceiling in the labour market. This would increase the number of disabled people who can pursue their desired careers and reach the top.

While the societal structure does have a significant influence on whether or not disabled people become a great occupational success, the successful disabled people in this book all perceived that their success was facilitated by their own personal traits and patterns of behaviour. As with non-disabled successful people, the disabled people in this book felt they were single-minded, had a strong need to achieve their ambitions, were determined and stubborn, persisted in the face of adversity, and were opportunistic and hard working.

Although all the disabled people in the study acknowledged that there are many ghosts to overcome – within themselves, within others and within society – they also considered themselves to have a sense of optimism, and a hope that the ghosts inherent in all of us would welcome the light, and not be terrified of it. As described by Henrik Ibsen in his play *Ghosts*:

> ...It's not just what we inherit from our mothers and fathers. It's also the shadows of dead ideas and opinions and convictions. They're no longer alive, but they grip us all the same, and hold us against our will. All I have to do is open a newspaper to see ghosts hovering between the lines. They are haunting the whole country, those stubborn phantoms – so many of them, so thick, they're like an impenetrable dark mist. And here we are, all of us, so abjectly terrified by the light. (cited in White *et al.*, 1992, p.229)

References

Abbot, D., Morris, J. and Ward, L. (2001) *The best place to be? Policy, practice and the experiences of residential placements for disabled children.* York: York Publishing Services and Joseph Rowntree Foundation.

Adams, J. S. (1965) 'Inequity in social exchange.' In L. Berkowitz (ed) *Advances in Experimental Social Psychology.* New York: Academic Press.

Aiken, M., Ferman, L. and Sheppard, H. (1968) *Economic Failure, Alienation and Extremism.* Ann Arbor, MI: University of Michigan Press.

Ajzen, I. (1988) *Attitudes, Personality and Behavior.* Milton Keynes: Open University Press.

Alderson, P. and Goodey, C. (1998) *Enabling Education: Experiences in Special and Ordinary Schools.* London: The Tufnell Press.

Allan, J. (1996) 'Foucault and special educational needs: a "box of tools" for analysing children's experiences of mainstreaming.' *Disability & Society 11,* 2, 219–233.

Allen, I. (1988) *Any Room at the Top? – A Study of Doctors and their Careers.* London: Policy Studies Institute.

Andrisani, P. and Nestel, G. (1976) 'Internal-external control as contributor and outcome of work experience.' *Journal of Applied Psychology 62,* 156–165.

Arthur, M. B. (1994) 'The boundaryless career: a new perspective for organisational enquiry.' *Journal of Organisational Behaviour 15,* 295–306.

Arthur, M. B., Inkson, K. and Pringle, J. K. (1999) *The New Careers: Individual Action and Economic Change.* London: Sage Publications Ltd.

Arthur, M. B. and Rousseau, D. M. (1996) *The Boundaryless Career: A New Employment Principle for a New Organizational Era.* New York: Oxford University Press.

Astin, H. S. (1984) 'The meaning of work in women's lives: A sociopsychological model of career choice and work behaviour.' *Counselling Psychologist 12,* 117–126.

Atkinson, J. W. (1964) *An Introduction to Motivation.* Princeton, NJ: Van Nostrand.

Audit Commission (2003) *National Report – Schools' View of Their LEA 2003: The National School Survey.* London: Audit Commission.

Bailyn, L. (1989) 'Understanding individual experience at work: comments on the theory and practice of careers.' In M. B. Arthur, D. T. Hall and B. S. Lawrence (eds) *Handbook of Career Theory.* Cambridge: Cambridge University Press.

Baldwin, S. and Glendinning, C. (1982) 'Children with disabilities and their families.' In A. Walker and P. Townsend (eds) *Disability in Britain: A Manifesto of Rights.* Oxford: Martin Robertson.

Ball, S. J., Bowe, R. and Gerwitz, S. (1994) 'Market forces and parental choice.' In S. Tomlinson (ed) *Educational Reform and Its Consequences.* London: Institute for Public Policy Research and Rivers Oram Press.

Bandura, A. (1982) 'Self-efficacy mechanism in human agency.' *American Psychologist 37,* 2, 122–147.

Barker, R. (1968) *Ecological Psychology.* Stanford, CA: Stanford University Press.

Barnes, C. (1991) *Disabled People in Britain – A case for Anti-Discrimination Legislation.* London: C. Hurst & Co. Ltd.

Barnes, H., Thornton, P. and Maynard Campbell, S. (1998) *Disabled People and Employment: A Review of Research and Development of Work.* Bristol: Policy Press and the Joseph Rowntree Foundation.

Bar-Tal, D. and Frieze, I. (1973) 'Achievement motivation and gender as determinants of attributions for success and failure.' Unpublished manuscript, University of Pittsburgh.

Barton, L. (ed) (1988) *The Politics of Special Educational Needs.* Brighton: Falmer Press.

Battle, E. (1965) 'Motivational determinants of academic task persistence.' *Journal of Personality and Social Psychology 2,* 209–218.

Baumann, E. (1997) 'Job search for women with disabilities: A qualitative study on the question: What role does gender and disability play in job search?' Unpublished thesis, The University of Wiesbaden and the World Institute on Disability.

Bax, M. and Smyth, D. (1989) *Health Care of Physically Handicapped Young Adults.* Oxford: Blackwell Scientific Publications.

BCODP (1986) *Disabled Young People Living Independently.* London: British Council of Organisations of Disabled People.

Bee, H. (1996) *The Journey of Adulthood* (3rd edition). New York: Prentice Hall.

Begum, N. (1990) *Burden of Gratitude: Women with Disabilities Receiving Personal Care.* Coventry: Social Care Practice Centre/Department of Applied Social Studies, University of Warwick.

Blau, P. M. and Duncan, O. D. (1967) *The American Occupational Structure.* New York: John Wiley & Sons, Inc.

Blaxter, M. (1976) *The Meaning of Disability.* London: Heinemann Educational.

Boardman, S. K., Hartington, C. C. and Horowitz, S. V. (1987) 'Successful women: A psychological investigation of family class and educational origins.' In B. A. Gutek and L. Larwood (eds) *Women's Career Development.* Beverly Hills, CA: Sage Publications.

Borsay, A. (1986) 'Personal trouble or public issue? Towards a model of policy for people with physical and mental disabilities.' *Disability, Handicap and Society 1,* 173–179.

Boudreau, J. W., Boswell, W .R. and Judge, T. A. (2001) 'Effects of personality on executive career success in the United States and Europe.' *Journal of Vocational Behaviour 58,* 53–81.

Bowe, F. (1983) *Disabled Women in America.* Washington, DC: Disability Rights Education and Defence Fund.

Bowles, S. and Gintis, H. (1976) *Schooling in Capitalist America.* London: Routledge and Keagan Paul.

Brown, D., Brooks, L. and Associates (1996) *Career Choice and Development* (3rd edition). San Francisco, CA: Jossey-Bass Publishers.

Brown, P. and Lauder, H. (1996) 'Education, globalization, and economic development.' In A. H. Halsey, H. Lauder, P. Brown and A. S. Wells (eds) *Education: Culture, Economy, Society.* Oxford: Oxford University Press.

Bulmer, M. (1984) *The Chicago School of Sociology: Institutionalization, Diversity, and the Rise of Sociological Research.* Chicago: University of Chicago Press.

Burchardt, T. (2000) *Enduring Economic Exclusion: Disabled People, Income and Work.* York: York Publishing Services – Joseph Rowntree Foundation.

Burgess, E. (2003) 'Are we nearly there yet? Do teenage wheelchair users think integration has been achieved in secondary schools in the UK? A Survey.' Cardiff: Burgess.

Callahan, E. J. and McCluskey, K. A. (eds) (1983) *Life-span Development Psychology: Nonnormative Life Events.* New York, London: Academic.

Campbell, P. H. (1987) 'The integrated programming team: An approach for coordinating professionals of various disciplines in programs for students with severe and multiple handicaps.' *The Journal of The Association for the Severely Handicapped 12*, 2, 107–116.

Campling, J. (1981) *Images of Ourselves: Women with Disabilities Talking.* London: Routledge and Kegan Paul.

Caplow, T. (1958) *The Sociology of Work.* Oxford: Oxford University Press.

Carr-Saunders, A. M. and Wilson, P. A. (1944) 'Professions.' *Encyclopaedia of the Social Sciences XX11*, 476–480. New York: The Macmillan Company Publishers.

Cassell, C. (1997) 'The business case for equal opportunities: implications for women in management.' *Women in Management Review 12*, 1, 11–16.

Chamberlain, A. M. (1993) *An Assessment of the Health and Related Needs of Physically Handicapped Young Adults.* Leeds: University Press.

Charles, N. and James, E. (2003) 'Gender and work orientations in conditions of job security.' *British Journal of Sociology 54*, 2, 239–257.

Clark, B. R. (1964) 'Sociology of Education.' In R. E. L. Faris (ed.) *Handbook of Modern Sociology.* Chicago: Rand McNally.

Clements, R. V. (1958) *Managers: A Study of their Careers in Industry.* London: Allen & Unwin.

Close, J. M. (1983) 'Dogmatism and managerial advancement.' *Journal of Applied Psychology 60*, 3, 395–396.

Colwill, N. (1984) 'Lucky Lucy and Able Adam: to what do you attribute your success?' *Business Horizons.*

Colwill, N. (1982) *The New Partnership: Women and Men in Organizations.* Palo Alto, CA: Mayfield.

Cook, T. Swain, J. and French, S. (2001) 'Voices from segregated schooling: towards an inclusive education system.' *Disability and Society 6*, 2, 293–310.

Cooper, C. and Hingley, P. (1985) *The Change Makers.* London: Harper & Row.

Cornes, P. (1988) 'The role of work in the socialisation of young people with disabilities in a post-industrial society.' Paper presented at OECD conference, *Adult Status for Youth with Disabilities.* Sweden: Sigtuna.

Cornwall, J. (1995) 'Psychology, disability and equal opportunity.' Disability and equal opportunity – Special Issue. *The Psychologist 8*, 9.

Costa, P. T. Jr. and McCrae, R. R. (1994) 'Stability and change in personality from adolescence through adulthood.' In C. F. Halverson, G. A. Kohnstamm and R. P. Martin (eds) *The Developing Structure of Temperament and Personality From Infancy to Adulthood.* Hillsdale, NJ: Lawrence Erlbaum Associates.

Cottone, P. L. and Cottone, R. R. (1992) 'Women with physical disabilities: On the paradox of empowerment and the need for a trans-symatic – a feminist perspective.' *Journal of Applied Rehabilitation Counseling 23*, 4.

Cox, C. and Cooper, C. (1988) *High Flyers: The Autonomy of Executive Success.* Oxford: Basil Blackwell.

Cox, C. J. and Cooper, C. L. (1989) 'The Making of the British CEO: childhood, work experience, personality, and management style.' *The Academy of British Management Executive III*, 3, 245–247.

Cox, T. and Blake, S. (1991) 'Managing cultural diversity: implications for organizational competitiveness.' *Academy of Management Executive, 5(3)*, 45–56.

Cox, T. H. and Harquail, C. V. (1991) 'Career paths and career success in the early stages of male and female MBAs.' *Journal of Vocational Behaviour 39*, 54–75.

Crandall, V. J. (1963) 'Achievement.' In H. W. Stevenson (ed) *Child Psychology: The 62nd Yearbook of the National Society for the Study of Education, Part I.* Chicago: University of Chicago Press.

Crandall, V. J. (1964) 'Achievement behaviour in young children.' *Young Children 20*, 77–90.

Crandall, V. J. and Rabson, A. (1960) 'Children's repetition choices in an intellectual achievement situation following success and failure.' *Journal of Genetic Psychology 97*, 161–168.

Croxen, M. (1984) *Overview, Disability and Employment.* European Community Information Service; Commission of the European Communities. Luxembourg: Washington, DC: Office for Official Publications of the European Communities.

Davidson, M. J. (1997) *The Black and Ethnic Minority Woman Manager – Cracking the Concrete Ceiling.* London: Paul Chapman Publishing Ltd.

Davis, J. M. and Watson, N. (2001) 'Where are the children's experiences? Analysing social and cultural exclusion in "special" and "mainstream" schools.' *Disability & Society 16*, 5, 671–687.

Davis, J., Watson, N. and Cunningham-Burley, S. (1999) 'Learning the lives of disabled children: Developing a reflexive approach.' In P. Christiensen and A. James (eds) *Research With Children: Perspectives and Practices.* New York: Falmer Press.

Davis, W. L. and Phares, E. J. (1967) 'Internal-external control as a determinant of information seeking in a social influence situation.' *Journal of Personality 35*, 547–561.

DCDP (1992) *A Point Prevalence Survey of Pressure Sores.* Derby: Derbyshire Coalition for Disabled People.

Deaux, K. and Emswiller, T. (1974) 'Explanations of successful performance on sex-skilled tasks; what's skill for the male is luck for the female.' *Journal of Personality and Social Psychology 29*, 80–85.

DeCharms, R. (1984) *Personal causation: the internal affective determinants of behaviour.* New York: Lawrence Erlbaum.

Department for Education and Employment (1996) *Bulletin 61, Designing for Children with Special Education Needs – Ordinary Schools Dept. of Education and Science Building.* London: HMSO.

Department for Education and Employment (2001) *Special Education Needs and Disability Act 2001.* London: HMSO.

Department of Education and Science (1978) *Report of the committee of enquiry into the education of handicapped children and young people (The Warnock Report).* London: HMSO.

Department of Education and Skills (1989) *Report of HMI Inspectors on Educating Physically Disabled Pupils.* London: Department of Education and Science.

Department for Education and Skills (2004) *Removing Barriers to Achievement.* Nottingham: DfES Publications.

Derr, C. B. (1986) *Managing the New Careerist.* San Francisco: Jossey Bass.

Derr, C. B. and Laurent, A. (1989) 'The Internal and External Career: A Theoretical and Cross-Cultural Perspective.' In M.B Arthur, B.S. Laurence and D.T. Hall (eds) *The Handbook of Career Theory.* Cambridge: Cambridge University Press.

Devereaux, E. C., Bronfenbrenner, U. and Rogers, R. (1969) 'Child rearing in England and the United States: a cross sectional comparison.' *Journal of Marriage and Family, 31*, 257–270.

Dickens, L. (1994) 'The business case for women's equality: is the carrot not better than the stick?' *Employee Relations 16*, 8, 518.

Disability Discrimination Act (1995) London: HMSO.

Disability Now (2000) December 2000 edition. London: Scope. www.disabilitynow.org.uk

Disability Rights Commission (2004) *Disability Discrimination Bill welcomed but DRC urges action on housing shortage.* London: Disability Rights Commission.

Disability Rights Commission (2000) *DRC Disability Briefing: November.* London: Disability Rights Commission.

Dobson, B. and Middleton, S. (1998) *Paying to Care: The Cost of Childhood Disability.* York: York Publishing Services and Joseph Rowntree Foundation.

Donelson, E. and Gullahorn, J. E. (1977) *Women: A Psychological Perspective.* New York: Wiley.

Doyle, B. (1995) *Disability, Discrimination and Equal Opportunities: A Comparative Study of the Employment Rights of Disabled People.* New York: Mansell Publishing.

Dreher, G. F. and Ash, R. A. (1990) 'A comparative study of mentoring among men and women in managerial, professional, and technical positions.' *Journal of Applied Psychology 75,* 539–546.

Driver, M. J. (1988) 'Careers: A review of personal and organizational research.' In C. L. Cooper and I. T. Robertson (eds) *International Review of Industrial and Organisational Psychology.* New York: John Wiley & Sons.

Dublin, R. (1956) 'Industrial workers' worlds: A study of the central life interest of industrial workers.' *Social Problems 3,* 131–142.

Dublin, R., Hedley, R. and Taveggia, T. (1976) 'Attachment to work.' In R. Dublin (ed) *Handbook of Work, Organisation and Society.* Chicago: Rand McNally.

Duckworth, S. (1995) 'Disability and equality in employment – imperative for a new approach.' Unpublished PhD Thesis. Southampton: Southampton University.

Dunn, L. M. (1968) 'Special education for the mildly retarded – is much of it justifiable?' *Exceptional Children 35,* 5–22.

Dweck, C. S. (1999) *Self-Theories: Their Role in Motivation, Personality, and Development.* Philadelphia: Taylor & Francis.

Eby, L. T., Butts, M. and Lockwood, A. (2003) 'Predictors of success in the era of the boundaryless career.' *Journal of Organizational Behavior 24,* 689–708.

Eby, L. T. and De Matteo, J. S. (2000) 'When the type of move matters: examining employee outcomes under various relocation situations.' *Journal of Organizational Behavior 21,* 677–687.

Eccles, J. S. (1987) 'Gender roles and women's achievement-related decisions.' *Psychology of Women Quarterly 11,* 135–172.

EOR (1994) 'Positive about disabled people: the disability symbol.' *Equal Opportunities Review 56,* July–August.

Eysenck, H. J. and Cookson, D. (1970) 'Personality in primary school children.' *British Journal of Educational Psychology 40,* 117–131.

Faltermaier, T. (1992) 'Developmental processes of young women in a caring profession: A qualitative life-event study.' In R. Young and A. Collin (eds) *Interpreting Career.* Westport, CT: Praeger Publishers (Greenwood Press)

Farmer, H. S. (1985) 'Model of career and achievement motivation for women and men.' *Journal of Counseling Psychology 32,* 3, 363–390.

Feather, N. T. (1966) 'Effects of prior success and failure on expectations of success and subsequent performance.' *Journal of Personality and Social Psychology 3,* 287–298.

Feldman-Saunders, S. and Kiesler, S. B. (1974) 'Those who are number two try harder: The effects of sex on attributions of causality.' *Journal of Personality and Social Psychology 6,* 846–855.

Fine, M., and Asch, A. (eds) (1988) *Women with Disabilities: Essays in Psychology, Culture, and Politics.* Philadelphia: Temple University Press.

Fitzgerald, L. F. and Betz, N. E. (1983) 'Issues in the vocational psychology of women.' In W. B. Walsh and O. H. Osipow (eds) *Handbook of Vocational Psychology.* Hillsdale, NJ: Lawrence Erlbaum.

Foster, S. and Mac Leod-Gallinger, J. (1999) 'Career pathways of successful deaf professionals.' Working Paper Presented at 12th Annual Meeting of the Society of Disability Studies, Washington DC.

Freeman, J. (1971) 'The social construction of the second sex.' In M. H. Garskof (ed) *Roles Women Play: Readings Toward Women's Liberation.* Belmont, CA: Brooks/Cole.

French, S. A. (1986) *Handicapped People in Health and Caring Professions: Attitudes, Practices and Experiences.* London: South Bank Polytechnic: MSc Thesis.

French, S. and Swain, J. (2000) 'Personal perspectives of the experience of inclusion.' In M. Moore (ed) *Insider Perspectives on Inclusion: Raising Voices, Raising Issues.* Sheffield: Phillip Armstrong.

Freund, E. D. (1973) 'Tasters and smellers in the food and fragrance industry.' *Rehabilitation Record,* March–April, 6–9.

Friedman, M. (1970) 'The social responsibility of business is to increase profits.' *The New York Times Magazine,* 13 September.

Friedmann, E. and Havighurst, R. (1954) *The Meaning of Work and Retirement.* Chicago: University of Chicago Press.

Frieze, I. H. (1975) 'Women's expectations for and causal attributions of success and failure.' In M. T. S. Mednick, S. S. Tangri and L. W. Hoffman (eds) *Women and Achievement and Motivational Analysis.* Washington, DC: Hemisphere Publishing.

Fuchs, D. and Fuchs, L. S. (1998) 'Competing visions for educating students with disabilities: Inclusion versus full inclusion.' *Childhood Education 74,* 5, 309–316.

Garfield, C. (1986) *Peak Performers.* London: Hutchinson.

Gattiker, U. E. and Larwood, L. (1986) 'Subjective career success: a study of managers and support personnel.' *Journal of Business and Psychology 1,* 2, 78–94.

Gattiker, U. E. and Larwood, L. (1988) 'Predictors for managers' career mobility, success and satisfaction.' *Human Relations 41,* 8, 569–591.

Gattiker, U. E. and Larwood, L. (1989) 'Career success, mobility and extrinsic satisfaction of corporate managers.' *Social Science Journal 26,* 75–92.

Gerson, K. (1993) *No Man's Land: Men's Changing Commitments to Family and Work.* New York: Basic Books.

Giddens, A. (1997) *Sociology* (3rd edition). Oxford: Blackwell.

Ginzberg, E. (1952) 'Toward a theory of occupational choice.' *Personnel and Guidance Journal 30,* 8, 19–30.

Ginzberg, S.W., Atelrad, S. and Herma, J.L. (1951) *Occupation Choice: an approach to a general theory.* New York: Columbia Press.

Glendinning, C. (1983) *Unshared Care: Parents and Their Disabled Children.* London: Routledge and Kegan Paul.

Goldberg, A. (1990) 'Information Models, Views, and Controllers'. *Dr. Dobb's Journal, 15,* 7, 54–61.

Goodale, J. G. and Hall, D. T. (1976) 'Inheriting a career: The influence of sex, values and parents.' *Journal of Vocational Behaviour 8,* 19–30.

Gottfredson, L. S. (1981) 'Circumscription and compromise: A developmental theory of occupational aspirations.' *Journal of Counselling Psychology Monograph 28,* 6, 545–579.

Graham, P., Jordan, D. and Lamb, B. (1990) *An Equal Chance or No Chance?* London: The Spastics Society.

Greenberg, J. and McCarthy, C. L. (1990) 'Comparable worth: A matter of justice.' In G. R. Ferris and K. M. Rowland (eds) *Research in Personnel and Human Resources Management 8,* 265–301.

Grover, R. and Gladstone, G. (1982) *Disabled People – A Right To Work.* London: Bedford Square Press.

Gunz, H. (1989) 'The dual meaning of managerial careers: organisational and individual levels of analysis.' *Journal of Management Studies 26,* 3, 225–250.

Gurin, P., Gurin, G., Loo, R. and Beattie, M. (1969) 'Internal-external control in the motivational dynamics of Negro youth.' *Journal of Social Issues 25,* 204–206.

Gutteridge, T. (1973) 'Predicting career success of graduate business school alumni.' *Academy of Management Journal 16*, 129–137.

Hackett, G. and Betz, N. E. (1981) 'A self-efficacy to the career development of women.' *Journal of Vocational Behaviour 18*, 326–336.

Hahn, H. (1988) 'The politics of physical differences: disability and discrimination.' *Journal of Social Issues 44*, 1, 39–47.

Hall, D. T. (1976) *Careers in organisations*. Santa Monica, CA: Goodyear.

Hall, D. T. and Mirvis, P. H. (1996) 'The new protean career: psychological success and the path with a heart.' In D. T. Hall and Associates (ed) *The Career is Dead – Long Live the Career*. San Francisco, CA: Jossey Bass.

Hall, R. H. (1969) *Occupations and the Social Structure*. London: Prentice-Hall International.

Hansen, J. C. (1984) 'The measurement of vocational interest: Issues and future directions.' In S. D. Brown and R. W. Lent (eds) *Handbook of Counselling Psychology*. New York: Wiley.

Haring, T. G. (1991) 'Social relationship.' In L. H. Meyer, C. A. Peck and L. Brown (eds) *Critical Issues in the Lives of People with Severe Disabilities*. Baltimore: Brooks.

Harpaz, I. and Fu, X. (2002) 'The structure of the meaning of work: A relative stability amidst change.' *Human Relations 55*, 6, 639–667.

Hasazi, S. B., Johnson, R. E., Hasazi, J. E., Gordon, L. R. and Hull, M. (1989) 'Employment of youth with and without handicaps following high school: Outcomes and correlates.' *The Journal of Special Education 23*, 3, 243–255.

Hawkridge, D., Vincent, T. and Hales, G. (1985) *New Information Technology in the Education of Disabled Children and Adults*. London: Croom Helm.

Hayslip, J. B. (1981) 'Developing career mobility for women with disabilities.' Doctoral dissertation: George Peabody College for Teachers; *Dissertation Abstracts International 42*, 4426A.

Heider, F. (1958) *The Psychology of Interpersonal Relations*. New York: Wiley.

Helmreich, R. L., Spence, J. T., Bean, W. E., Lucker, G. W. and Matthews, R. A. (1980) 'Making in academic psychology: Demographic and personality correlates of attainment.' *Journal of Personality and Social Psychology 39*, 896–908.

Hendey, N. (1999) *Young Adults and Disability: Transition to Independent Living?* PhD Thesis, University of Nottingham.

Hendey, N. and Pascall, G. (2001) *Disability and Transition to Adulthood: Achieving Independent Living*. Brighton: Pavilion Publishing.

Hennig, M. and Jardim, A. (1978) *The Managerial Woman*. London: Marton Boyars.

Herr, E. L. (1996) 'Towards a convergence of career theory and practice: mythologies, issues and possibilities.' In M. Savickas and W. Welsh *Handbook of Career Counselling Theory and Practice*. Palto Alto, CA: Davis-Black Publishing.

Hetherington, E. M. and Morris, W. N. (1978) 'The family and primary groups.' In W. H. Holtzman (ed) *Introductory Psychology in depth: Developmental Topics*. New York: Harper & Row.

Himmelweit, H. T., Halsey, A. H. and Oppenheim, A. N. (1952) 'The views of adolescents on some aspects of class structure.' *The British Journal of Sociology 3*, 148–172.

Hodkinson, P. (2003) 'Learning careers and careers progression.' *Learning and Skills Research Journal 6*, 3, 24–26.

Hodkinson, P. and Sparkes, A. (1997) 'Careership: a sociological theory of career decision making.' *British Journal of Sociology of Education 18*, 1, 29–44.

Hoffman, L. W. (1972) 'Early childhood experiences and women's achievement motives.' *Journal of Social Issues 28*, 2, 129–155.

Holland, J. L. (1958) 'A personality inventory employing occupational titles.' *Journal of Applied Psychology 42*, 336–342.

Holland, J. L. (1962) 'Some explorations of a theory of vocational choice: One- and two-year longitudinal studies.' *Psychological monographs,* 76 (26, Whole No. 545).

Horner, M. S. W. (1972) 'Towards an understanding of achievement related conflicts in women.' *Journal of Social Issues 28,* 2, 157–175.

Howard, A. and Bray, D. (1988) *Managerial Lives in Transition: Advancing Age and Changing Times.* New York: Guilford Press.

Hyatt, C. (1990) *Shifting Gears.* New York: Fireside.

Inner London Education Authority (1985) *Educational Opportunities for All (The Fish Report).* London: HMSO.

Jahoda, A., Markova, I. and Cattermole, M. (1988) 'Stigma and self-concept of people with mild mental handicap.' *Journal of Mental Deficiency Research 32,* 1, 103–115.

Jaskolka, G., Beyer, J. M. and Trice, H. M. (1985) 'Measuring and predicting managerial success.' *Journal of Vocational Behaviour 26,* 189–205.

Jenkinson, J. C. (1997) *Mainstream or Special? Educating Students with Disabilities.* London: Routledge.

John, P. (1996) 'Damaged goods? An interpretation of excluded pupils' perceptions of schooling.' In E. Blyth and J. Milner (eds) *Exclusion from School: Inter-P Issues for Policy and Practice.* London: Routledge.

Johnson, S. (1983) 'Employment discrimination and the disabled woman.' Doctoral dissertation. Southern Illinois University at Carbondale; *Dissertation Abstracts International 44,* 2115A.

Jolly, D. (2000) 'A critical evaluation of the contradictions for disabled workers arising from the emergence of the flexible labour market in Britain.' *Disability and Society 15,* 5.

Jowett, S., Hegarty, S. and Moses, D. (1988) *Joining Forces: A Study of Links Between Special and Ordinary Schools.* Windsor: NFER-Nelson

Judge, T. A. and Bretz, R. D. (1994) 'Political influence behaviour and career success.' *Journal of Management 20,* 43–65.

Judge, T. A., Cable, D. M., Boudreau, J. W. and Bretz, R. D. (1995) 'An empirical investigation of the predictors of executive career success.' *Personnel Psychology 48,* 485–519.

Kandola, R. (1995) 'Managing diversity: New broom or old hat?' *International Review of Industrial and Organisational Psychology 10,* 131–167.

Kanter, R. M. (1989) 'Careers and the wealth of nations: a macro-perspective on the structure and implications of career forms.' In M. B. Arthur, D. T. Hall and B. S. Lawrence (eds) *Handbook of Career Theory.* Cambridge: Cambridge University Press.

Katkovsky, W., Crandall, V. C. and Good, S. (1967) 'Parental antecedents of children's beliefs in internal-external control of reinforcements in intellectual achievement situation.' *Child Development 28,* 765–776.

Kauffman, J.M. (1999) 'Commentary: today's special education and its messages for tomorrow.' *The Journal of Special Education 32,* 2, 244–254.

Kettle, M. (1979) *Disabled people and their employment.* London: RADAR.

Keys, D. (1985) 'Gender, sex role and career decision making of certified management accountants.' *Sex Roles 13,* 1–2, 33–46.

Kidd, J. M. (1984) 'Young peoples' perceptions of their occupational decision making.' *British Journal of Guidance and Counselling 12,* 7, 25–38.

Kimball, M. M. (1989) 'A new perspective on women's math achievement.' *Psychological Bulletin 105,* 198–214.

King, Z. (1999) 'Job for life or job for kicks? Intended career paths of younger employees.' *The British Psychological Society Book of Proceedings,* January, 204–209.

Kluckhohn, F. R. and Strodtbeck, F. L. (1961) *Variations in Value Orientations.* Evanston, IL: Row, Peterson.

Korman, A. K. (1980) *Career Success/Personal Failure.* Englewood Cliffs, NJ: Prentice-Hall.

Korman, A. K., Wittig-Berman, U. and Lang, D. (1981) 'Career success and personal failure: alienation in professionals and managers.' *Academy of Management Journal 24,* 2, 342–360.

Kotter, J. P. (1982) *The General Managers.* New York: The Free Press.

Kukla, A. (1972) 'Attributional determinants of achievement-related behaviour.' *Journal of Personality and Social Psychology 21,* 166–174.

Kutner, N. G. (1984) 'Women with disabling health conditions: The significance of employment.' *Women and Health 9,* 4, 21–31.

Labour Force Survey (1998) Department for Education and Employment Disability Briefing. Winter 1998.

Labour Force Survey (2001) DRC Disability Briefing. December 2001. Website: www.drc.gb.org/InformationAndLegislation/Page356.asp.

Lang, M. A. (1982) 'Creating inclusive, nonstereotyping environments: The child with a disability.' Unpublished manuscript.

Larson, D. (1977) *The Rise of Professionalism.* Berkeley, CA: University of California Press.

Larwood, L. and Gutek, B. A. (1987) 'Working towards a theory of women's career development.' In B. A. Gutek and L. Larwood (eds) *Women's Career Development.* Newbury Park: Sage.

Lefcourt, H. M. (1982) *Locus of Control* (2nd edition). Hillsdale, NJ: Lawrence Erlbaum.

Legge, K. (1995) *Human Resource Management: Rhetorics and Realities.* Basingstoke: Macmillan.

Leicester, M. (1999) *Disability Voice – Towards an Enabling Education.* London: Philadelphia: Jessica Kingsley Publishers.

Lent, R. W., Brown, S. B. and Hackett, G. (1996) 'Career development from a social cognitive perspective.' In D. Brown, L. Brooks and Associates (eds) *Career Choice and Development* (3rd edition). San Francisco, CA: Jossey-Bass Publishers.

Lent, R. W., Larkin, K. C. and Brown, S. D. (1989) 'Relation of self-efficacy to inventoried vocational interests.' *Journal of Vocational Behavior 34,* 279–288.

Lerner, R. M. and Busch-Rossnagel, N. A. (1981) 'Individuals as producers of their development: conceptual and empirical bases.' In R. M. Lerner and N. A. Busch-Rossnagel (eds) *Individuals as Producers of Their Development. A Life-span Perspective.* New York: Academic Press.

Lewin, K. (1951) *Field Theory in Social Science.* New York: Harper & Row.

Lewis, M. (1998) *Reflections on Success.* Herpenden: Lennard Publishing.

Lloyd-Smith, M. and Tarr, J. (2000) 'Researching children's perspectives: a sociological dimension.' In A. Lewis and Lindsay G. (eds) *Researching children's perspectives.* Buckingham: Open University Press.

Locke, E. A. (1976) 'The nature and causes of job satisfaction.' In M. D. Dunnette (ed) *Handbook of Industrial and Organisational Psychology.* Chicago: Rand McNally.

Lofland, J. and Lofland, L. H. (1984) *Analysing Social Settings: A Guide to Qualitative Observation and Analysis* (2nd edition). Belmont: Wadsworth.

London, M. and Stumpf, S. A. (1982) *Managing Careers.* Reading, MA: Academic Press.

Low, J. (1996) 'Negotiating identities, negotiating environments: an interpretation of the experiences of students with disabilities.' *Disability and Society 11,* 2, 235–248.

Lysaght, R., Townsend, E. and Orser, C. L. (1994) 'The use of work schedule modification to enhance employment outcomes for persons with severe disability.' *Journal of Rehabilitation,* 26–29.

Makin, P. (1987) 'Career commitment, personality and career development in organisations.' PhD Thesis. University of Bradford.

Marcia, J. E. (1966) 'Development and validation of ego identity status.' *Journal of Personality 3*, 5, 551–558.

Marginson, P. (1994) 'Multinational Britain: employment and work in an internationalized economy.' *Human Resource Management Journal 4*, 4, 63–80.

Marshall, J. (1995) *Women Managers Moving On*. London: Routledge.

Matthews, G. F. (1983) *Voice From the Shadows: Women with Disabilities Speak Out*. Toronto: The Women's Press.

McCall, M. W. and Lombardo, M. M. (1983) *Off the Track: Why and How Successful Executives Get Derailed*. Technical Report No. 21. Greensboro, NC: Center for Creative Leadership.

McCarthy, H. (1988) 'Attitudes that affect employment opportunities for persons with disabilities.' In H. E. Yuker (ed) *Attitudes Towards Persons with Disabilities*. New York: Springer Publications Co.

McClelland, D. C. (1951) *Personality*. New York: William Sloane.

McClelland, D. C. (1955) 'Measuring motivation in fantasy.' In D. C. McClelland (ed) *Studies in Motivation*. New York: Appleton.

McClelland, D. C. (1961) *The Achieving Society*. New York: Van Nostrand.

McClelland, D. C., Atkinson, J. W., Clark, R.A. and Lowell, E. L. (1953) *The Achievement Motive*. New York: Appleton-Century-Crofts.

McCrudden, C. (1982) 'Institutional discrimination.' *Oxford Journal of Legal Studies 2*, 303–367.

McDonald, A. P. (1971) 'Internal-external locus of control: parental antecedents.' *Journal of Consulting and Clinical Psychology 37*, 1, 141–147.

Melamed, T. (1995) 'Career success: the moderating effect of gender.' *Journal of Vocational Behaviour 47*, 35–60.

Middleton, L. (1999) *Disabled Children: Challenging Social Exclusion*. Oxford: Blackwell Science Ltd.

Miller, G. (1991) 'The challenge of upward mobility.' *Journal of Visual Impairment and Blindness* October, 332–334.

Minuchin, P. P., Shapiro, E. K. (1983) 'The school as a context for social development. In E.M. Hetherington (ed) *Handbook of child psychology: Vol.4. Socialization, personality, and social development*. New York: Wiley.

Mirvis, P. H. and Hall, D. T. (1994) 'Psychological success and the boundaryless career.' *Journal of Organisational Behaviour 15*, 365–380.

Morris, J. (1989) *Able Lives: Women's Experience of Paralysis*. London: The Women's Press.

Morris, J. (1990) *Our Homes, Our Rights: Housing, Independent Living and Physically Disabled People*. London: Shelter.

Morris, J. (1997) 'Gone missing? Disabled children living away from their families.' *Disability & Society 12*, 2, 241–258.

Morris, J. (2002) *Moving into Adulthood – Young People Moving into Adulthood*. York: Joseph Rowntree Foundation.

Morse, N. and Weiss, R. (1955) 'The function and meaning of work and the job.' *American Sociological Review 20*, 191–198.

MOW International Research Team (1987) *The Meaning of Work*. London: Academic Press.

Mrug, S. and Wallander, (2002) 'Self-concept of young people with physical disabilities: does integration play a role.' *International Journal of Disability, Development and Education 49*, 3, 268–280.

Murray, H. A. (1938) *Exploration in Personality*. New York: Oxford University Press.

Mussen, P. H., Conger, J. J. and Kegan, J. (1979) *Child Development and Personality*. New York: Harper Row.

National Information Center for Children and Youth with Disabilities (1990) 'Having a daughter with a disability: is it different for girls?' *News Digest* October, 14.

Norburn, D. (1986) 'The Chief Executive: a breed apart; Working paper 85.18.' *Strategy and Enterprise Working Paper Series.* Cranfield: Cranfield School of Management.

Norwich, B. (1994) *Segregation and Inclusion: English LEA Statistics.* Bristol: Centre for Studies in Inclusive Education.

Norwich, B. (1997) 'Exploring the perspectives of adults with moderate learning difficulties on their special schooling and themselves: Stigma and self-perceptions.' *European Journal of Special Education 12,* 1, 38–53.

O'Donnell, M. (1981) *A New Introduction to Sociology* (2nd edition). Surrey: Thomas Nelson & Sons Ltd.

Oliver, M. (1990) *The Politics of Disablement.* London: Macmillan.

Oliver, M. (1996) *Understanding Disability.* London: Macmillan Press.

OPCS (1988) *Surveys of Disability in Great Britain Report 4: Disabled Adults: Services, Transport and Employment.* London: HMSO.

O'Reilly, C. A. and Chatman, J. A. (1994) 'Working longer and harder: a longitudinal study of managerial success.' *Administrative Science Quarterly 39,* 12, 603–627.

Osipow, S. H. (1983) *Theories of Career Development* (3rd edition). Englewood Cliffs, NJ: Prentice Hall.

Parker, H. and Arthur, M. B. (2000) 'Careers, organizing, and community.' In M. A. Peiperl, M. B. Arthur, R. Goffee and T. Morris (eds) *Career Frontiers: New Conceptions of Working Lives.* Oxford: Oxford University Press.

Parker, J. G. and Asher, S. (1987) 'Peer relations and later personal adjustment: are low-accepted children at-risk?' *Psychological Bulletin 102,* 357–389.

Parsons, T. (1956) 'A revised analytical approach to the theory of social stratification.' In R. Bendix and S. M. Lipset (eds) *Class, Status, Power: A Reader in Social Stratification.* Glencoe, IL: Free Press.

Pearse, P. (1996) 'Integration or segregation: a personal account of school.' Unpublished Diploma in Disability Studies; University of Leeds.

Peluchette, J. van E. (1993) 'Subjective career success: the influence of individual difference, family and organisational variables.' *Journal of Vocational Behaviour 43,* 198–208.

Perry, D. (1984) *More Equal than Some.* London: Lady Margaret Hall Settlement.

Pfeiffer, D. (1991) 'The influence of socio-economic characteristics of disabled people on their employment status and income.' *Disability, Handicap and Society 6,* 2, 103–112.

Pitta, V. and Curtin, M. (2004) 'Integration versus segregation: the experiences of a group of disabled students moving from mainstream school into special needs further education.' *Disability and Society 19,* 4, 387–401.

Porter, L. W. and Lawler, E. E. (1968) *Managerial Attitudes and Performance.* Homewood, IL: Irwin.

Powell, G. N. and Mainiero, L. A. (1992) 'Cross-currents in the river of time: conceptualising the complexities of women's careers.' *Journal of Management 18,* 2, 215–237.

Preece, J. (1995) 'Disability and adult education – the consumer view.' *Disability and Society 10,* 87–102.

Priestley, M. (1998) 'Childhood disability and disabled childhoods.' *Childhood – A Global Journal of Child Research 5,* 2, 207–223.

Raynor, J. O. (1974) 'Motivation and career striving.' In J. W. Atkinson and J. O. Raynor (eds) *Motivation and Achievement.* New York: Halstead.

Reid, I. (1981) *Social Class Differences in Britain* (2nd edition). London: Grant McIntyre Limited.

Reiser, R. and Mason, M. (1990) *Disability Equality in the Classroom: A Human Rights Issue.* London: Inner London Education Authority.

Roe, A. (1956) *The Psychology of Occupations.* New York: John Wiley.

Rosenthal, R. and Jacobson, L. R. (1968) 'Teacher expectations for the disadvantaged.' *Scientific American 218*, 19–23.

Rotter, J. B. (1966) 'Generalised experiences for internal versus external control of reinforcement.' *Psychological Monographs: General and Applied 80*, 609.

Rowe, A. (ed) (1990) *Lifetime Homes: Flexible Housing for Successive Generations.* London: Helen Hamlyn Foundation.

Russo, H. (1988) *Disabled, Female, and Proud!* Boston, MA: Exceptional Parent Press.

Russo, N., Kelly, R. M. and Deacon, M. (1991) 'Gender and success-related attribution: beyond individualistic conceptions of achievement.' *Sex Roles 25*, 5–6, 331–350.

Saborine, E. J. (1985) 'Social mainstreaming of handicapped students: Facing an unpleasant reality.' *Remedial and Special Education 6*, 2, 12–16.

Saunders, S. (1994) 'The residential school: a valid choice.' *British Journal of Special Education 21*, 2, 64–66.

Schein, E. H. (1979) *Organizational Psychology* (3rd edition). Englewood Cliffs, NJ: Prentice Hall.

Sewell, W. H. and Shah, V. P. (1968) 'Social class, parental encouragement and educational aspirations.' *American Journal of Sociology 73*, 559–572.

Shah, S., Arnold, J. and Travers, C. (2004) 'The mark of childhood on disabled professionals.' *Children & Society 18*, 179–193.

Shakespeare, T. and Watson, N. (1998) 'Theoretical perspectives on research with disabled children.' In G. Fairbairn and S. Fairbairn (eds) *Integrating Special Children: Some Ethical Issues.* Aldershot: Avebury.

Shapero, A. (1975) 'The displaced uncomfortable entrepreneurs.' *Psychology Today*, November, 83–88.

Shearer, A. (1981) *Disability – Whose Handicap?* Basil Blackwell.

Shepherd, G. (1997) 'Vocational rehabilitation in psychiatry: a historical perspective.' In G. Grove, M. Freudenberg, A. Harding and D. O'Flynn (eds) *The Social Firm Handbook: New Directions in the Employment, Rehabilitation, and Integration of People with Mental Health Problems.* Brighton: Pavilion.

Simpson, G. (1984) 'The daughters of Charlotte Ray: The career development process during the exploratory and establishment stages of black women attorneys.' *Sex Roles 11*, 113–138.

Simpson, P. (1990) 'Education for disabled children – today and tomorrow.' *Contact 64*, 9–11.

Slappo, J. and Katz, (1989) 'A survey of women in nontraditional careers.' *Journal of Rehabilitation* January/February/March, *23–30*.

Sloper, P. and Turner, S. (1992) 'Service needs of families of children with severe physical disability.' *Child-care, Health and Development 18*, 259–282.

Sonnenfeld, J. and Kotter, J. P. (1982) 'The maturation of career theory.' *Human Relations 35*, 19–46.

Spillane, R. (1985) *Achieving Peak Performance: A Psychology of Success in the Organisation.* Sydney: Harper & Row.

Stogdill, R. M. (1974) *A Strong Drive For Responsibility: Handbook of Leadership.* New York: Free Press.

Strauss, A. (1962) 'Transformations of identity.' In A. M. Rose (ed) *Human Behaviour and Social Processes: An Interactive Approach.* London: Routledge and Kegan Paul.

Sturges, J. (1996) 'What it means to succeed: personal conceptions of career success held by male and female managers at different ages.' PhD thesis. Cranfield School of Management, Cranfield University.

Sturges, J. (1999) 'What it means to succeed: personal conceptions of career success held by male and female managers at different ages.' *British Journal of Management 10*, 239–252.

Sullivan, S. (1992) 'My school experience.' In R. Rieser and M. Mason (eds) *Disability Equality in the Classroom: A Human Rights Issue*. London: Jessica Kingsley Publishers.

Sullivan, S. E. (1999) 'The changing nature of careers: a review and research agenda.' *Journal of Management 25*, 457–484.

Super, D. E. (1957) *The Psychology of Careers*. New York: Harper & Row.

Super, D. E., Savickas, M. L. and Super, C. M. (1996) 'The life-span, life space approach to careers.' In D. Brown and L. Brooks (eds) *Career Choice and Development* (3rd edition). San Francisco, CA: Jossey-Bass.

Sutherland, A. (1981) *Disabled We Stand*. London: Souvenir Press.

Swain, J., Finkelstein, V., French, S. and Oliver, M. (eds) (1993) *Disabling Barriers – Enabling Environments*. London: Sage in association with the Open University.

Swinyard, A. W. and Bond, F. A. (1980) 'Who gets promoted?' *Harvard Business Review* September–October, 6–18.

Thomas, C. (1998) 'Parents and family: disabled women's stories about their childhood experiences.' In C. Robinson and K. Stalker (eds) *Growing Up With Disability*. London: Jessica Kingsley Publishers.

Thomas, D. (1978) *The Social Psychology of Childhood Disability*. London: Methuen.

Tinklin, T. and Hall, J. (1998) *Students First: The Experiences of Disabled Students in Higher Education; Research Report*. Glasgow: Scottish Council for Research in Education.

Tomlinson, S. (1982) *The Sociology of Special Education*. London: Routledge & Kegan Paul.

Tomlinson, S. (1995) 'Machines and Professional Bureaucracies: Barriers to Inclusive Education.' Paper presented at the Sociology and Disability Conference, Hull, October.

Trice, A. D., Hughes, A. M., Odom, C., Woods, K. and McClellan, N. C. (1995) 'The origins of children's career aspirations IV: testing hypothesis from four theories.' *The Career Development Quarterly 43*, 307–32.

Tyler, B. B. (1958) 'Expectancy for eventual success as a factor in problem solving behavior.' *Journal of Educational Psychology 9*, 166–172.

UNESCO (1994) *The Salamanca Statement on Principles, Policies and Practice in Special Needs Education*. Paris: United Nations Education, Social and Cultural Organisation.

United Nations (1989) *Convention on the rights of the child*. Geneva: UN

Useem, M. and Karabel, J. (1986) 'Pathways to top corporate management.' *American Sociological Review 51*, 184–200.

Valle, V. A. and Frieze, I. H. (1976) 'Stability of causal attributions as a meditator in changing expectations for success.' *Journal of Personality and Social Psychology 3*, 2, 217–236.

Van Maanen, J. and Schein, E. H. (1977) 'Career development.' In J. R. Hackman and J. L. Vernon (1977) *Human Motivation*. Cambridge: Cambridge University Press.

Veroff, J., Atkinson, J. W., Feld, S. and Gurin, G. (1960) 'The use of thematic apperception to assess motivation in a nation-wide interview study.' *Psychological Monographs 74*, 12.

Vernon, A. (1997) 'Reflexivity: the dilemmas of researching from the inside.' In C. Barnes and G. Mercer (eds) *Doing Disability Research*. Leeds: Leeds Disability Press.

Vondracek, F. W., Lerner, R. M. and Schulenberg, J. E. (1983a) 'The concept of development in vocational theory and intervention.' *Journal of Vocational Behaviour 23*, 179–202.

Vondracek, F. W., Lerner, R. M. and Schulenberg, J. E. (1983b) 'On aspiring to present a developmental theory of occupational aspirations: A reader's guide to Gottfredson.' *Journal of Vocational Behaviour 23*, 213–218.

Vondracek, F. W., Lerner, R. M. and Schulenberg, J. E. (1986) *Career Development: A Life-Span Development Approach*. London: Lawrence Erlbaum Associates Publishers.

Vroom, V. H. (1964) *Work and Motivation*. London: John Wiley & Sons.

Waddel, F. T. (1983) 'Factors affecting choice, satisfaction and success in the female self-employed.' *Journal of Vocational Behaviour 23*, 294–304.

Wagner, M. and Shaver, D. M. (1989) *The Transitional Experiences of Youth with Disabilities: A Report From the National Longitudinal Transitional Study.* Menlo Park, CA: SRI International.

Wallace, C. and Jones, G. (1992) *Youth, Family and Citizenship.* Berkshire: Open University Press.

Warner, W. L. and Abegglen, J. C. (1955) *Big Business Leaders in America.* New York: Harper and Row.

Warnock, H. M. (1978) *Report of the Committee of Enquiry into the Education of Handicapped Children and Young People.* London: HMSO.

Warr, P. (1985) 'Twelve questions about unemployment and health.' In B. Roberts, R. Finnegan and D. Gallie (eds) *New Approaches to Economic Life.* Manchester: Manchester University Press.

Watson, L. (1997) *High Hopes: Making Housing and Community Care Work.* York: Joseph Rowntree Foundation by York Publishing Services.

Watson, N., Shakespeare, T., Cunningham-Burley, S., Barnes, C., Corker, M., Davis, J. and Priestley, M. (1999) *Life as a Disabled Child: A Qualitative Study of Young People's Experiences and Perspectives: Final Report.* Universities of Edinburgh and Leeds.

Wedge, P., and Prosser, H., (1973) *Born to Fail.* London: Arrow Books.

Weiner, B. (1972) *Theories of Motivation.* Chicago, ILL: Rand McNally.

Weiner, B. and Potepan, P. A. (1970) 'Personality correlates and affective reactions toward exams of succeeding and failing college students.' *Journal of Educational Psychology 61*, 144–151.

Weiner, B., Frieze, I., Kukla, A., Reed, L., Rest, S. and Rosenbaum, R. M. (1971) *Perceiving the Causes of Success and Failure.* New York: General Learning.

Werts, C. E. and Watley, D. J. (1972) 'Parental influence on talent development.' *Journal of Counseling Psychology 19*, 367–372.

Wheatley, E. (1994) 'Dances with feminists: truth, dares and ethnographic stares.' *Women's Studies International Forum 17*, 4, 421–3.

White, B. L. (1989) 'A study of the characteristics of female managers and female entrepreneurs.' Unpublished MSc Dissertation. UMIST.

White, B., Cox, C. and Cooper, C. (1992) *Women's Career Development – A Study of High Flyers.* Oxford: Blackwell Publishers.

Wood, M. (1973) *Children: The Development of Personality and Behaviour.* London: Harrap.

Wood, P. (1981) *International Classification of Impairments, Disabilities and Handicaps.* Geneva: World Health Organization (WHO).

Woodhams, C. and Danieli, A. (2000) 'Disability and diversity – a difference too far.' *Personnel Review 29*, 3, 402–416.

Wright, B. (1960) *Physical Disability: A Psychological Approach.* New York: Harper & Row.

Young, G. (1981) 'A woman in medicine: reflections from the inside.' In H. Roberts (ed) *Women, Health and Reproduction.* London: Routledge and Kegan Paul.

Zigler, E. and Hall, N. (1995) 'Mainstreaming and the philosophy of normalisation.' In J. M. Kauffman and D. P. Hallahan (eds) *The Illusion of Full Inclusion.* Austin, TX: Pro-Ed.

About the Author

Dr Sonali Shah is a postdoctoral research fellow in the School of Sociology and Social Policy at the University of Nottingham. She is currently working on a three-year qualitative research project, funded by the European Social Fund, entitled 'Future Selves: The Career Choices of Young Disabled People'.

Sonali has a type of cerebral palsy. She attended special education for 17 years before going to Loughborough University. She graduated from there in 1996 with a BSc(Hons) in Computing & Management. She was awarded her PhD in Occupational Psychology and Disability in 2002, by Loughborough University.

She has worked at the Centre for Disability Studies at Leeds University as the lead researcher on two qualitative projects about disability, ethnicity and health. She has written for *Disability Studies Quarterly, Children and Society, British Journal of Special Education* and the *Journal of Research on Special Educational Needs*. She has also presented work at national and international events including the *Eleventh International Literacy and Education Research Network Conference on Learning*. Her research interests are connected with disabled young people, career choices and transitional development, ethnicity, education, health and illness.

She is a trustee for Share Music, an international performance arts organisation for young people with physical disabilities.

Sonali lives in Nottingham with her partner, Jonathan Legge.

Subject index

Note: page numbers in *italics* refer to information contained in tables.

Author Index